THE 11TH
DURHAM LIGHT
INFANTRY
IN THEIR OWN NAMES

THE 11ᵀᴴ DURHAM LIGHT INFANTRY

IN THEIR OWN NAMES

MARTIN BASHFORTH

AMBERLEY

First published 2011

Amberley Publishing
Cirencester Road, Chalford,
Stroud, Gloucestershire, GL6 8PE

www.amberleybooks.com

British Library Cataloguing in Publication Data.
A catalogue record for this book is available from the British Library.

ISBN 978-1-4456-0265-3

Typeset in 10pt on 12pt Sabon.
Typesetting and Origination by Amberley Publishing.
Printed in the UK.

Contents

11th Durham Light Infantry, In Remembrance, 1914–1918. (*Patricia Bashforth*)

Introduction

The United Kingdom government has been continuously involved in war for more than a decade now, a period longer than the First and Second World Wars combined. Hundreds of young men return every year in coffins, badly injured or severely traumatised. The wars themselves have been contentious. We will shortly commemorate the centenary of the First World War, the 'war to end all wars'. Descendants of the generation that fought then, a major proportion of the UK population, cannot help but ask questions, both about the involvement of our forebears in war and about the more recent conflicts that seem to have connections with that past. This book originated with such questions and seeks to find new ways of understanding.

Most of the men who fought in the First World War were born between 1875 and 1899. Their world was 'Late Victorian' or 'Edwardian'. They witnessed a period of profound social, political and cultural upheaval that makes those labels seem exotic a century later. The event that marked the passage from their world to what we regard as ours was the war in which they were (or felt) obliged to fight. The First World War involved all classes and communities, though most numerously it was the men of the working class and lower middle class who provided the physical manpower. These men were individual human beings. They had families behind them and were part of wider communities, not nameless people subsumed under the titles of the military units in which they served. Many histories have featured a selection of infantry battalions, especially the Pals battalions, so savagely mauled on the first day of the Battle of the Somme. More recently there have been books about the Army Service Corps, tunnellers and the Royal Naval Division. Almost every battle in every theatre has been covered to some degree, increasingly with the use of personal testimony from those who served. Published memoirs and diaries have provided a flavour of experience from an individual viewpoint, while the last surviving veterans have provided a late flow of reminiscence. Considerably less has been published regarding the average units that remain unsung, because they played only minor parts in the greater dramas. There has also been no real attempt to move beyond the military experience, to portray the soldiers in their social context. This book attempts to correct that imbalance.

At the centre of this story is the experience of a battalion recruited from volunteers in August and September 1914: the 11th (Service) Battalion, Durham Light Infantry (Pioneers). Unlike the Pals battalions, the recruits did not all hail from one town, or from one workplace, though evidence suggests that the early volunteers came from a catchment area that included the whole of County Durham, as well as parts of Northumberland and North Yorkshire. They would, in the course of the war, be replenished by men from farther afield. Their officers included both local men and others from across the British Empire. It is the individual men who are at the heart of this book.

The purpose is to reconstruct the human story of this unit, in order to explore an average experience of an average soldier in an average battalion. The sources include contemporary letters and newspapers, as well as the surviving fragments of personal records lodged in a variety of record offices. A range of battalion, brigade and divisional war diaries are used, as well as histories published shortly after the end of the war. A substantial source is the collection of pension and service records of men who served during the First World War, now made available online by the National Archives in conjunction with Ancestry.co.uk. I have also drawn on the activities of others, like myself, whose ancestors served in 11th DLI. In that sense this book is a reflection of the need of present generations to fulfil a desire for remembrance.

We who remember, from the perspective of the early twenty-first century, have been shaped by social and cultural influences very different from the experience of the men we celebrate. The verb 'remember' is technically inaccurate, since we can in no way recall the actual events from our own experience, and rarely knew firsthand the men who provide us with such fascination. Occasionally we have known survivors and the widows of those who did not make it home and their bereaved sons and daughters. An act of remembrance in itself, this book also reflects on what remembrance means, almost a century onwards, at the personal, social and political level.

My first debt is to those people who have made contact with me during the course of my research and have contributed so much to what has been a painstaking and difficult task. Gaynor Greenwood and Kenneth Banks provided access to, and permission to quote from, the surviving letters of Robert Bennett, without which this would have been a less human book. Gaynor Greenwood also provided numerous images from around France and Belgium as part of her travels, assisted by her friend Jon Miller. David Kelly provided photographs and information relating to Thomas Bonney. Sean Gregory provided similar information about John Cummins. Emma Laycock told me about John Doyle. Mike Lavelle provided the link to Hugh Lavelle, who survived. All provided encouragement.

My research would not have been possible without the support of those professionals working in museums, archives and record offices. Stephen Shannon, formerly of the Durham Light Infantry Museum, invited me to give a talk at the museum, which caused me to raise my ambitions. The Durham Light Infantry Trust and Durham County Records Office provided access to material in their archives relating to 11th DLI and permission to reproduce examples. The Liddle Collection at the University of Leeds provided information from related military units. The National Archives proved an informative source in the early days of research and, in partnership with the Ancestry.co.uk website, made substantial amounts of material accessible online, making my task easier and speedier, while quantitatively a challenge. I am grateful for permission to quote from texts and to publish illustrations from the above organisations, as well as the *Northern Echo*. I also thank the Imperial War Museum for their generosity in allowing me to use several photographs from their fine collection.

My former colleagues, Professor Colin Divall of the Institute for Railway Studies and Transport History and Tim Procter of the National Railway Museum, helped me to critically review and reassess the content and style of the book in preparation for publication. My cousin, David Bashforth, has helped with family photographs. My wife Patricia has been a patient witness to moments of both obsession and despair, and has helped me shape my ideas through hours of discussion over twelve years. Without her support and intelligent interest, this book would have been much the poorer.

The team at Amberley Publishing have been generous in their support during the preparation of this book. I would particularly like to thank Alan Sutton for agreeing to take it on in the first place, Joseph Pettican for his courtesy and skill in bringing the project to a successful conclusion, and the design team for their work with the illustrations and cover. Any remaining faults in the book are mine.

In terms of initial inspiration, I would like to thank three people. My late cousin, Thomas Sidney Bashforth, researched the family history in the days before computers and provided the first evidence of my grandfather's war service. My late father, Ray Bashforth, whose discomfort with his father, whom he never knew, was too painful to discuss until his own final years, when he gave me a postcard photograph and provided me with a personal challenge. My grandfather, Sergeant 14956 Thomas Bashforth, remains the principal inspiration behind this work. His photograph in uniform has watched over me throughout the research and writing of this book. He was just a plasterer who put his hand up and volunteered, a man among millions.

Martin Bashforth, November 2010

Private Thomas Bashforth, newly recruited, 1914.
(*Collection of M. Bashforth*)

Abbreviations Used in the Text

Battalions are generally referred to in the following format:

11th DLI	11th Durham Light Infantry
10th KRRC	10th King's Royal Rifle Corps
10th RB	10th Rifle Brigade
7th KOYLI	7th King's Own Yorkshire Light Infantry
7th DCLI	7th Duke of Cornwall's Light Infantry
7th SomLI	7th Somerset Light Infantry
6th KSLI	6th King's Shropshire Light Infantry
6th OBLI	6th Oxfordshire and Buckinghamshire Light Infantry
12th King's	12th King's Liverpool Regiment

Other abbreviations:

Bde	Brigade
C-in-C	Commander-in-Chief
CWGC	Commonwealth War Graves Commission
DCM	District Court Martial
Div	Division
FA	Field Ambulance
FGCM	Field General Court Martial
FP1	Field Punishment Number One
FP2	Field Punishment Number Two
GOC	General Officer Commanding
HQ	Headquarters
IWM	Imperial War Museum
NCO	Non-commissioned Officer

OTC	Officer Training Corps
RAMC	Royal Army Medical Corps
RFA	Royal Field Artillery
SSFA	Soldiers and Sailors Families Association
WO	War Office

CHAPTER ONE

Past Imperfect, Future Conditional

Thursday 11 October 1888 was an unremarkable date. At 8 Cranbourne Terrace, Workington, a child was born, also nothing out of the ordinary – children were being born all the time. Life expectancy was not great, but if you survived childhood you might live forty or fifty more years. However, many male children born around this time would have their lives cut short in early adulthood. This boy would not see his thirtieth birthday. He was called Thomas after his grandfather. The mother was seventeen, a domestic servant and unmarried. She was the second of four children living with their widower father, Thomas Bashforth, a foundryman at Cammell's steel works. Young Thomas was my grandfather.

Elements of an individual Victorian family's records may seem an unlikely place to start the story of a First World War battalion. However, the details of such families in the decades leading up to 1914 provide an insight into the lives of those who experienced the war directly. The types of records used by family historians tend to be avoided by academic historians. In isolation they are seen as anecdotal, while the volume of records across a mass of families is difficult to manage. However, the family historian is able to populate the generally accepted record with examples of individual experience and discover elements of detail perhaps overlooked by more conventional approaches. The use of family records across a broader range of families can help us appreciate our predecessors a little better as individual human beings and as particular groups.[1]

The birth of Thomas Bashforth is one of many personal entry points that might be used to illuminate the origins of the men who would later serve in the 11th Battalion Durham Light Infantry in the First World War. While no single man's background can be held up as typical, because there were so many different experiences, Thomas Bashforth's life is emblematic of the milieu from which the volunteers and conscripts of the First World War were largely taken. Family history illuminates kinship networks and draws attention to the variety of household economies from which recruits were drawn and their place within them. It can disclose patterns of both settlement and migration, throw light onto the detail of local communities and help identify some of the sources of cultural influence on recruits during childhood and schooling. We can learn more about the family influences that may have motivated the First World War recruits. As the story of this unremarkable battalion unfolds, aspects of the lives of many more men will be explored, most of them working-class like Thomas, several from middle and lower middle class backgrounds and occasionally from among the families that held positions in county society or were engaged in the business of building the British Empire abroad.

The story of young Thomas Bashforth's family begins in the region around Sheffield in the 1870s, among people trying to survive during a depression that badly hit the metal-working industries. The father of the family, also called Thomas Bashforth, struggled to find jobs as a blacksmith or foundryman. He had been born in Sheffield to a father from Barnsley, but moved to Derby with his father for a time, then lived in Birmingham with relatives and later returned to Barnsley.[2] In 1871, he was unemployed and living in Barnsley, with his second wife Bridget, two sons from his first marriage (William and James), Bridget's son from her previous marriage (James McDonald), and the couple's first daughter Mary Anne, aged one. He moved to Birmingham in search of work that same year and Ellen, the second daughter, was born there. By 1873, the family was in Sheffield, where Bridget, the third daughter, was born in the Union Workhouse, suggestive at least of continued poverty if not a further period of unemployment. They had rooms at the back of the Arundel Castle pub in Arundel Street, Sheffield, when Matthew the last of the children was born in 1876.

In 1881, the family (less the three older boys) were in Dronfield, where Thomas had found work at the Wilson Cammell & Company steelworks. However, in 1883 the company was uprooted to a new site at Moss Bay in Workington, Cumberland. Most of the steel rail manufactured in Dronfield went for export, and the logistics of obtaining materials and distributing the finished product from this site was too difficult, time-consuming and expensive. In modern times, it might be expected that a family would have been paid relocation costs, but not so for Cammell's employees. If they wanted work, they had to find their own way to Workington. Because of the difficulties of finding homes in the town and the lack of any pay during the period of temporary unemployment, fathers often went ahead of their families, bringing them later when things were settled. Given the distance involved, most travelled by train, if they could muster enough savings for the fares and carried only a few possessions. The descendants of these immigrant workers are still known in Workington as 'Dronnies', an indication of the impact of their arrival on the local community and of the numbers who made the journey. There were estimated to be between 400 and 500 families involved.[3] For the Bashforth family to face this kind of upheaval was not unusual and was preferable to remaining behind with a high risk of unemployment.

In Workington, the family moved from one rented house to another. On 5 November 1884, the mother, Bridget, died of cancer of the liver at only forty-six years of age, leaving her eldest daughter Mary to take up the household duties at the age of fifteen. The second daughter, Ellen, went into domestic service, to add what she could to the family income. In 1888, she was helping in the house of a Manxman, Matthew Kelly.[4] It was he who allegedly made Ellen pregnant. The source of this information was Ellen herself and the story has been passed down the family line ever since. In itself, it is one of those anecdotes that historians rightly treat with suspicion, especially as details can be misremembered or embroidered in the retelling. The detail of the name would hardly be worth noting, but for an event yet to happen, some thirty years later.[5] Ellen Bashforth did not marry Kelly. We do not know whether he offered, or if he was in a position to do so. Having a child out of wedlock was not as socially acceptable as now, though it was not uncommon. We do not know what Ellen's father thought about the pregnancy, but at least she had her child at home and named him after her father. It suggests a degree of family tolerance and acceptance.

When Thomas senior died on 30 August 1889, Ellen's older sister registered the death. Mary Anne had by then married James McIlheron but was still living at her father's home in Cranbourne Street. It must have been a crowded household: old Thomas, three daughters, a son Matthew, a son-in-law and now a grandson. Two years later the family unit had moved to 2 Bridge Terrace, with James McIlheron recorded in the census as the head of the household, an ironworks labourer aged thirty and from Ireland. He and Mary Anne had a daughter, Mary McIlheron, aged two months. Staying with them were sister-in-law Ellen, aged nineteen, general servant, and her son Thomas, aged two. Living in a separate part of the house was an old couple, described as 'receiving parish relief', the nearest equivalent to an old age pension in those days and preferable to the workhouse. Seven people in a two-up, two-down terrace house was not untypical for working-class families in an industrial town with uncertain levels of employment.

It was equally typical that Thomas' aunt Bridget, aged sixteen, was now a general servant in the household of railway engine driver William Bird.

Matthew Bashforth, aged fourteen, was living in Birmingham, in a back-to-back courtyard, with his 35-year-old half-brother James Bashforth, a blacksmith. Matthew was working as his assistant, a common way for a young man to make his way in the world. James had, like his father before him, used kinship connections to find work in the Midlands, and now Matthew was following the same pattern. As well as James, his wife and daughter, and Matthew, they also had a female lodger. These back-to-backs were small and the living conditions were cramped. The household make-up demonstrates that, although enforced migration to find work may have stretched family networks, they continued to keep in touch. Even in the absence of surviving letters and postcards it suggests that there was a sufficient level of literacy to maintain connections through the late Victorian postal network.

Over the next ten years the McIlheron family moved several times to search for work. They moved to Wigan during 1891 or 1892, taking the two younger Bashforth sisters with them. Two more children were born in Wigan: Hugh, in about 1894, and Thomas, in about 1897. By 1901, James and Mary MacIlheron and their family were living in Barrow-in-Furness, where James was an iron founder. Their brother Matthew Bashforth had come back from Birmingham and was also in Barrow, where he was employed as a labourer in the shipyard gun shop. The two younger sisters had married in the meantime.

On 7 November 1892 Ellen Bashforth, then living in Ince-in-Makerfield, married John McGlasson. He would be influential as Thomas' father from the age of four. His family originated in Carlisle and moved to Workington following the death of John's father and the need for the sons to find work. John McGlasson was an iron moulder and his older brother a plasterer. The younger brothers would split between the iron trade and plastering, though eventually all the sons would gravitate towards plastering. John took a detour via the Army. After a brief experience with the militia (3rd Border Regiment), he signed up as a regular in Carlisle, aged twenty, on 4 November 1885. His attestation form describes him as 5 feet 6 and 4/10 inches tall, weighing 125 lb, with a chest measurement of 34 inches, grey eyes, fair hair and a fresh complexion. He had a scar behind his left ear and a blue spot on his left thumb. He gave his religion as Church of England. He had been vaccinated in childhood against smallpox. Almost exactly the same form would be used to record all recruits involved in the First World War, with the same sets of personal information.[6] He went on to serve in Ireland, India and Burma until he returned to England in 1890, to be stationed at Dover. The medical records suggest that he took advantage of local female company wherever he went, much to the detriment of his health. On 3 November 1892, he was transferred from active service to the Army Reserve. In the two years since arriving back in England, John McGlasson had made Ellen's acquaintance. They had most likely met in Workington, before the McIlheron household moved to Wigan, possibly through the mutual acquaintance of Edward McGlasson and James McIlheron, who were both ironworks labourers, perhaps at the same place. John McGlasson wasted no time in getting to Wigan to marry Ellen Bashforth. The marriage took place only four days later.

Work in the 1890s was hard to find and families frequently had to move. It was often doubly difficult for former soldiers, who were basically unskilled. They were frequently reduced to menial labouring jobs. Between 1892 and 1901, the McGlasson family moved back to Workington and then on to Gosforth, north of Newcastle-upon-Tyne, where John worked as a plasterer, after the fashion of his older brothers. In 1901, as well as Thomas Bashforth, aged twelve, there were three McGlasson daughters, Laura aged seven, Margaret Ellen aged five and Dora aged one. The last of their children, Edwin, was born in 1908. The McGlasson family and Ellen's sisters would be the main network of support for the younger Thomas Bashforth and his later family, though Thomas also kept in touch with his cousin and childhood playmate, Mary McIlheron. The McGlassons were still in Gosforth at the time of the 1911 census, though Thomas Bashforth was not living with them. He was on the road looking for work and must have arrived in Darlington around that time, a little prior to his eventual marriage in 1912.

According to my father's recollections, Thomas Bashforth learned his trade as plasterer with his stepfather John and his uncle Edward.[7] Edward was reputedly in great demand as a plasterer, travelling as far as London on contracts. As well as teaching Thomas the specific skills, which did not require an apprenticeship, he taught him some of the cultural elements of the trade, such as how to play cards and the virtues of the economical use of physical energy. Edward's plastering contracts were on piecework. There was a fixed price for the job to be done to the specified quality and by the agreed time. The estimate agreed left sufficient leeway for the McGlasson clan to practice their game of cards so long as there were no outside observers. The work was done in the last few days of the contract. Such knowledge would become very handy for a junior non-commissioned officer in a Pioneer battalion on the Western Front, but that was some way in the future. Whether or not the details of this family tale are true, it is suggestive of the working culture Thomas experienced. Of importance in his upbringing might have been his stepfather's tales about serving in the Army in Ireland, India and Burma, though they may not have included John McGlasson's dubious medical experiences.

Thomas Bashforth's uncle, Edward McGlasson, was a witness at his marriage to Florence Wood on 27 May 1912, at St Hilda's church,

Darlington. Not unusually for the times, the bride was probably already pregnant, as their first child, Ethel, was born less than six months later on 17 November 1912. Two sons were born during wartime. The eldest, called Thomas after his father, was born on 20 March 1915 before his father went overseas. The youngest son, John Raymond (my father), was born on 5 November 1917, the product of two weeks' home leave earlier in the year. He would never know his father. The family lived at 6 Bridge Terrace, Bank Top in Darlington. These were old back-to-back houses dating from before the 1850s. Entrance was along a passage and round to the back behind No. 7, where the Ingledew family lived. On the corner was the Royal Oak public house. Opposite the passageway was a set of stone steps leading down to the main road through the bricked retaining wall of an embankment. Through the back door was a kitchen area and stairs leading up to two bedrooms. It would have been manageable enough with a couple and three very young children.[8]

The detailed life cycle of the Bashforth family demonstrates something of the range of experiences in working-class communities, but Thomas Bashforth was just one future recruit to 11th DLI from a much broader context. Others were drawn from across all parts of County Durham and the great majority were miners. The principal towns in Durham from which the battalion's recruits came in 1914 were Gateshead, Sunderland, West Hartlepool, Darlington, Bishop Auckland and the city of Durham itself. The larger towns included many miners as well as a wide variety of working-class trades. Equally important in terms of volunteers were the more dispersed mining communities around Consett, Stanley, Chester-le-Street, Birtley, Heworth and Felling. Although spread out over a number of separate townships, in otherwise rural areas, these mining villages were collectively significantly populous.

Population growth in the first decade of the twentieth century had ceased to be dramatic but remained significant. Between 1901 and 1911, the population of County Durham (including its associated County Borough towns) rose from 1,187,474 persons to 1,369,860 persons.[9] This was an increase of about 15 per cent in ten years. The global figure hid some wide discrepancies. Darlington, a prosperous industrialised market town in the south of the county grew by 25 per cent in the same period, the product of a diverse economy embracing finance, retail, engineering and agriculture. By contrast, Gateshead-on-Tyne in the north grew by only 6 per cent. On the coast, Hartlepool's population actually fell slightly and neighbouring West Hartlepool grew by a fraction. Population growth in pit areas lay between the county average and that of Darlington. Coal was still king, although challenged by newer, more skilled engineering trades.

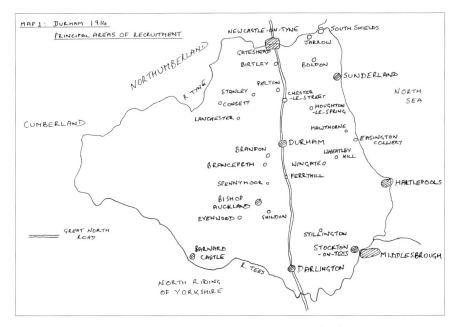

Durham 1914: principal areas of recruitment. (*Martin Bashforth, 2010*)

Even outside the towns, the main recruiting areas were thoroughly industrial and thoroughly working-class. Although individual pits might be situated among green fields, the next pit was often within view and agriculture was hardly picturesque. A. D. Hall toured Britain in 1910–1912, and noted in this part of the world the 'violent contrast, so rapidly does one exchange purely pastoral or agricultural country for densely populated colliery areas or that still more dreary land where the coal has been won and farming is being resumed in a half-hearted way'.[10]

The majority of men of working age were in employment and wages were just about adequate for daily subsistence, subject to the vagaries of sickness, occasional lay-offs and too many mouths to feed. All but the most skilled workers in regular employment lived a relatively hand-to-mouth existence on the edge of debt. Undernourishment and poor health were a problem for the very young, the very old and for growing young families.[11] Despite the material hardship, where communities pooled their resources life need not be without its compensations. Paul Thompson quotes the daughter of a furnaceman from Darlington: 'The Co-operative Movement in those days was not just a shopping movement, it was also an educational movement. Looking back there was far more culture, what I would call cultural activities in Darlington than there are now. It's very starved of cultural activities now.'[12] In the main towns society was highly stratified by class. This was geographically evident in Darlington, for example. The most prosperous middle-class housing was (and remains) largely confined to a tree-lined south-west quadrant of the town. Almost the whole of the housing in the remaining three quarters of the town comprised various types of terrace housing, most of it for the families of those employed in the neighbouring factories and works, and at best, two-up, two-down with a small backyard.

By contrast, the pit villages of Durham had a more unified sense of community. Horizons were narrow around the older pits, though some of the more recently sunk pits towards the coast attracted inward migration from Wales and South Yorkshire. Thomas Bonney made the rank of Sergeant in 11th DLI and would lose his life within a day or two of Thomas Bashforth. When he enlisted he was a miner, a male tradition in the family. In 1901, he was a five-year-old boy living at Urpeth, near Beamish, County Durham. His road, Nicholson Terrace, consisted of a single row of twelve terrace houses. The dominance of the local colliery as the main employer was evident. Of thirty working people in the street, twenty-four were miners of one grade or another. There were two railway workers, a butcher, an electrical engineer, a bricklayer and a domestic servant. All but two heads of household were colliery workers. The exceptions were directly or indirectly dependent on the pit for their livelihood. Most came from the home area or elsewhere in Durham, two from Northumberland and one each from Yorkshire and Ireland. While the self-employed butcher and his wife were the sole occupiers of their terrace house in Urpeth, it probably also served as their shop. The Bonney household, by contrast, was nine strong, including parents, two girls, three boys and two adult male boarders. This was a fairly typical pattern as young children earned no money, but had to be fed and clothed. Boarders provided a useful addition to the family income and allowed the mother to make a financial contribution. One wage between seven would have been a struggle. By 1911, the family had moved to Ouston Square, Birtley, County Durham, and three of the sons (Richard, William and Thomas) were working in the pit alongside their father. The family still had a lodger, another miner, who was a widower. Two more sons had been born and, though the household still numbered nine, with more wage earners contributing to the household income there was a little more prosperity.

The backgrounds of those who became officers in 11th DLI were extremely varied. Thomas William Applegarth was born 18 September 1893 in Piercebridge, just to the west of Darlington. In 1901 his father, Thomas Applegarth, owned and drove a threshing machine, though he must have had other sources of income than this seasonally useful piece of equipment. He was sufficiently well-off to be able to send his son to Queen Elizabeth Grammar School in Darlington and then to Emmanuel

College, Cambridge. The future officer was at school in 1911, by which time his father gave his employment as 'stone breaker, above ground', which indicates another source of his income. While the family had no servants, there were two young teenage nieces and a one-year-old 'nurse child', indicating some attempt to supplement the household finances. The young man later became a secondary school teacher and was still living with his family, then resident at Evenwood near Bishop Auckland, when he enlisted in 1914. Given his father's working-class occupation, it is not a surprise that his first posting was as a private soldier and driver in the Army Service Corps. His university education was no substitute for his lower-class background at this stage of the war.

By contrast, Ernest Rowan Butler Clough, born 11 June 1894, was cut out for officer class from the start. His father was Lieutenant Colonel Alfred Herrick Butler Clough of the Royal Munster Fusiliers. As a student aged seventeen, still at home at the time of the 1911 census, Clough was at The Grange, Alveston, in Gloucestershire, with his retired father, mother and sister, and two family servants. Educationally he was not on the same level as Applegarth, using a 1912 London University matriculation certificate as his qualification for a commission. But his family background ensured his immediate enlistment as an officer. Similarly, there was no obstacle to Richard Laurence Stapylton Pemberton. Not only was he the son of John Stapylton Grey Pemberton, barrister, MP, and Recorder for County Durham, but his family network included connections to the Indian Army. The Pembertons were major owners of mines and land in County Durham and overseas – rather more substantial than owning a threshing machine and breaking stones. R. L. S. Pemberton himself was educated at Eton and a graduate of New College, Oxford. Former employees from his family's coal mining interests probably served under him in 11th DLI.

If Clough and Pemberton were emblematic of the upper classes as they existed at the outbreak of war, Applegarth was more typical of the struggling lower end of the middle classes, who provided the substantial numbers of officers demanded by the size of the Army that eventually had to be built and replenished several times during the Great War. Despite their different starting points, however, all these young men had to prove themselves in action and work their way up according to their abilities. They were supplemented by men with strong connections to the Empire, such as William John Endean. Although born 1 April 1888 in St Austell, Cornwall, to a mine manager, Endean was educated both privately and at Grafton School, Auckland, New Zealand. At the time of his original enlistment he was working as a clerk in South Africa and initially joined the 3rd South African Infantry in 1915, before being sent to England for a commission.

If we look back across this mixture of experiences, both in the depth of detail accorded to my grandfather's kinship networks, and in the more summary descriptions of other families, we can detect something of the varied texture of life in the thirty years or so before the outbreak of the First World War. For working-class families the driving force was household survival in difficult economic circumstances, with minimal support from the state or employers, and a cultural dependency on kinship and local community. Of these two supports the former was the most vital, as communities were powerless in the face of the exigencies of trade and the decisions of businesses. The local community could do little to help the workers at Wilson Cammell & Company in Dronfield, in 1883, and the town suffered as a whole.

Periodic cyclical changes in economic circumstances rendered employment precarious, forcing families into recurrent poverty and the frequent need to move home, not just within the locality but much further afield. Individual men might choose to escape by joining the Army, but that strategy carried risks of its own. There was adventure, but there was the threat of injury, death and disease. Young women had fewer choices – domestic work was the most common source of income. Whether living in with employers or as daily domestics, there was the risk of sexual predation and its potential consequences. Life expectancy was not high and healthcare was frequently beyond the means of even the employed working classes. It was not uncommon for people to die before the age of fifty. This happened to both the wives of Thomas Bashforth senior, the first from consumption at the age of twenty-seven, the second from cancer of the liver at forty-six. He himself died at fifty-eight from a combination of pneumonia and congestion of the liver. Throughout all the vicissitudes of the life cycle it was the families that provided the support: accommodation when seeking work, despite aggravating the overcrowding; employment opportunities when previous means of earning a living declined; and care during illness, old age and in the event of single motherhood.

To understand the decision of young civilian men volunteering as soldiers in unprecedented numbers in 1914, it is helpful to appreciate the family backgrounds from which they came. For those who became officers, the opportunities for absorbing ideas about loyalty to a British imperial ideal were much stronger for men of their class, education and experience. Among recruits from all classes, the influences were possibly more personal and may have been more contingent on events. It is profitable to balance these influences with local and communal factors, especially the effects of compulsory education, to understand both why so many did volunteer, and why so many more did not. These influences, both in the decades before the war and at the time of its outbreak, will be the focus of the next chapter.

NOTES TO CHAPTER ONE

1   A number of recent academic studies have recognised the possibilities inherent in the use of family history methods. Tim Brennan suggested this in his chapter 'History, family, history' in *Seeing History: Public History in Britain Now*, edited by Hilda Kean, Paul Martin and Sally J. Morgan (Francis Boutle Publishers, London, 2000). Hilda Kean further developed the potential in *London Stories: Personal Lives, Public Histories* (Rivers Oram Press, London, 2004) and has encouraged this kind of work among her students at Ruskin College. Martin Bashforth has raised the possibilities of a collective approach to the use of family history techniques in the chapter 'Absent Fathers, Present Histories' in *People and their Pasts: Public History Today*, edited by Hilda Kean and Paul Ashton (Palgrave Macmillan, Basingstoke, 2009).

2   Details of the family's history have been obtained from the use of census material, and records of births, marriages and deaths, using standard genealogical methods. Table 1 at the end of this chapter provides a simplified illustration of the family connections related to Thomas Bashforth.

3   See J. Austin and M. Ford, *Steel Town: Dronfield and Wilson Cammell 1873–1883* (Sheffield, 1983), pp. 97–104, for details of the impact on the workforce.

4   Matthew Kelly remains unidentified in genealogical records. In 1891, there were a small number of families in Workington from the Isle of Man called Kelly, Kelley or Killey, including a nearby shopkeeper, but no members called Matthew.

5   See chapter 11. Following the publication of a memorial notice of Thomas Bashforth's death in the local press in 1918, the widow was visited by Kelly to offer support.

6   The National Archives, WO 97/3364.

7   As with many stories coming down the family line by hearsay, the story may be inaccurate in some of its details. At the time of the 1911 census, Edward McGlasson was still in Workington employed in the steelworks.

8   The house is as described by my father, Ray Bashforth.

9   *Census of England and Wales, 1911*, Table 10 (HMSO 1913).

10 Hall, 1913, p. 124.

11 A broad account of working-class family economy, especially among miners, is provided by José Harris, *Private Lives, Public Spirit: Britain 1870–1914* (Penguin Books, Harmondsworth, 1993), pp. 71–73.

12 Thompson, 1992, p. 32.

Table 1:
Family Trees Related to Thomas Bashforth

1.1 The family of Thomas Bashforth, born Sheffield 1831

Thomas Bashforth (1831–1889) = (1) 1852, Mary Brown, died 1859
- William, b. 1853, Barnsley
- James, b. 1856, Barnsley
                              = (2) 1869, Bridget McDonald, died 1884
- (James McDonald, b. 1863, previous marriage)
- Mary Ann, b. 1869, Barnsley
- **Ellen, b. 1871, Birmingham**
- Bridget, b. 1873, Sheffield Workhouse
- Matthew, b. 1876, Sheffield

1.2 The family of John McGlasson, born Carlisle 1865

Edward McGlasson = Margaret, died 1891
- James, b. 1857, Carlisle
- Betsy, b. 1861, Carlisle
- Jane, b. 1863, Carlisle
- **John, b. 1865, Carlisle**
- Mary, J. b. 1867, Carlisle
- Margaret, b. 1869, Carlisle
- Edward, b. 1872, Silloth
- Robert, b. 1874, Carlisle

1.3 The immediate family of Thomas Bashforth (1888–1918)

John McGlasson = 1892, Ellen Bashforth, died 1935
- **(Thomas Bashforth, b. 1888, illegitimate)**
- Laura, b. 1893, Workington
- Margaret Ellen (Maggie), b. 1895, Workington
- Dora, b. 1900, Byker
- Ellen Victoria Alexandra (Nellie), b. 1902, Gosforth
- Edward, b. 1908, Gosforth

CHAPTER TWO

For King and Country

If family and kinship provided the primary network of influences and support for the working classes in the early decades of the twentieth century, then the main secondary influence was the local community. This chapter will describe some of the internal dynamics of communities in County Durham in the early twentieth century and how these influenced the 1914 volunteers.

It has been suggested that the period between 1870 and 1914 was one in which working-class communities became more settled, and developed the sense of close-knit neighbourhoods that has popularly been regarded as typical and traditional.[1] The experience of families in the previous chapter does not entirely support this view. Movement remained a common feature throughout the period, whether over the longer distances followed by the Bashforths and McGlassons, the movement of collier families like the Bonneys from pit to pit within a region, or the movement of agricultural workers such as the Applegarths within a limited area of Teesdale. Migration does not preclude the formation of strong neighbourhood networks, but suggests there had to be influences at work of a more dynamic nature than confined geographical mobility.

There were such features among the Durham mining families who provided the bulk of recruits to 11th DLI. In general terms, the period from 1870 to 1914 saw a general increase in trade union membership, from approximately half a million to four million, with a corresponding increase in militancy. This was equally true of the miners, though in County Durham the culture and forms of organisation were peculiar to the region. The Durham Miners' Association developed within a society dominated by a few paternalistic, but occasionally ruthless, coal-owners and the pervasive influence of the Church, both the established Church centred on the Bishopric of Durham and the alternative influence of Methodism.[2] Union organisation was highly local, based on the independent lodge – the name itself indicating the concept of the mutual friendly society. The Lodge took its place alongside the Chapel, Church Mission, Co-operative store, Institute and other clubs and societies. These associations reflected the way in which the hewers banded into small teams of mates or 'marras', and their dependence on custom and practice. They were represented by the elected checkweighman, who was the go-between on rates and weights between men and employers. While families might, therefore, come and go, there was a strong, independently minded, traditionally organised social fabric within which the newcomer could earn their place. Though different in detail and kind, this was not different in principle from the working-class neighbourhood of the larger towns and cities, with its culture of behavioural standards, respectability and internal hierarchies of gossip and degrees of belonging.[3]

Other events and institutions would help cement these social networks. In 1912, the Durham pits played a significant role in a national strike. The dispute, over the minimum wage, was resolved through political reform. Of more general significance was the solidarity around smaller, more local disputes over working conditions. The Durham Miners' Association owed its origins to the collective struggle of local lodges against the system of annual bonded service that previously characterised the Durham pits. The annual Big Meeting, when the lodges gathered in Durham City with parades, family fun and friendly rivalry, was as much a celebration of working-class freedom as of communal pride.[4] Alongside such celebratory examples of solidarity was the response to the ever-present dangers of pit life. Accidents were commonplace, mostly affecting one or two men at a time and not always fatal. In the ten years preceding the outbreak of the First World War, the Durham pits suffered 26 dead at Wingate Grange in 1906, 14 dead at the Glebe Pit near Washington in 1908, and the disaster at West Stanley in 1909 in which 168 men lost their lives. It is an interesting feature of Wingate village today that the 26 men who died in the pit disaster are commemorated on a highly visible roadside memorial, while the 137 men who lost their lives in the war are remembered on a plaque inside the church opposite, now frequently locked and with its windows grilled against vandalism; yet there are family names that link the two.[5] This suggests that the community took greater pride in the local pit disaster, something more unique to their experience, than in the casualties of a war they shared with neighbouring villages.

Less easy to identify with empirical evidence are the looser influences of neighbouring families in the same street, families overlapping through intermarriage and the normal friendships among men, women and children that characterised the day-to-day relationships within a community. These everyday bonds are a feature of reminiscences about growing up in working-class communities. Sid Chaplin's memories of south-west Durham focused on the cheaply constructed houses, the shared sanitation, the epidemics of childhood diseases, the constant battle by the women for cleanliness, and, above all, the outdoor community of street life, gossip and games played by adults (usually associated with petty gambling) and children. It was an experience he described in tones of ambivalence, describing it on the one hand as 'sufficient' but also as 'insular', a culture in which you were simultaneously embraced and imprisoned.[6]

With the introduction of compulsory schooling for children from 1870, education became a major influence on the way people grew up and on their thinking. The state could imbue a captive population with its dominant ideology of empire. Conventionally, the period before 1914 is regarded as the high point of the British Empire. Its values are assumed to be shared across the classes. What is perhaps not readily appreciated is the extent to which the sense of Imperial might was a fairly recent cultural construction. Before 1870, the monarchy was not especially popular, Queen Victoria having largely cut herself off from society following the death of Prince Albert. The ideological concept of Empire was cultivated by Disraeli and the associated pomp and circumstance grew significantly in the period between the declaration of Victoria as Queen Empress of India and the outbreak of war in 1914. High points were the Jubilee celebrations, the Boer War (especially the relief of Mafeking), the Delhi Durbar of 1911 and, as a last gasp, the call to arms of autumn 1914.

The extent to which imperial ideals influenced popular thinking prior to 1914 is still a matter of fierce debate. There were contrary movements – aspects of the Boer War were controversial and the issue of Home Rule for Ireland posed a threat to the fragile status quo, while the organised working classes flexed their industrial muscle in a wave of militancy, perceived by some as potentially revolutionary. But none of this found much of a unifying political philosophy. Socialism had little hold on working-class thought, except in a few isolated areas. The recently formed Labour Party and the trade unions tended to be pragmatic rather than ideological; Durham miners in particular were slow to switch from voting Liberal to Labour until after the war. Imperial ideals of superiority and beneficence were inculcated in schools and the mass media. The sense of British superiority was made manifest in London and other big cities, in the form of a wave of splendid building. However, little of this is likely to have penetrated to the industrial villages of Durham like Brandon Colliery or Stillington, and probably not far into the consciousness of school children in particular. While one recent study of the cultural influence of the elementary school on working-class children has demonstrated how schools consciously sought to inculcate ideas about the superiority of the Anglo-Saxon race and their elevated place in the world, actual evidence of the processes involved and above all the level of success are hard to prove.[7]

One particular example of how those who propounded the imperialist message sought to gain an influence on the mind of children was the Earl of Meath's Empire Day Movement. From 1902, the movement attempted to establish the celebration of Empire Day annually on 24 May, particularly targeting schools. Evidence from school log books in County Durham would suggest that success was limited. School log books were sometimes rather cryptic summaries of points of interest, more often filled in weekly than daily, paying little attention to curriculum matters as opposed to absent teachers, epidemics and inspections. But some contain indications of the relative significance of Empire Day. From 1902 to 1910, years in which the younger volunteers of 1914 attended school and might have been influenced by the propaganda aspects of Empire Day, the celebration frequently fell on weekends or during the Whitsuntide holiday break. In 1906, it coincided with Ascension Day, when the many Church-run schools considered the religious celebration to be of more significance. In 1910, the date fell close to the funeral of King Edward VII on 20 May, which would have provided its own patriotic context. For simple practical reasons, Empire Day was frequently not part of the school experience.

Between 1904 and 1910, the log book for Chester-le-Street Victoria Boys National School mentions the celebration on only two occasions. In 1907, the log book records: 'Today being Empire Day appropriate Reading, History, Geography, Composition, Moral Lessons and Scripture Lessons were given in all classes and the National Anthem sung.' This was a Friday, as was the second mention in 1908 when Empire Day fell during the following weekend. There is a detailed description of how the local community became involved.

> Sunday next being Empire Day I gave an address to the whole school on the lines suggested by the Earl of Meath in pamphlets, &c. The Map of the Empire was displayed on the wall of the Central Room, flanked by portraits of the King and Queen (kindly presented by Mr Black, Manager of the Co-operative Stores). The Union Jack was described as in Baden-Powell's *Scouting*. The size and extent of the Empire was given and the responsibilities and duties of a British Citizen inculcated broadly, and the National Anthem took the place of the evening hymn. On Monday all lessons will be made to bear on the subject of Empire.[8]

There was, however, no mention at all in the log books for Castle Eden National Boys School (available to 1906), Brandon Church of England School (between 1906 and 1914), Evenwood Church of England Junior School, Consett British Mixed School or Wheatley Hill Infants School.[9] Brandon school log book did mention Empire Day during the war itself, in 1916, but only to say that there would be no alteration to the timetable. At Consett, because of the proximity of the Whitsun holidays, the head teacher regretted the impossibility of keeping the children in school in the afternoons, when the circus was in town. The occasional school made reference to having an afternoon off for Royal Oak Day on 29 May, which had officially ceased to be a recognised holiday in 1859, but obviously retained some local significance.[10]

Easington Church of England Infants School came late to the celebration of Empire Day, but showed that even the youngest could be involved. In 1908, the children were given a holiday for Empire Day.[11] On 25 May 1917, it was recorded that 'yesterday being Empire Day, appropriate little talks with the children took place'. By 1918, there was a more evident curricular interest at the school when the log book noted that 'being Empire Day the children wore their Overseas Club Flags and sang two Patriotic Songs'. It was similar at Shotton Colliery Council Boys School. The first mention in the school log book was 24 May 1911, when it fell midweek: 'special lessons on our Empire, Patriotism etc are being given today to all our classes'. Special lessons for Empire Day were not mentioned again until 1916.[12]

From such a small sample of an incomplete record it is possible only to derive very provisional conclusions. Empire Day itself played a small part in inculcating an imperial ideology into young children's heads before the Great War. Nevertheless, schools seem to have felt that it was part of their duty to encourage thoughts about Empire and patriotism. Size of school, age range or relationship to the established Church did not seem to matter. In some cases, as at Easington, the organisation of children into Overseas Clubs to encourage an interest in the Empire and Dominions seems to have been part of an all-year-round activity. What is perhaps more certain is that this celebration was probably too sporadic and ill-organised before 1914 to have had much impact on the mindset of potential recruits, particularly the younger volunteers and conscripts who might have been exposed to it. If such young men were motivated by some form of 'Imperial Ideology', then it derived from more general cultural influences than school activities alone.

For older recruits schooled before the celebration of Empire Day there may nevertheless have been influences from within the family, as well as the more generally pervasive background culture. Thomas Bashforth may have been influenced by his stepfather, John McGlasson, who had served as a regular soldier in the outposts of Empire. He was not alone in that respect among 11th DLI recruits. William Bennett was the father of Robert Bennett, whose letters provide insight into the early months of the battalion,[13] and his military record shows that he served in the Army from 1885 until 1897, including a spell in the Indian subcontinent, in which he received the India General Service Medal with Burma Clasp.

Perhaps what guided men to join the Army in 1914 was less educational conditioning than immediate events and contingent influences around the time that war was declared. Throughout July 1914, the front pages of the *Northern Echo* followed the darkening series of events that threatened war. Despite some foreboding, the summer bank holiday on Monday 3 August went on as normal. Many people enjoyed the fine weather at the seaside and in country beauty spots. Tuesday's paper listed the local Members of Parliament who were liable to be called up for war service as officer reservists and speculated on what that might mean to the parliamentary processes.

Late July was the traditional time for the Territorial Army training camps. Membership of Territorial Army units was popular among young working-class men, attracted less by patriotism than by the social life, physical fun and excitement, parading around in uniform and a general reinforcement of masculinity.[14] The Territorial units of the Durham Light Infantry were in camp in North Wales for their annual fifteen days' training. The 5th Battalion was at Deganwy with the York and Durham Brigade, while the 6th, 7th and 8th Battalions were at Conwy. Newspaper reports on Tuesday 4 August described a flurry of activity at Territorial Army camps. The Durham Territorials at Conwy Camp were woken with reveille at 4 a.m. and quickly organised on to special trains. Chester station saw sixty of these pass through by 4 p.m. the same day. The 5th Battalion, which included many Darlington men, was recalled to its Stockton base on 3 August and sent to dig coastal defences at Hartlepool and the South Gore, before gathering at a training camp at Ravensworth Park near Gateshead. The 6th Battalion went into camp at Bishop Auckland, the 7th at Sunderland, the 8th at Durham and the 9th at Gateshead.[15] Closer to Darlington there was a parallel mobilisation. The 2nd Brigade of the Duke of Wellington's West Riding Territorial Regiment had been at camp near Marske. From here, more than 3,000 men were shipped out through Saltburn station, using specially commissioned rolling stock. There were similar scenes at Scarborough further down the coast, where the West Riding Brigade was stationed.

Enthusiasm for the war in Darlington was muted and patchy. Old soldiers and reservists found their way to recruiting offices. The St John's Ambulance and Red Cross teams held meetings to discuss what they should do. The newspapers reported concerns about the impact on the Tyne coal trade and fears for ships already en route across the North Sea towards German ports. The Kingston Unity of Oddfellows passed a resolution deploring 'the present agitation and unrest in Europe'. A huge meeting addressed by Keir Hardie in Trafalgar Square was reported and illustrated, alongside photos of the Royal Naval Reserve being mobilised. The *Northern Echo* for Wednesday 5 August reported the declaration of war on the front page and covered a meeting of 1,000 protestors in Darlington Market Place the previous evening, called by Darlington Trades Council. W. G. Loraine of the National Union of Railwaymen had moved a moderately worded motion urging the government to maintain British neutrality. Crowds cheered on troops as they were mobilised and the Darlington Territorials were pictured in Wednesday's paper on their way to the station, while Thursday's edition suggested that Darlington was calm with no demonstrations of war fever. Bank Top station coped with trainloads of troops and reservists, along with 300 men of the 2nd Northumbrian Royal Army Medical Corps, by restricting civilian passengers to a single file at the ticket barriers. The sports page of the newspaper featured the beginning of what became a long discussion on whether or not to cancel the football leagues.

By Friday 7 August, the headline reports suggested the Germans were being severely battered on sea and on land: an impression which was to continue for weeks under the effect of censorship, regardless of the realities. On Saturday 8 August, there was even a report that the Germans had asked for a truce. Meanwhile the local Labour Party announced that it was abandoning peace meetings, while a letter from the Territorials Association asked for patience from would-be volunteers awaiting a response from their applications, as they were overwhelmed with the workload. The seemingly unhurried local process to recruit volunteers can be seen by the front-page report of the *Northern Echo* on Saturday 8 August, which stated:

> Recruiting has been progressing busily in Darlington since Wednesday for on each of the last three days about ten men have been enrolled among the Regulars. The recruiting sergeant told our representative last night that had he had assistance in his work he would have been able to have enlisted twice or even thrice times that number. No recruiting is at present being sought in respect of the local Territorial force.

Meanwhile, half of the back page carried a 'Message from the Society of Friends' addressed to 'Men and Women of Goodwill in the British Empire' still expressing hope for a peaceful resolution.

The Territorial battalions were not called upon to volunteer for foreign service until 15 September, so early recruitment in the Darlington area concentrated on bringing back experienced and trained soldiers for the Regular Army. The front page of the *Northern Echo* on Monday 10 August carried the following notice:

> An officer of the 5th Durham Light Infantry will attend at the Drill Hall, Darlington, tonight between seven and nine o'clock to enlist men willing to serve in the above regiment. Only men with four years' service between the ages of 18 and 35, and who are in possession of their discharge certificates, can be taken.

By way of encouragement, the Darlington company of the National Reserve, consisting of about 150–200 men, paraded in the streets, among them Private J. Pottage of 52 Dodd Street wearing his South African War medals.

Lord Kitchener, not content with the slow progress of recruitment, decided to bypass the cumbersome processes of the locally based Territorial units. As early as 7 August 1914, he published his first appeal for 100,000 volunteers to be recruited directly into the Regular Army to form a Second Army (the so-called K1 battalions). Second and third appeals followed on 28 August and 13 September. The process of involving the local public was slow. On Friday 14 August, a reader employing the pseudonym '*Ich Dien*' complained in the letters column of the *Northern Echo* that he had tried to enlist under Kitchener's call at Darlington, but had been told that 'no official orders had been received from the War Office to that effect' and that he would have to travel elsewhere in the county to enlist. On the other hand, a Distress Committee had been formed to assist soldier's wives and families as a result of the loss of their men's incomes. From Monday 17 August, newspaper advertisements called on women to knit 'Soldier's Nightcaps' and by the following Saturday 'huge stocks of flannel helmets' were reported to have been collected.

Occasionally, reports in the newspaper suggested that the French and British forces were not having things their own way, but the overwhelming majority of reports gave the impression of rousing victories in the field. While on Wednesday 12 August, the newspaper reported a disaster to a French division in Alsace, Friday's headline was, 'Allied Armies Making a Clean Sweep in Belgium. German Troops in Full Retreat.' Gradually, during the third week of war the mood and tone of newspaper reports became more alarming. On Thursday 20 August, under a banner headline that the 'Kaiser Gives the Order for a General Advance', appeared the first reports of local British casualties: two officers and one man dead. By

Friday, 'Belgian Capital Occupied by German Troops' was the banner, and on Saturday, 'Germany Demands £8,000,000 War Levy from Brussels.' Reports of alleged German atrocities had begun to appear. The *Northern Echo* itself began advertising for subscriptions to its forthcoming *War Book of Facts* for 2s 9d. The mood was becoming more serious, reflecting the growing realities of the situation.

Only in the fourth week did local recruitment of Kitchener's volunteers gather pace. On Monday 24 August, a full-page advertisement for the Middlesbrough Recruiting Area appeared on page three of the *Northern Echo*, while page eight carried a smaller advertisement from the Newcastle recruiting office. These were repeated throughout the week. While the headlines continued to present an upbeat attitude, the news itself belied the spin. On Tuesday, British Forces were in a 'Great Battle on the Belgian Frontier', on Wednesday they were displaying 'Splendid Marksmanship at Mons', while on Thursday a mixture of headlines included 'Germans Occupy Lille', 'Three French Towns Said to be Taken' and 'Staggering Rumour of Enemy's Advance'. The *Echo Book of Facts* was published the same day. The war came even closer to home on the Friday when it was reported that five ships had been blown up by German mines off the mouth of the Tyne. Despite 'British Soldier's Valour Withstands All German Assaults', the precarious state of the Allied forces in Belgium and France was beginning to penetrate the official censorship.

Friday 28 August saw the first attempts towards general recruitment in Darlington. A small advertisement appeared on page two, announcing that the Earl of Durham was to address a mass meeting in the Market Square on Saturday 29 August at 6.30 p.m. and calling on 'every young man who can' to join now for the period of the war. Tucked away on the letters page was an appeal from George G. Plant, '(Late) 1st Volunteer Battalion Durham Light Infantry and Supervising Recruiting Darlington and District, at the Recruiting Office, Prebend Row, Darlington,' asking 'Is Darlington Patriotic?'

Sir – There must be hundreds if not thousands of men in Darlington and district of suitable age for the most part unmarried and without grave responsibility.

With a view to bringing home to such that their country needs them urgently, I have been instructed by the representatives of the War Office to arrange on short notice the biggest possible meeting to awaken the citizens of Darlington to the gravity of the present position and the need for men.

A mass meeting will therefore be held in the Market-place, Darlington, at 6.30 on Saturday evening next, when his Worship the Mayor of

Darlington, will, as chief citizen, preside, and the meeting will be addressed by the Earl of Durham as Lord Lieutenant of the county.

All public men who have already been approached and are able to do so have promised to support his Worship and the Earl of Durham on the platform. As the arrangements for the meeting have had to be made at a few hours notice, it is desirable that those wishing to take their places on the platform will send their names to me at the above address at once so that arrangements may be made, as far as possible, for their accommodation and that the platform may be worthy of the occasion.

I am persuaded that when the gravity of the situation, and the urgent need of men is made clear, an appeal of this kind to the loyalty and patriotism of Darlington will not be made in vain.

The *Northern Echo* headlines on the morning of Saturday 29 August once again put a positive spin on events. The primary headline featured the sinking of two German cruisers and two destroyers by the British Fleet, while secondary headlines reinforced this impression with 'British Fleet Win First Sea Fight' and 'British Army Holds Up Enemy'.

The public meeting in Darlington Market Place that evening was designed to stir up emotions. Proceedings were opened by Revd J. A. G. Birch, chaplain to the local Territorials, with the hymn 'O Lord our help in ages past', accompanied by the Cockerton Silver Band. The Mayor, Councillor J. G. Harbottle, and the Earl of Durham made speeches, while every conceivable local dignitary and personality was on the platform to lend their support. The Mayor warned that atrocities being committed in Belgium might one day be committed in the peaceful town of Darlington and proclaimed to the young men of the town that 'it is time you left your cinemas and your football: your duty is not there, your duty is on the tented field'. Loud cheers met his call for volunteers. The Earl of Durham declared that only the gallant action of the British Fleet in the Straits of Dover and the small Army in France had so far averted the threat of invasion. He called upon everyone 'to use all the influence in your power with your relatives and friends and those whom you see hanging back and induce them at this grave crisis to come forward in the service of their country'. Other speakers followed, each met with cheers. Mr A. F. Pease assured married men that their wives and families would be looked after. Colonel Sir Mark Sykes claimed that this was a 'sacred war, a crusade in the service of mankind'. George Beadle, professing to be no lover of militarism, urged workers to rise up for liberty against 'one of the greatest tyrants that ever lived' and 'do your duty, face the foe, and if you die, then die like men and not like cowards'.

It was announced that both the council chamber and the recruiting office in Prebend Row were open to take volunteers and, with the singing of the

National Anthem, the meeting was closed. Monday's paper reported that a hundred men had enlisted after the meeting. Volunteering continued for several days afterwards. It was commented on Tuesday 1 September that this had dispelled any 'adverse reflection at the part Darlington has begun to play in the recruiting field'. By contrast, a similar meeting in the city of York's Guildhall was reported as having missed the opportunity to recruit hundreds, as no facilities were made available and no spontaneous call was made.[16]

Thomas Bashforth answered the call for volunteers at the Darlington meeting on 29 August 1914, and was assigned to the Durham Light Infantry as number 14956. His attestation form records that he was precisely 25 years and 322 days old, a plasterer and had inhabited rateable property for at least a year. He was married, had not been apprenticed and had not been imprisoned. He was not already or previously a member of the armed services, nor had he been rejected as unfit for military service. He was willing to be vaccinated and to be enlisted for General Service. He signed, agreeing to serve for three years or the duration and took the oath:

> I, Thomas Bashforth, swear by Almighty God, that I will be faithful and bear true allegiance to His Majesty King George the Fifth, His Heirs and Successors, in Person, Crown and dignity against all enemies, and will observe and obey all orders of His Majesty, His Heirs and Successors and of the Generals and Officers set over me. So help me God.

Among the several witnesses to his signature was that of the Justice of the Peace, Alderman Leach.

The inside sheet of the same form contains several hieroglyphic references to other Army forms dated 1918, concerning the process of documentation following his eventual death. Dying was of course something he did not agree to when he signed up, any more than other volunteers. It may have crossed his mind, but we have no means of knowing. Although it was not until the day after Thomas had signed up that the *Sunday Times* and the *Mail* broke the news that the British Expeditionary Force was in headlong retreat after the Battle of Mons, it is more than probable that rumours were already spreading and public concern growing. The simple accumulation of reports of what was happening will have built up a level of general excitement, curiosity and anxiety.

If we do not know about his thoughts and reasons on signing up, we do know something of Thomas' physical condition. On 31 August, still in Darlington, he was subjected to a medical. According to Army Form B178, we find him to have been 5 feet 4¾ inches tall, weighing 119 lb, with a

33-inch chest fully expanded from its basic 31 inches. He was described as having good physical development with a pulse rate of seventy-five. He had three vaccination marks in his right arm dating from his infancy. He had perfect vision in both eyes and no marks that might suggest any 'congenital peculiarities or previous disease'. He was described as having a fresh complexion, brown eyes and light brown hair, no distinguishing marks and adhering to the Church of England. He was certified fit for service from a medical point of view, fit for service from a military point of view by the recruiting officer, and the process of completing all the correct forms for enlistment was approved by a captain. From that day forward he was a private soldier, duly posted. The process had taken two days.

On the evening of 31 August, after the medicals, there was a smoking concert for the new recruits, held at the Temperance Hall, presided over by Mr J. F. Latimer. The management of the Empire Cinema provided film views of the war and songs were contributed by numerous artistes. The men were given pipes, tobacco and cigarettes, and were sent off to the singing of 'It's a long, long way to Tipperary' and the National Anthem.

Nationally recruitment had been rising on a steady curve since the first week in August, though at a level lower than originally required. By the time of Darlington's recruiting campaign, only some 80,000 men had enlisted rather than the 100,000 called for. Those encouraged by patriotic appeals or personal feelings and circumstances alone in these early weeks may have included men like Thomas Bashforth, but their numbers were to be dwarfed in the following two weeks. Almost 180,000 men enlisted during the week after 30 August, before voluntary recruitment dropped back to a steady average of 20,000 a week.

It is difficult to explain this extraordinary peak without firsthand knowledge of the individual motives of the volunteers. Attempts have been made to provide assessments from statistical data, linked for example to unemployment statistics and low pay rates.[17] Undoubtedly trade was hit at the start of the war and there were threats of lay-offs, while prices rose by 10 per cent. Propaganda became fierce and peer group pressure would have been considerable, especially in larger firms or in smaller communities such as pit villages. Set against this were fears of the unknown as well as problems about making ends meet for families on Army pay, evidenced by the local campaigns to get employers to assist wives and families of recruits and the setting up of Distress Committees.

That men discussed the issue both among their mates and with their immediate families we may take for granted, but we must equally assume that arguments went in both directions. There is evidence of what might have been discussed, to be found in some of the attestation forms from County Durham. The phenomenon is most noticeable at Brandon Colliery where a number of men altered the declaration on the attestation form. Typical of these was Lance Corporal 15313 James Brown who enlisted at Brandon on 28 August 1914. The amendment to the declaration was as follows:

> For a term of three years, ~~unless the War lasts longer than three years, in which case you will be retained until the War is over.~~ If employed with Hospitals, depots of Mounted Units, and as Clerks, etc., you may be retained after the termination of hostilities until your services can be spared, but such retention shall in no case exceed six months.

The section struck through was amended to read: 'If however the war is over in less than 3 years you will be discharged with all convenient speed.'

The war lasted longer than three years, some such signatories lost their lives in the meantime, and it is doubtful what validity the alteration would have had.[18] However, it illustrates discussion among the men about the implications of volunteering, including, perhaps, the influence of local union leaders and the lack of deference to authority that characterised the Durham pitmen. While more common among surviving attestation forms from Brandon men, it was not restricted to them. Lance Corporal 16268 John George Dobson from Stanley also altered the terms of engagement in this way when he enlisted on 28 August 1914. These men were not prepared to sign away their freedom totally.

While it is remarkable that about 25 per cent of available men did volunteer, it is important to recognise that 75 per cent did not. It may suggest that the early peak in recruitment reflected a concentrated burst of propaganda, linked to short-term economic uncertainties, combined with a working-class conviction in the values of fair play and a desire to help out in time of collective crisis. In these early weeks of September, the truth about what was happening to the British Army, in full retreat from Mons, was finally acknowledged in public. An instinctive sense of solidarity was awakened among those responsive to such feelings, but, for the majority, the priority remained to make ends meet and leave the adventuring to others. The decision to volunteer may have been influenced by peer groups, by local community pressures, or by any number of contributory factors, but it remained personal.

NOTES TO CHAPTER TWO

1   See for example, Andrew August, *The British Working-Class 1832–1940* (Pearson Longman, Harlow, 2007).

2   Beynon and Austin, 1994.

3   August, 2007, pp. 95–96.

4   Grodnitzky, 2005, University of York (unpublished thesis).

5   There are five matching surnames and a definite family link can be established between Thomas Pace of 5th DLI, killed in action aged twenty-one in 1917, and his great uncle Henry Pace, killed in the Wingate Grange explosion in 1906 aged forty-six.

6   Chaplin, 1971.

7   Heathorn, 2000.

8   Durham County Records Office, D/X 1053/3, School Log Book, Chester-le-Street Victoria Boys National School, 1903–1931. Entry for 22 May 1908.

9   Durham County Records Office, School Log Books, respective references: E/E2, E/C7, E/SW49, E/SW/C35, E/NW8, E/E81.

10 Royal Oak Day was established in 1664 by Charles II to celebrate the restoration of the monarchy and his hiding in an oak tree at Boscobel in 1651 after the Battle of Worcester.

11 Durham CRO, E/E50, School Log Book, Easington Church of England Infants School.

12 Durham CRO, E/E74, School Log Book, Shotton Colliery Council Boys' School.

13 See chapters 3 to 6.

14 August, 2007, p. 151.

15 Ward, 1962. Chapter X.

16 All quotations are from the *Northern Echo* for Monday 31 August 1914.

17 Statistics and some of this discussion are based on an article in Midland History, vol. 24, pp. 167–186 (University of Birmingham, 1999). John Hartigan, *Volunteering in the First World War: The Birmingham Experience, August 1914–May 1915.*

18 Private 16233 John James Cornish died of a gunshot wound to the head on 11 September 1916. He also altered his attestation form on 31 August 1914 at Brandon Colliery.

CHAPTER THREE

From Civilian to Soldier

The military historian John Bourne has commented that: 'The British soldier of the Great War was essentially the British working man in uniform.'[1] Somehow, this complex variety of working men had to be transformed into individuals approaching the standards, values, professionalism and discipline of what had previously been essentially a colonial police force, and then fit them for what would become a new form of industrial warfare. Bourne has argued that the process, though it took years to complete, was eminently successful, transforming both the men (including more or less unwilling conscripts) and the Army itself. The early training of 11th DLI illustrates many features of the process. A remarkable set of letters written home to his family by a former Durham miner provides an intimate insight into the process of this transformation of himself and his comrades.

Recruitment outstripped resources. The main depot for the DLI was at Fenham Barracks, Newcastle-upon-Tyne, but it was unable to cope with the influx of recruits. Local landowners and businesses offered space for accommodation and training: Lord Durham at Cocken Hall and the Co-operative Society in West Hartlepool. The *Northern Echo* for Wednesday, 3 September reported Mr Ernest W. Ormston's efforts to raise a 'Pal's Battalion' based on the North Eastern Railway Company's Wagon Works. The rate of recruitment into the DLI accelerated during late August and the early weeks of September. The first batch of Kitchener recruits left Newcastle on 22 August to become the 500-strong core of the 10th (Service) Battalion at Woking, attached to the new 14th Division. They were quickly joined by further detachments to make up the full battalion strength of just over 1,000 men. Enough for two battalions had been recruited by the end of the month, many of these eventually forming the 11th Battalion. A further 2,180 men left Newcastle on 16 September to

Pirbright, to make up the 12th and 13th Battalions. On 21 September, 710 men left, to be later joined on 24 September by 400 more to form the 14th Battalion. The Surrey area was overwhelmed with new armies, so the 15th Battalion assembled at Halton Park near Aylesbury in Buckinghamshire from 26 September to 1 October with a further 1,040 men. Some, including Thomas Bashforth, remained in Durham before joining the 16th and 17th training battalions near Rugeley in Staffordshire. Within six weeks over 6,000 men from County Durham had been assigned to new army battalions.[2]

It was easier to get men to volunteer than it was to get uniforms and equipment, or experienced officers to provide training. Many in the ranks were pitmen and other specialised manual workers, hard-working, but independent-minded and possessed of a sense of their own rights. Typically, the Kitchener battalions were brought together under the command of a mixture of retired veterans and serving officers. There were more than 500 of the latter home on leave from India who were quickly commandeered to help form the new units.[3] Colonel G. M. Davison had retired from command of 2nd DLI in 1906, and now took over the 11th Battalion with only three experienced officers to assist him. One of these was Lieutenant Geoffrey Hayes from the 1st Battalion DLI, on home leave from India at the outbreak of war. He was assigned to the 11th Battalion as adjutant. Not even the colonel had a uniform and he began drilling the men dressed in a suit and bowler hat. This probably added to the difficulties of instilling serious army culture into the civilian recruits.

One of these recruits was Robert David Bennett, a pitman from Shotton Colliery, who wrote more than eighty letters home to his family. Born 1 June 1894, Robert came originally from Llanberis in North Wales and was the son of Catherine and William Bennett.[4] His father had been a regular soldier and had served in Burma, before becoming a miner. In 1903, the family left Wales, first to Lancashire and then to Shotton Colliery in County Durham. William was somewhat authoritarian and Robert tended to be closer to his mother. When he was old enough, Robert too went down the pit. The family story is that Robert joined up when a recruiting van turned up at the pit head at the end of a shift. Though his father considered him too gentle for the Army, Robert was one of those who signed up on the spot. Private 17203 Bennett attested on 1 September 1914 before Captain H. B. Ostler and was assigned for training with 11th DLI, serving with D Company.

Robert's letters are full of the novelties that were the common experience of thousands of new recruits in their new surroundings. His first letter home was sent from tents at Inkerman Barracks, Woking, in Surrey, where the 11th Battalion was first billeted.

Private Robert Bennett, the letter
writer, during training, 1915.
(*Collection of G. Greenwood*)

Dear Mam and Dad

I am now close against Aldershot we came here on Saturday we were 1½
hours in the train. I have seen Humphres down here also Knocker Surtees
and Harry Williams. Humphres is a lance corporal and Harry Williams
as well. We are well off as regards food we get tinned Salmon sardines
Herrings we have had no pay yet, it is a good [job] I took the four bob
what Dick West gave me. There is some more coming from Newcastle
because they are putting new tents up. It is full of orchards here and we
are sick of apples pears and plums the toffs stand at the gates and hand
these out. We get plenty of drill from 6 in the morning till 7 at night
the old soldiers say we are doing a weeks drill in a day. I believe we are
stopping here for 13 weeks then going to Malta or Giblarlter it hot down
here like being in a furnace. Humphres told me to tell me dad that he
was asking after him. We have not had our uniform yet but we have had
a pair of dawres like dads and a shirt to change and two pairs of socks
but these home boots is giving me gip yours with love

R. Bennett

The letter illustrates the sense of improvisation and the speed with which
recruitment was pushing the logistics of training, equipping, feeding and
paying the new army.[5] It picks up on the novelty of the area, populated

by 'toffs' with southern accents, and the natural instinct to keep in touch with pals from home. His second letter, written on YMCA paper, mentions the gradual process of being kitted out and the rumours about where they might be going. The importance of the postal services is very apparent, as is the possibility of meeting other recruits from home stationed nearby.

Dear Mam and Dad
I am writing to tell you that there is a parcel on the rail I have only sent the jacket and muffler I got a jacket and a shirt off a lad in our tent. The coat might fit me dad there is nothing to pay on the parcel because the clerk in the parcel office at Woking station said so. We had to burn all our other clothes. I believe we are to be vacsinated next week or something of the sort to gaurd against enteric fever. I forgot to tell you that I have never had the letter you sent to Newcastle some lads have had letter from Newcastle. How is Peggy going on now I bet she would not know me now.[6] Our Leutenant is mad to go to the front because he has a brother there he says we will not go to Malta and such places the terriers are going there.[7] The 12th and 13th Battalions are camped about 2 miles from here against Bisley rifle range I am send you 3/1 P.O. and a penny stamp I bet this crosses your letter again I have no more news to tell you this time with love to all
yours with love
R. D. Bennett
P.S. I am afriad I am a poor letter writer
xxxxxxxxxxxx

Pay during training did not stretch very far. Recruits were charged for laundry facilities and for at least some meals. Support from home was absolutely essential to raise the men's spirits.

Dear Mam and Dad
I am writing in answer to your letter. I got a letter from Emrys with 2 post cards in with his photo in. I am sending them to you and I sending you the photo of my mate he is a nice lad a tetotalar like me. He belongs to Barnsley by rights but was at Stanley when he enlisted[8] they are all nice lads in our tent. There is one from Newcastle a Scotch lad he is always getting hampers sent him from his uncle at Newcastle what has plenty of money and he shares them round the tent. I think it is cheaper to get the clothes washed here all the Company washing goes to-gether it costs me 4 pence to get me socks shirt drawers and towel thats a penny each. We get a change every week so it would amount to more if I sent it to you, the postage there and back I mean. I kept the cakes for tea and I

wrote the last letter before I got the tabs[9] and I thank you for them now. We have plenty of blankets one on the boards and 3 on top of us we are as warm as toast at night. theres been a lot of wives been here this last week from Newcastle. There husbands are National Reserve men[10] and they have just had there £10-0-0. I am sending you the photo of my mate with this letter. I have benn nockilated it's a sort of vacsination. Its in the breast. We get 48 off after we get done. Some of them have been very bad but I have champion to some of them. It leaves no sort of mark after it, you cannot see nothing now and I only got done on Thursday. you feel bad just like I was after I got my arm put right. They are only paying 2 and 3 shillings a week now you have not much left after you pay for washing and 2d for supper every night. I must finish now with love to all.

yours with love, R. D. Bennett

Training was largely improvised. Inexperienced officers might use a manual and swot up in advance of attempting to deliver instruction. Old sweats used methods more appropriate to the South African veldt. Drill and exercise was a daily feature, as much to keep recruits active as to instil some element of military discipline. Until rifles were issued in adequate numbers, musketry took second place. Everybody got plenty of experience digging trenches, holes and making rudimentary fortifications. An elementary defensive practice at this stage, by the end of the war trench-making was a skilled craft in its own right.[11]

Crucial to the training and development of infantrymen were the non-commissioned officers, who spent most of their time in direct association with the private soldiers. How men were found in the early days varied according to circumstances. Any reservists or retired veterans would be useful in the first instance. Many were simply chosen from those who were prepared to volunteer, almost as they arrived at the training camps. Robert Bennett's first letter refers to two of his pals being promoted to lance corporal. According to Bennett family stories, one of these, whom Robert referred to as 'Humphres', who survived the war and returned to Shotton Colliery, was regarded as being something of a 'wide boy' and would therefore have instinctively sought out his own benefit. Married men with children might volunteer for promotion to earn an extra few pennies, and that might have influenced my grandfather, Thomas Bashforth, while still at his first depot in Barnard Castle, before he was posted to the 16th Battalion. Although his experience as a plasterer had taught him to conserve his own effort, it is difficult to see how that might have prepared him to handle new recruits in the mass, especially men from highly unionised backgrounds, such as miners.

Sergeants of 10th and 11th DLI at Woking, September 1914. (*DLI Trust and Durham CRO, Reference D/DLI 2/10/10(1)*)

Much of the training concentrated on drill and in time the men began to take a pride even in this routine. A visit by Kitchener seems to have impressed Private Bennett, as did the prospect of a royal visit, though he expressed concerns about pay and food.

Dear Mam and Dad
I am writing to thank you for the parcel of cakes they are nice. I am sorry I cant send you anything this weekend I did not get much pay they say that it will be settled at the quarters end. I sent the pictorial letter yesterday and I got the letter and the parcel this morning as I said, I sent a letter to Nain and I got a parcel of cigarettes and a letter by return of post, I am sending their letter to see who is the other lad besides Emrys I don't know him. I sent a letter to Emrys at Southampton I have not had an answer yet. The King and Queen are coming here on Tuesday to inspect us, Kitchener was here yesterday and said the Durhams were the steadiest on parade. There were about 8 different Batallions of different regiments so it gives us a good name. Humphres is cook here now over the D Company cooks he must have plenty of money I was talking to him the other day when a chap come to him and asked for the lend of 2 bob and he asked me did I want anything but I had a shilling myself he

says his wife got £5-10-0 from the War Office the other day. It is very hot
here now but chilly at night.
I am
yours with love
R. D. Bennett

However, food seems to have been much more of a comforting
preoccupation than good words from those on high, closely followed by
contact with family and the prospect of a trip home.

Dear Mam
I am writing in answer to your letter I got today. I am very sorry to
hear that little Mary is bad I hope she is a lot better by the time you
get this. I believe Humphres is coming home for 4 days he has been
good to me giving me coffee and ham and bread and sometimes tea of
course it does not come out of his own pocket he being corporal over the
cooks. I got the parcel alright but the tomatoes was smashed the cake
was champion. I am saving my money to come home at Xmas it costs
22/9 for us to Durham and the fare to Shotton will amount to about 25
shillings return. I am expect a letter from Nain and Emrys also Lizzie. I
kept Lizzie waiting for a letter last time I thought it was her turn to write
when it was mine. Theres been a chap here taking living pictures of us
today he says they will be on the pictures in the North so it might be on
at Shotton gaff. I have no more news to tell you this time
I am xxxxxxxxxx
yours with love
R. D. Bennett

As the weather worsened towards autumn 1914, the prospect of remaining
in tents began to pall on recruits like Bennett, as evidenced by his letter to
Kitty.[12]

Dear Kitty
I am writing in return to your kind letter hoping you are in good health
as it leaves me at present I am sorry to hear that Mary is bad I hope she is
better, you are getting on champion with your writing it is good writing
it has been raining very much here to-day and raining hard at that all
day. I will try to bring some-thing at Xmas for writing the letter to me
tell Mam I am expecting a letter from her and I don't know when we are
going to be shifted from the tents it looks gloomy they are putting a big
Y.M.C.A. up with a wooden floor so it does not seem likely we will be
shifted for a bit unless some more are going to take our place here. We

will have to go somewhere to a rifle range and the nearest is at Bisley
about 15 miles away and it is dew this month for our shooting I have no
more news this time with love to you all and to Mam
yours with love xxxxxxxxxxxxxxxxxx
R. D. Bennett
write back

Maintaining discipline was an ongoing problem with men used to their
freedoms and trying to make the most of any available scam or dispensation
that presented itself.

Dear Mam
I am writing in answer to the crossed letter I got this morning – Sunday. I
am thanking you for the tabs, Humphres has not come back yet I doubt
there is something the matter because there is only 4 day passes given
out but I don't want you to say anything. I am glad that Mary is better.
A chap in our tent got a such in he wrote to his wife to send a telegram
to say that she was very bad and he tried for a pass but they sent a
chap from Newcastle to see and he found her washing and this chap got
wrong so they have stopped the passes through that and chaps stopping
away and never coming back. I have not much news to tell you this time
but write back I am putting a penny stamp in
I am
yours with love
R. D. Bennett

In the very next letter he confirmed that Humphreys had overstayed his
pass by four days and had lost his lance corporal's stripe, and with it his
privileges and perquisites. Robert's letter indicates a small problem with
men going absent. Humphreys continued his decline; a later letter of
Robert's mentioned that he had been given 168 hours imprisonment but
asked that the news not be passed to Humphreys' wife in case she should
be worried. Robert may not have realised that Humphreys' wife would
have been affected by the loss of pay that the imprisonment would also
have incurred.

Robert did not get home for Christmas 1914, but had to settle for a
barracks festivity. At least by December his company found themselves
out of their tents. His next surviving letter is addressed from No. 13
Platoon Hut, D Company, 11th Service Battalion DLI, Pirbright Camp
near Woking, Surrey. The battalion had moved there at the end of
November.

Dear Mam

I am writing to thank you for the parcel of cakes and bacca I bet you will be sorry to hear that I will not be able to get to Xmas dinner at Home we are the last batch to go away but one. I went to the Quarter Master Sergeant about the paper you sent me he says that you have to send me regt. no. and what Battalion I am in I am sending it. I think I have plenty of money saved up I have 18/– in the bank beside the ration money I will get when I go away they say that we are going to get a free warent any way they have taken our addresses and where we want to go book to so that I am going to get a pass to Shotton bridge thats where I booked to I have no more news to tell except that Nain was poorly when I got a parcel from her I hope she is better by now. They say that we are going to get a good dinner on Xmas day. My Regimental Number is 17203 and say that I am in the 11th Battalion DLI and in D Company. I have no more to tell you this time.[13]

I am yours with love

Robert xxxxxxxxxxxxxxxxx

The long period of training may have been a tedious experience but it had its share of incidents. A depressing example was recollected by Second Lieutenant Ian Melhuish, 7th Battalion, Somerset Light Infantry, another unit of the 20th Division, in a letter to his mother,[14] though this lamentable event does not appear in the divisional history. On 24 January 1915, the divisional troops were marched out in snow, sleet and rain to a parade ground between seven and ten miles away from the camps. The various units came from deployments across a wide area, with the main brigades at Blackdown, Deepcut, and Aldershot, and the engineers and ambulance units split between Chatham and Aldershot. After more than two and a half hours marching they arrived, then stood waiting for another two and a half hours, expecting to be reviewed by Kitchener and his guest. They drove past in a closed car without any acknowledgement. Twelve thousand men had been dragged through these appalling conditions to no good purpose, with inadequate back-up, leaving many lying in the slush. Scores of men collapsed. Many suffered from exposure. Two men died. If the young lieutenant felt bitter, it would not be hard to imagine the feelings of the working-class men who formed the backbone of the division. Robert Bennett was lucky to be excused the event, as he intimated in one of his letters home.

I will be expecting it's a good job I have been off this week because there was a inspection of the army the lads had to walk 10 miles away to where they had to go and it was raining all the time and sleet as well.

That French chap was there (President Pioncarre) and Kitchener and they never got out of their motor car to see them the lads were standing up to the knee in water for an hour and a half.

The 11th Battalion had already suffered its first fatalities during training. Private 18866 F. Newman died on 6 December 1914 and was buried at Brookwood Cemetery. Private 16024 T. Kane, aged thirty, the son of John Henry and Martha Kane from Felling, died on 13 January 1915 and is buried in Heworth, County Durham, where he had lived with his wife Ellen.[15] One wonders to what degree any early euphoria had begun to dissipate under the rigours of training and discipline, often in appalling winter conditions such as this. Sometime around Christmas, the 11th DLI had been issued with emergency blues, and it is probably these they were wearing at the review.[16]

The 11th DLI had originally been assigned to the 61st Brigade of the 20th (Light) Division as an ordinary infantry battalion. However, in December 1914, the War Office decided that each division should have its own dedicated battalion of Pioneers. These units were intended to provide both skilled and unskilled labouring support to the divisions. On 6 January 1915, the 11th DLI were assigned to this role for the 20th Division, some men were exchanged between them and the 10th Battalion to get the right mix, and they were replaced in the 61st Brigade by the 12th King's Liverpool Regiment. Some specialist officers were also assigned to the 11th DLI during March 1915. Robert Bennett's letter home indicates

No. 9 Platoon, C Company, 11th DLI, at Woking, September 1914. (*DLI Trust and Durham CRO, Reference D/DLI 2/11/3*)

that he was less than impressed by the battalion's new role, despite the extra pay that came with it.

Dear Mam

I am writing in answer to the parcel you sent me it is a good one I have not tasted it yet I am writing straight away you need not be sorry about the 2/– I am sending another 2/– its pay Friday today. Ive had a rotten foot it turned into an abbsess but its healing now Ive done nothing for a fortnight only going to the doctor every morning. I'll get to work on Monday and I suffered some pain its not holes in stockings what makes it its marching. The blister came on after a 25 mile march its the first time Ive had bad feet and we have done 25 before. What I want you to send bacca is because you get all dry bacca here and it burns away like anything and we dont get weight in the canteen an ounce is not half an ounce because its cut up ready and its not weight and not cut at the mark on the bacca they'll take you down with your eyes open here. Did you get the Insurance card I sent you I am expecting a letter from me dad. Our captain was telling us today that we have another 3 months training to go through yet as pioneers its bridge building and making shit houses and the champion job of cleaning them out I said many a time I would not have a shit cleaners job for a pension but that's what we will have to do. Its all labourers and scavengers jobs we have to do anyway its 2d a day extra. We have not much to do now only tieing knots with a rope hundreds of different kinds. I have no more to tell you this time expecting a letter about Wednesday

Yours with love

Robert

xxxxxxxxxxxxxxxxxxxxxx

for Hilda xxxxxxxxxxxxx

In February, the Pioneers were moved to new billets at North Chapel in West Sussex for a week, before rejoining the division at its new, unified camp a few miles north at Witley. Some of the men were employed building roads and drains. Their efforts were greatly welcomed by the rest of the division, as the Witley camp was by then a sea of mud with damp and leaky huts.[17]

While near North Chapel, Robert Bennett's No. 13 Platoon was very cosily billeted in part of an unusual building in Shillinglee Park.

Dear Mam

I am writing to let you know I am alright but I have a tale to tell. We marched 5 miles from the nearest station we are 2½ miles from a shop

and it does not sell bacca only tabs and Ginger would lick it up its that
big. You have to catch the postman coming from Haslemere where the
station is where we marched from. I expect dad has got home alright. We
have got a good billet to what some have got we are in a tower and there
is a family on the ground floor and we are upstairs we are champion to
what some have got. 14 Platoon are in a hay loft and rats running over
them all night others are in barns. I heard some lads saying that there
was cattle in before we came. We have got the best of the lot it is a clean
house. Would you send me some bacca as sharp as possible and I will
pay you for it with the next letter we get the same food as at Pirbright
it is in big marques we get no food at all in our billets I think there is no
more to tell you this time so
I remain
your loving son
Robert
xxxxxxxxxxxxxxxxxx

He described the tower in more detail in another letter. It was a tall, square
building with turrets on each corner. It was the gamekeeper's family home
on the estate of Lord Douro. Robert wrote: 'I saw his wife yesterday and
she was riding in a motorcar she got out and she had mens riding breetches
on our landlord says she is the youngest of the Coates them that makes all
the thread.' The park was about an hours' walk from North Chapel from
where Robert collected his writing paper. The Deer Tower, as it is known
by its present owners, has since been enlarged to create an impressive
family home set in acres of beautiful parkland.[18]

While stationed at North Chapel, Robert heard that his family were
struggling financially and made arrangements to send home four shillings
a week to help. Many working-class families were highly dependent, not
just on the father of the house, but on all members of the household to
contribute to the joint income to keep the rents paid and everybody fed,
including those too young or infirm to earn their own keep. The allowance
would go some way to compensating for the loss of Robert's contribution
to the household economy.

The battalion was issued with khaki clothing some time before late
March or early April. Robert Bennett described them: 'these new clothes is
a lump different to the blue ones they are a lot warmer and the overcoat is
a ton weight as warm as toast'. The uniform provided the chance to pose
for postcard photographs to send home to families and loved ones. Robert
had his photo taken in Woking, costing 2s 6d for a dozen.[19]

In the spring of 1915, the battalion, along with the rest of 20th Division,
moved to Larkhill on the edge of Salisbury Plain, not far from Stonehenge.

'The Tower,' right foreground, was used by Robert Bennett's platoon in 1915. Shillinglee House is visible in the distance. (*Susan and Michael Taylor*)

They marched the sixty-three miles in a creditable four days in warm, dry and dusty conditions. There were no doubt economic reasons for making the journey on foot, avoiding the costs of transport by rail and the logistical problems of using motorised transport that was in short supply, but the experience was also designed to bring together the many units into the greater whole and to consolidate all the drill and fitness-building that had gone before. There followed three more months of hard training before the units were posted overseas.

Private Bennett wrote home giving his new address as Machine Gun Section, D B Coy Lines No. 1 Camp, Lark Hill. Because his letters are undated it is somewhat difficult to disentangle the likely order, though the letters from Lark Hill are among the most interesting. By this stage, he had gained confidence in writing and no longer used the formal 'R. D. Bennett', but signed off using his first name. Tobacco remained a constant source of Robert's interest. In the interests of economy, he took to smoking a pipe but found that he could only get 'shag' locally, which was dry and tended to burn up quickly and expensively at four pence and five pence an ounce. He warned his folks that they should send tobacco by registered post as it tended to go missing. In return, he bought small pieces of 'crested China' for his mother, usually at sixpence each, but a more expensive item at a shilling was unfortunately broken in the post – he blamed his own clumsy attempt at packing.[20] Robert was also trying to work out the best way to support the family from his pay. He had explained to the authorities that he had been paid twenty-eight shillings a week as a miner, from which his mother had allowed him three shillings pocket money. Now he was sending only four shillings a week and was trying to arrange for a sixpence a day deduction.

A row brewed up among the men at the camp about their treatment in relation to payment for road marking, compensation for the loss of civilian clothes and charges for alleged barrack room damages.[21] Robert described the events in a letter home.

> There is a devil of a row here somebody has written a letter to a Member of Parliament complaining of the treatment the officers are giving us and we have not had any money for the civilian clothes we came up in. Other battalions have had 8/– or 12/– for them. And getting money for marking the roads and it was kepted off for barrack room damages at Pirbright. Barrack room damages was abolished some time ago. The member went to the War Office for the men. The War Office wanted the names of the 200 men what had signed it. The Member of Parliament refused. The officers don't know what to do threatening court martial and all sorts of things to get to know the men. So the officers have been getting some money thats my opinion but I think we will get it now.

This was much more serious than the usual complaints about food. Robert mentioned that they were not getting the food they should have, especially meat. One day they were served only rice pudding with dates. The problem was quickly resolved, as he later reported: 'we are getting very good food now ... different sorts of pudding and a bottle of Allysloper on the table between twelve of us, all sorts of tinned fruit for tea'.[22]

The men were up to all sorts of ideas for time off. Robert considered going to the doctor with an itch problem to get sick furlough. Rumour had it that it was possible to insist on going home to see your own doctor for treatment. 'I've got the itch right enough, all fares paid and ration money paid is champion I think.' He changed his mind when it was rumoured that leave might be in the offing, once the battalion started shooting practice. Cost of return home was a big issue. Although the men got papers allowing them return fare for the price of single, it was 37s 11d to Newcastle – more than a week's pay. They made do with passes to local towns such as Salisbury – only a shilling – or visiting mates who were stationed at nearby places such as Tidworth. Nevertheless, Robert did eventually make it home, as he described a typical journey back to barracks in one of his letters.

I got back alright. I had a lot of changing to do. I changed at West Hartlepool, Eaglescliffe and at Darlington then I got a express to Kings X it only stopped at York. I got here at between 2 and 3 in the morning. It did not matter being 1 or 2 hours late so I am alright as far as that goes.

There was still the slight hope that the war might not come to anything. Having bought a set of postcards that he thought might look nice in a fretwork frame; Robert suggested that it might not be long before he was home to make it, if Italy entered the war. In fact, the battalion would soon be on the Western Front and found themselves practising for a march past for a royal visit in June – usually a sign of imminent departure overseas.

We have been practising a march past today for the King is coming tomorrow. Dad will know what I mean. We have about 7 miles to march on the parade ground. We are all in a line, the King comes along the line on a horse, the line is 3½ miles long, the line is like this [draws a dotted oval line]. We have to march along the dotted line and marching to attention all the way, our rifles at the trail. Your arms are fit to drop off I can tell you because a rifle is not a light thing.

How serious the training was is shown by a letter in which Robert explains that:

We hardly do any work in the day time now, we work at night. We went out on Tuesday night at 7 oclock and came back on Wednesday morning at 8 oclock. We did no work on Wednesday at all. I went to bed on Wednesday morning at 10 oclock and I did not wake till late at night so you tell I was tired for want of sleep. I was sorry for our Colonel. We were warm enough digging trenches but he looked frozen and he is that old he is 68 years old I felt sorry for him.

The last of the men went off on their pre-embarkation leave. On 20 July 1915, the 20th Light Division set out for France. Their training was by no means complete, as they had yet to experience conditions on the Western Front and what it was really like living in the trenches and moving in and out of frontline service. It would take several more years before they reached the full degree of professional development as described by John Bourne, but even at this early stage, while 'their values and inspiration remained obstinately civilian',[23] the men were now 'marked by a pragmatic and contingent attitude to authority, by a distinctive work ethic and by an extraordinary degree of mutuality'.[24] The process of change would accelerate with experience.

Postcard photograph of Corporal Thomas Bonney, back row second on the right, posing with other NCOs, at Larkhill, 1915. (*Collection of David Kelly*)

The reverse of the postcard has a message from Bonney and some inaccurate notes made by a later member of the family. (*Collection of David Kelly*)

We can get an indication of how difficult it was to change the behaviour of civilians and convert them into disciplined soldiers by looking at their recorded conduct. The data is based on the service records of seventy-three men who died on active service. They had been assigned to 11th DLI on enlistment or shortly thereafter, trained with the battalion, and went out to France with them on 20 July 1915. Their conduct sheets have survived along with their service records. The seventy-three men were responsible for 152 offences in total, making an average of a little over two offences per man. Of those men committing three offences or more there were twenty-two (30 per cent). By far the majority committed two offences or less. Fifteen had no offences recorded on their conduct sheet. The figures indicate that 20 per cent of men were very well behaved and a further 50 per cent were relatively well behaved. Those in this middle group were mainly charged with minor absences, occasionally aggravated by drink or disorderly behaviour.

By far the most common offences were overstaying passes (thirty-four), absent off pass (twenty-three) and absent or late for parade or tattoo (twenty-seven). These accounted for 55 per cent of all offences. While treated seriously enough, they were generally dealt with by a few days' confinement to barracks and an admonishment. That might vary if there were repeated offences, if the perpetrator was a non-commissioned officer or if there was felt to be a need to make an example as a warning to others. The last course was pursued when a large number of men overstayed passes during Christmas 1914, to the detriment of other men going on leave; though those overstaying embarkation leave passes in summer 1915 were treated rather more leniently.

Out of 213 punishments awarded for the 152 offences, by far the most common was confinement to barracks (three days being common) and the loss of a few days' pay, frequently in combination for the various types of absence and the length of sentence depending on the length of absence. They accounted for approximately 57 per cent of all the awards. Admonishment and reprimand were occasionally all that was given. When an example was to be made, however, the result was Field Punishment. The two types, FP Nos 1 and 2, had replaced flogging as the publicly administered punishment, but were as heartily disliked by the men. Both involved being lashed to a static object for varying periods of time per day over a number of days. FP1 was the most severe. The miscreant was lashed to something like a wheel in a crucifix position; though in practice this position was not always used and there were periods of rest laid down in the King's Regulations and a limit to the number of days that could be awarded. FP2 generally involved being tied to a post. Both were designed to publicly humiliate the man involved, though it is just as likely that the punishment evoked sympathy from at least some comrades.

Of the seventy-three men, only three offenders are worthy of particular note: John Brady, Patrick Connolly and John Iveson. Private 21547 John Farrell first tried to join up in Scotland. He was discharged immediately – for having a misshapen toe! On being refused he set off for London, where he succeeded in enlisting with 7th Duke of Cornwall's Light Infantry under the name of Brady. He was transferred to 11th DLI when they became a Pioneer battalion, due to his being a skilled bricklayer. He was persistently accused of absence, both with 7th DCLI and 11th DLI, was drunk and disorderly on one occasion and had a tendency to speak back to NCOs. He later died of wounds in Belgium on 13 March 1916, one of several hit by heavy shelling while working on improvements to the frontline trench system near Elverdinghe.

Private 16202 Patrick Connolly appears as the archetypal disorderly Irishman, with a conduct sheet running to several pages. The vast majority of his offences involved periods of absence, aggravated by breaking out of camp when confined to barracks. His behaviour earned him a District Court Martial, where he was given a 56-day detention order. No sooner had it expired than he went absent again – by which time the battalion was due overseas. Even abroad his indiscipline continued with three more awards of field punishment and loss of pay running up to 27 August 1916. He died of wounds a few days later on 5 September 1916, on the face of it undisciplined to the last, but wounded during a courageous assault that led to the capture of the German strongpoint at Guillemont.

Private 20731 John Iveson was a miner from Birtley. Aged twenty-four, he was an early volunteer, enlisting on 12 August 1914. His parents were both dead and he was the youngest of seven children, two of whom had emigrated to Canada. His 39-year-old sister, Mrs Sarah Bell of Bewick Main, Birtley, was his designated next of kin. Iveson served with C Company, 11th DLI, and was brought to book on nine occasions between December 1914 and his first days in France in July 1915. While he overstayed his pass on two occasions, most of his offences were due to insubordinate behaviour – improper dress on parade, inattention, ignoring or refusing to obey orders. Six times confined to barracks and three times having pay deducted did nothing to improve his behaviour, nor did two awards of FP2. He was given twenty-eight days' imprisonment by a District Court Martial in the UK; his behaviour had gone beyond what could be dealt with inside the battalion. Yet still he went absent without leave on arrival in France and was awarded his second period of FP2 and the loss of two days' pay before he finally seems to have settled down. He died of wounds at 34th Casualty Clearing Station, 20 September 1916, when working at night under heavy fire near Bernafay Wood on the Somme, and is buried at the Grove Cemetery, Méaulte.

Accepting the limitations of this data and the occasional individual exception, the working-class recruits had adapted very well to military discipline. They brought with them behaviours established in their neighbourhoods and places of work. Service records indicate that several men had a degree of religious faith and some, like Robert Bennett, were teetotal. Miners worked in teams and depended on each other, a characteristic that probably also featured among men from engineering workshops, shipyards, steelworks and other large industries. In small firms the size of a military section or platoon, the close proximity to the boss would have inculcated a degree of respect and self-discipline. Military standards were difficult to inculcate in relation to restrictions on the men's freedom as civilians, outside of 'work hours', hence the predominance of problems relating to drink, lateness, and absence, occasioned by visits to family, friends and local hostelries. Serious indiscipline, at least when not aggravated by alcohol, was very rare. While the evidence of this small number of records from one battalion cannot be taken as conclusive, it suggests that wider study of conduct sheets might overturn any assumption that there was a particular problem in shaping working-class civilians into soldiers. They were already well adapted to 'labour discipline' and imbued with the values of being respected by family, friends and neighbours. They transferred these standards to their new work as soldiers – values that helped them survive the rigours of war. A sense of themselves as 'free men' was a strength, not a problem, especially among those, like miners, from a vibrant community background.

As 11th DLI set off overseas in July 1915, the elderly Brevet Colonel Davison remained CO, with Major A. E. Collins as his second-in-command. Captain Geoffrey Hayes was adjutant, later replaced by Captain A. W. Dawson. They were assisted by two more officers, one as quartermaster and the other as medical officer, along with a small number of NCOs and other ranks who formed the Battalion Headquarters section. The remainder of the battalion was organised in four companies designated with the letters A to D, each comprising approximately 200 men, with a major or captain in charge and a captain or lieutenant in support. Each company was subdivided into four platoons numbered sequentially from one to sixteen, each comprising approximately fifty men under the command of a lieutenant or second lieutenant. Each platoon was divided into four sections under NCO command.

It is sometimes possible from the war diary and other records to identify the officers and NCOs in command of particular parts of the unit, though there was frequent change. At one point Major Collins was in charge of A Company rather than at HQ. During the first two months in France, the Quartermaster Sergeant was called Paynter, Captain H. P. Lloyd commanded C Company with Lieutenant W. G. Cunningham as his second-in-command, and Second Lieutenant C. G. Sturt commanded a platoon in the same company. Lieutenant Palmer led the machine gun section, assisted by Second Lieutenant Wood. Captain Hayes and Lieutenants Gaine and Pemberton were each involved in the command of a company, while Second Lieutenants MacLaren, Tait, Douglas, Ward and Floyd headed out platoons. But new batches of men were coming in every month – officers, NCOs and privates – and the personnel was constantly in flux due to transfers, promotions and training courses.[25]

Table 2.1
The Structure of 20th (Light) Division

There would be many changes to the organisation of the 20th Division over the coming years, some minor, some quite far-reaching. In July 1915, it was made up of twelve battalions of light infantry organised into three brigades of four battalions each, with a variety of support troops under command of divisional HQ. As light infantry, the troops were armed with rifles and other weapons that were easily carried around the person, while a specialised few managed light machine-guns such as the Lewis gun. These were the core fighting arm of the division. The aim was that the division would be able to manoeuvre at short notice, without relying on heavy equipment, and this principle was carried through into the formation of the divisional support units.

2.1.1	Infantry Brigades:
59th Infantry Brigade	10th Battalion, King's Royal Rifle Corps 11th Battalion, King's Royal Rifle Corps 10th Battalion, Rifle Brigade 11th Battalion, Rifle Brigade
60th Infantry Brigade	12th Battalion, KRRC 12th Battalion, Rifle Brigade 6th Battalion, Oxfordshire and Buckinghamshire Light Infantry 6th Battalion, King's Shropshire Light Infantry

61st Infantry Brigade	12th Battalion, King's Liverpool Regiment 7th Battalion, Prince Albert's Somerset Light Infantry 7th Battalion, Duke of Cornwall's Light Infantry 7th Battalion, King's Own Yorkshire Light Infantry

The support units were structured so that they could be deployed from divisional HQ as best suited to any particular operation. They could, if necessary, be separated from the division altogether and deployed for special purposes to support other divisions. The artillery comprised light, horse-drawn guns that could be quickly disassembled and moved on demand to provide direct support to the division, independent of the quite separate heavy artillery units behind the lines. The Pioneer unit was trained to act as light infantry with rifles and Lewis guns as well as providing skilled labour to complement the units of more specialised engineers. Transport was largely horse-drawn, supplemented with small lorries from time to time.

2.1.2   Divisional Troops:

Artillery	90th, 91st, 92nd and 93rd Brigades, the Royal Field Artillery
Pioneers	11th Battalion, the Durham Light Infantry
Engineers	83rd, 84th and 96th Field Companies, the Royal Engineers 20th Divisional Signal Company, the Royal Engineers
Transport and Supply	20th Divisional Train
Medical	60th, 61st, 62nd Field Ambulance Units, the Royal Army Medical Corps

NOTES TO CHAPTER THREE

1 Cecil and Liddle, 2003, chapter 25, 'The British Working Man in Arms', John Bourne, p. 336.
2 Most of these details are obtained from Miles, 1920, and cross-referenced with Ward, 1962.
3 Middlebrook, 2000, p. 43.
4 According to the 1911 census the Bennett family was as follows:

   Father: William Bennett, Stone Man in Coal Pit, forty-six, born Mold, Flintshire
   Mother: Catherine Bennett, forty-one, born Llanberis, Caernarvon
   Children: Robert David, sixteen, Pit Boy, born Llanberis, Caernarvon
              Elizabeth, fourteen, Apprentice Dressmaker, born Llandeiniolen, Caer'n
              David, nine, born Llanberis
              Catherine, seven, born Denaby Main, Yorkshire
              Hilda, six, born Shotton Colliery, Durham
              Peter, one, born Shotton Colliery, Durham

   One child, John Bennett, is shown in the 1901 census for Llanberis aged two, and must presumably have died before 1911. The birthplace for Catherine illustrates how William Bennett had previously worked in the South Yorkshire coalfield. Elizabeth is referred to as 'Lizzie' in Robert's letters, while Catherine is referred to as 'Kitty'. David started work in the local pit while Robert was serving in France.
5 There is virtually no punctuation in the original letters. Except to occasionally help understanding, the spelling and grammar remain unaltered, in order to keep the texture and tone of the original. Most of the letters are undated, but internal clues were used to set them in approximate order.
6 Peggy has not been identified by the remaining family and may have been a personal friend of Robert.
7 The term 'terriers' refers to the Territorial battalions.
8 Several men from Barnsley are listed among those who lost their lives with 11th DLI. Private 12934 Edward Collins, died 5 April 1918, originally from Barnsley enlisted at Newcastle-upon-Tyne. It is unlikely that Collins is Bennett's mate as he was no teetotaller, being pulled up for being drunk and disorderly during training.
9 Slang for cigarettes.
10 These would be former regular soldiers, called up in 1914 as part of the National Reserve, and allocated to the Kitchener battalions to provide a salting of experienced soldiers. Several would have been non-commissioned officers.

11 For examples see Mitchinson, 2000, Appendix IV.

12 Kitty was Robert's younger sister Catherine, aged ten. She married Cyril Banks in 1925 and was responsible for preserving her brother's letters following her mother's death in 1930. Her son, Kenneth Banks has provided permission to quote from the letters in this book.

13 Previous letters had mainly been written on YMCA headed paper, but this was the first of several written on paper from the Wesleyan Soldiers' Homes, Aldershot Command.

14 Quoted in Brown, 1999, page 20, from microfilm copies of twenty-seven of his letters at the Imperial War Museum, reference 11994 PP/MCR/69, private papers of 2nd Lt I. V. B. Melhuish.

15 The Commonwealth War Graves Commission's records attribute 2526 Private James Briddick to 11th DLI. As he was killed on 26 April 1915, before the unit went overseas, and is recorded on the Menin Gate at Ypres, he was in one of the Territorial Battalions of DLI fighting in the Second Battle of Ypres.

16 The men in the photograph of 9 Platoon are wearing 'blues'.

17 Inglefield, 1921, p. 5.

18 Photograph by permission of the present owners, Susan and Michael Taylor.

19 The photograph of Robert reproduced in this chapter may be one of these.

20 None of these pieces have survived (note from Gaynor Greenwood).

21 See above where Robert describes in a letter having many of their civilian clothes burned.

22 'Allysloper' referred to one of several types of bottled brown sauce or relish. Ally Sloper was the principal character in a comic paper, popular since the 1880s, *Ally Sloper's Half Holiday*. So popular was the character that he became the focus of a mass-marketing campaign, branded to sell numerous goods, from cigars and pills to bicycles and musical instruments.

23 Cecil and Liddle, 2003, p. 340.

24 Ibid., p. 342.

25 No official embarkation list has survived for 11th DLI. It would be technically feasible to reconstruct an approximation of the names of those who went out to France on 20 July 1915 by cross-referencing the list of recipients of the 1914–1915 Star for the Durham Light Infantry [The National Archives, WO 329/2789–2792] with the lists for those receiving the British War Medal and Victory Medal [The National Archives, WO 329/1601–1631] and the War Medal Index cards, which provide an embarkation date.

CHAPTER FOUR

Into the Line of Fire

Troops leaving England for the first time in 1915 marched out of one new world, to which they had become accustomed, and into another one utterly different. As well as confronting changes in language and culture, the men learned that they were no longer playing at soldiers. Proximity to the front line demanded changes in discipline (now taken much more seriously), codes of behaviour (such as what might be written in letters home) and daily subsistence (rations, trench life, rough billets), not helped by the unnerving experience of working under artillery fire.

Each unit serving overseas kept its own record of daily experiences in a war diary. In a battalion it was collated on Army Form C2118, usually in pencil, by the adjutant to the commanding officer from reports provided by each company.[1] Other Army records provide additional insights. Registers of Field General Courts Martial listed the names of offenders sent up to divisional HQ for more serious offences, and the results of the case. Where the service records have survived for those men who lost their lives, some remarkable stories are revealed. Sometimes the records combine fortuitously to give us new insight into the frontline experience of serving soldiers.

The troops of the 20th Light Division gathered at Amesbury in Wiltshire on 20 July and were shipped out through Folkestone to Boulogne or from Southampton to Le Havre. 11th DLI went via the latter route, leaving Salisbury Plain at noon and arriving at Southampton at 8 p.m., having marched the thirty miles to the embarkation point. A six-hour voyage across the Channel brought them to Le Havre at 2 a.m. on 21 July. There were 30 officers and 922 other ranks, with Captain R. F. Higgins left behind sick. By 7 a.m., they had disembarked ready to march to their first Rest Camp.

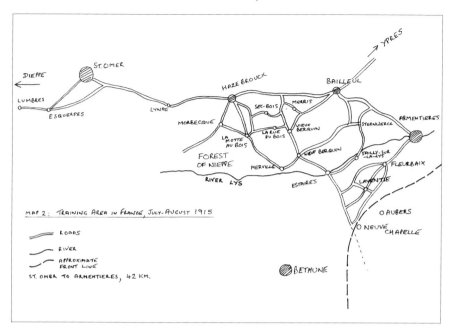

Training area in France, July–August 1915. (*Martin Bashforth, 2010*)

The adjutant soon had a story for the battalion war diary. There was a steep hill from the harbour, representing a challenge for any British unit wanting to impress the locals. In columns of four they marched briskly out in light infantry fashion. As they crossed a river bridge, a driverless wagon led by two panicking draught horses came hurtling towards them. Scattering to the sides of the bridge, the soldiers managed to avoid any serious injury. One poor man lost his rifle in the river below and had to face a court of enquiry, but it was decided that he was not at fault and would not be liable for the cost of replacing the rifle.[2]

Over the next few days they did little else but march about the countryside from billet to billet. At 8.30 a.m. on 22 July they marched on, caught a train at noon and arrived at St Omer at 9 a.m. the next day. By two o'clock that afternoon, they had marched in a south-westerly direction to Esquerdes, where they were billeted in some cottages. There was a ten-mile route march on 26 July. Two days later, they were marched in the opposite direction from Esquerdes to Lynde, south-east of St Omer. They were woken at 3 a.m. on 29 July and marched to Merris, further east beyond Hazebrouck. Here at last, after marching about like the Grand Old Duke of York's men, they began the task of defeating the enemy with picks and shovels. By 26 July 1915, the rest of the 20th Division had been concentrated in the vicinity of Lumbres and were attached to III Corps,

First Army between Neuve Chapelle and Armentières. The various units were billeted around Hazebrouck, Bailleul, Steenwerck and Neuf-Berquin with divisional HQ at Merris.

Robert Bennett took the first opportunity to write home after arriving in France. He recalled his late return from pre-embarkation leave, but had not been disciplined for it, possibly because he had an unblemished conduct record and the circumstances of rail travel may have warranted some leniency. His concerns were unchanged: the lads were getting plenty to eat and he was short of tobacco, though a friendly civilian on his train back to Wiltshire had given him 'a big box of cigarettes and 2/– for my breakfast'. His billet in a loft was comfortable enough and he was clearly anxious to keep in touch with his family: 'I don't think I've any more to say to you this time but will be expecting a reply every day.' As with most of his mates, this was the first time Robert had been overseas.

Letters from home soon began to arrive, including one from his sister Lizzie. Robert complained that he had not received a parcel sent to Wiltshire by a neighbour, Mrs Hartley. Until he got writing paper from home, Robert had to borrow from his mates. The tone of his writing was less free than during training. He had to be careful what he wrote, as letters were censored. He could say little, other than ask after everyone's health and talk about the weather: a mixture of hot days, showers and thunderstorms. Continually on the lookout for friends from home among other troops, he commented: 'I saw a lad I knew by sight belonging Shotton the other day but I had not time to speak to him as we were on the march.' Eventually a parcel arrived with one of those little home luxuries: 'the Oxo comes in handy for supper'.

The simple little delights received, as well as the problems with the mail service that appeared in these first exchanges between the family and Robert overseas, illustrate the vital part played by the postal service in maintaining morale. The Army Postal Services were run by the Royal Engineers (Postal Section), staffed by serving soldiers augmented by Territorials and volunteers from the GPO. At Regents Park in London, a 5-acre site was covered by a complex of wooden sheds where some 2,500 women sorters arranged outgoing mail by unit, which was despatched to bases in France such as Boulogne, Calais and Le Havre, also staffed mainly by women. The London depot was supported by several regional distribution centres in major cities. Mail had to be addressed by name, rank, regimental number and unit. The postal services were kept informed of the movement of units, though there were occasional delays and hitches in such arrangements. Mail was despatched via railheads and lorries to Divisional Postal Units, from where they would be broken down to individual units. An NCO saw to the final distribution to the men in each section. Mail the other way went through Field Post Offices – letters free, but parcels charged for. Regents Park was the main centre for onward sorting and distribution. It has been estimated that 2 billion letters and 114 million parcels were despatched between 1914 and 1918.[3] If there was an occasional mismatch or delay with mail for men like Robert Bennett and their families, it is hardly surprising.

Time for writing was precious. On 30 July, A and B companies were sent to La Rue du Bois, a tiny hamlet two miles south-west towards the Forest of Nieppe, where they worked improving roads and clearing ditches that allowed water to be drawn from the canal for the use of artillery en route to the front. They were joined next day by C Company, and all three companies were kept at work throughout Sunday 1 August, while D Company and HQ Company (including Robert Bennett in the Machine Gun Section) went on church parade.

The battalion soon had its first overseas casualty. On 4 August, C Company was at Fleurbaix (close to the front line between Armentières and Laventie) assisting 25th Brigade, 8th Division, in the construction of some forts. Private 17199 James Alexander Bowlt was killed in an accident. Bowlt had been a dock labourer in West Hartlepool before joining up on 29 August 1914. Originally from Bill Quay near Felling, he was aged thirty-three when he died. He had brown eyes, dark brown hair, stood 5 feet 5½ inches tall and was slight at 114 pounds. He left a wife Ellen at home at 102 Cumberland Street, West Hartlepool, with five children to bring up: James, John, Tom, Nellie and Winifred. She remarried, becoming Mrs Ellen Reynolds.

The battalion diary does not describe details of the accident, but the bizarre details have survived in Bowlt's service papers. A court of inquiry was convened at Fleurbaix, headed by Captain H. P. Lloyd commanding C Company, assisted by Lieutenant W. F. Cunningham and Second Lieutenant C. G. Sturt on 4 August 1915. Witness statements describe how Bowlt had fallen out of an upstairs window. He was found at 1 a.m. by Private 13421 John Ramshaw, lying on his back in a pool of blood in front of the billets used by 9 and 10 platoons. 'He was fully dressed with the exception of his coat and boots.' The Corporal of the Guard noted that he was directly under a window and went to fetch Lieutenant Cunningham from the house opposite. Private 16818 William Sheehan, who had been sleeping next to Bowlt on the first floor of the billet, reported that Bowlt had been perfectly sober and had fallen asleep first. The last of the witnesses, Private 15082 R. McKenzie, reported that 'two months ago at Lark Hill Pte Bowlt told me he was in the habit of walking in his sleep'.[4]

The strange circumstances surrounding Bowlt's death led to a considerable delay in settling the widow's right to a pension. It was not

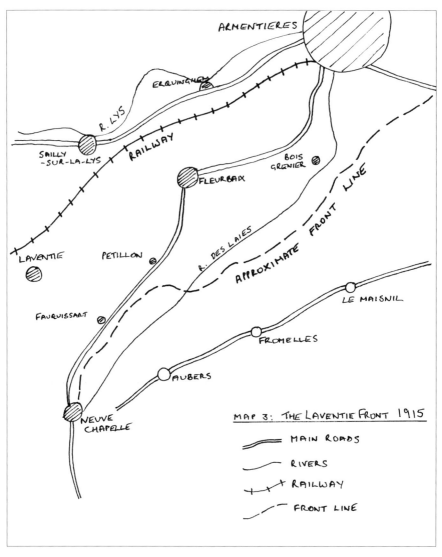

The Laventie Front, 1915. (*Martin Bashforth, 2010*)

finally agreed until 22 May 1916, after the intervention of the Hartlepool Branch of the Soldiers and Sailors Families Association the previous October. Mrs Bowlt was awarded 27s a week, backdated to 14 February 1916. Bowlt has no known grave and is commemorated on the Ploegsteert Memorial. His original grave must have been lost over the following years, though it was recorded at the time and precise details forwarded to the widow. He was 'buried at Fleurbaix in a corner of a field opposite the Mairie, 145 yards NW and 45 yards SW of the Mairie entrance marked by a wooden cross' as per reference map 1/10000 Hazebrouck 5a.

During August and September, work was mixed with training. As well as constructing fortifications at Fleurbaix, D Company were making hurdles in the wood at La Motte au Bois, a skill that was passed on to any new recruits as quickly as they arrived. Others, especially the ex-miners, were seconded to mining and tunnelling companies. There was always plenty of work on roads and ditches, as well as munitions and supplies to unload from barges.

The proximity of the front line figured for the first time in Robert Bennett's letters home. Previously keen to reassure that there was no fighting anywhere near, he remarked: 'I saw the bonniest sight tonight I think I ever saw. It was just after dusk and there was a big action on and I went upstairs and I could see it. Shrapnel and all sorts bursting all over us. I thought it the prettiest sight I ever saw, Manchester fireworks was not in it.' A parcel arrived containing socks, shaving brushes and soap and, best of all, some 'champion tea'. A tempting sandwich he put off until tea-time and he would report what it was like in his next letter. The parcels often contained newspapers from home, with photos and news of friends and neighbours to keep him in touch with life there. He asked for his dad's old pipes, regretted that he was not home to help him with his garden and promised to bring home some souvenirs, especially for his fourteen-year-old brother Davy who had now started at the pit.

The battalion continued working on the defences or in reserve as working parties for III Corps. On 22 August, the 20th Division was ordered into the line, though C and D companies of 11th DLI remained in reserve until early September. The general rule was that two battalions remained in the line with one in reserve on a ten-day rotation. But this varied for each company or even platoon, especially for the useful Pioneers. The Laventie area was badly waterlogged and it was not possible to dig trenches to full depth. Instead the shallow trenches were crudely fortified with sandbags as breastworks and whatever could be mustered to shelter behind from exploding shells. Most of the work was carried out at night, working in front of the trenches themselves and was accordingly very dangerous. Groups of men would work while others kept watch and provided defence.

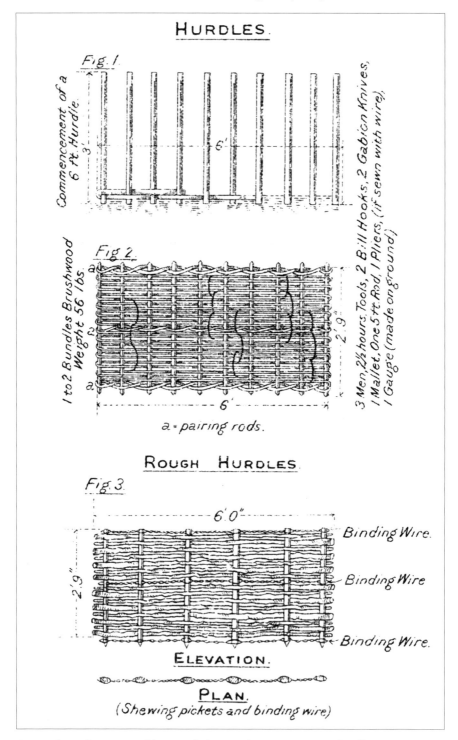

A page from the 1912 Field Manual showing how to construct hurdles.
(*Collection of Martin Bashforth*)

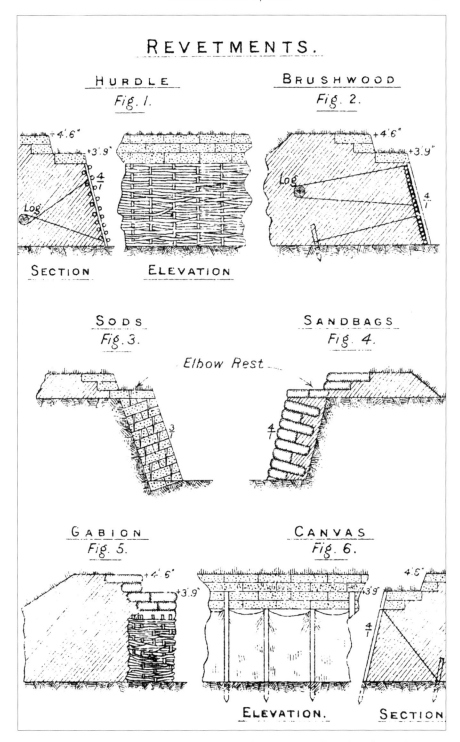

A page from the 1912 Field Manual showing how to revet the sides of trenches. (*Collection of Martin Bashforth*)

View of waterlogged trenches at Laventie, 1915, with soldiers of the Royal Scots. (*Imperial War Museum, Q 17421*)

Robert Bennett missed some of this early work. The first of his letters bearing a date was on 18 August 1915. It was full of appreciation for the things sent out in a parcel received the previous Wednesday. He had enjoyed the sandwiches, but suggested that they send a whole loaf of bread and a tin of tongue so that the bread didn't dry out. His eleven-year-old sister Kitty had sent some chocolates as a treat. A letter sent from home on 9 August had only just arrived. Shotton Colliery had apparently had a visit from a Zeppelin but it had not done any damage there. Robert gave the first hint of criticism of those still at home. Some people he had written to had not responded. He asked whether Jack and Arny Gray were medically unfit, clearly implying they should have signed up by now. Meanwhile he scotched rumours that had got home about him being unwell. He was, as he wrote, 'never better in my life'.

This was not exactly true. On the same day as this letter was sent he was admitted to 26th Field Ambulance with scabies. This was a common problem and features occasionally in the war diary, as well as many of the surviving service records. Scabies in civilian life was associated with overcrowding and poor domestic hygiene, conditions replicated in military billets. Quarters were rudimentary and opportunities for bathing infrequent. Lice and other mites were a constant problem and affected officers as well as the men. Scabies results from the activities of a mite burrowing under the skin and causing outbreaks of itching that are difficult to treat and control. Clothes had to be disinfected and the skin had to be treated with pesticide-based ointments. Robert remained under treatment in hospital until the end of August. Fortunately letters were sent on from his unit as a relief to his misery and embarrassment. He received a parcel with lots of tobacco, chocolates and a dozen boxes of matches. As he commented ironically: 'that's what we need most here, plenty of bacca in your pocket and no matches to light it with'. Not for the first time he grumbled about not having been paid and the problems that caused when trying to buy basic essentials. Private Bennett rejoined his unit after eleven days in hospital, waiting for his mail to catch up with him. The moving around had also disrupted the flow of letters from himself and he explained in one of his letters the items he had sent back, suggesting that one letter might even have been 'destroyed at base', presumably under censorship regulations as he may have written something he should not.

Throughout August, units from 20th Light Division were retrained. In England, they had been schooled in the ways of open warfare, but trench warfare called for very different skills. Officers and NCOs were sent for training to other divisions, returning to their units to train others. Lieutenant R. S. Rigby, for instance, taught the men, in groups of twelve privates and one NCO per company, the art of throwing bombs. More officers were added to the list of instructors when Lieutenant Gaine and Second Lieutenants MacLaren, Tait and Douglas came back from Grenade School and Lieutenant Pemberton went off for the same training with Second Lieutenants Ward and Floyd. Several groups of machine-gunners (possibly including Robert Bennett) were sent to Estaires, a small town on the River Lys away from the front line. The diary does not record what they did there, but it was almost certainly part of the continuing process of upgrading fighting skills for the new conditions. Everyone was drilled in the practice of using helmets and respirators, gas having been used by the Germans at Ypres not many weeks before. Conditions were producing their share of illness. When the battalion moved from La Rue du Bois to La Motte au Bois on 29 August 1915, they left behind the sick with the intention that they rejoin their companies at Fleurbaix later.

Further drafts of men arrived from the 16th and 17th Reserve Battalions. Some of these require little comment, other than the date of their arrival. Fifty arrived on 12 August from 16th Battalion and a further fifty on 22 August from 17th Battalion. The battalion diarist grumbled about one such draft of fifty NCOs and men arriving from 16th Battalion on 2 September, as being 'not suitable men for a pioneer battalion'. They were passed on to C and D Companies for instruction. Among the new draftees was Corporal Thomas Bashforth, arriving in France on 25 August 1915. One would expect him to have been able to get from Le Havre or any other port to join his unit within a day or two, suggesting that he joined B Company around 27 August 1915.

The diary highlights recorded by Captain Dawson in these first weeks may seem a little dull because the events being recorded were largely routine. There were the bare facts of church parade every Sunday, usually followed by drill. There were the comings and goings of groups of men in their various duties, rarely mentioned by name unless they were officers. On 6 September, B Company had a busy day, travelling first to Estaires to join the rest of the division, then on to Le Nouveau Monde for some unspecified pioneer work, before going into the trenches at night at Laventie. A rather pragmatic comment in the diary suggests that this last experience had not been exactly quiet. The entry stated that 'B type ammunition found unsuitable for rapid fire: withdrawn and sent to Machine Gun Section'. Robert Bennett wrote home to say that his Machine Gun Section from D Company had been up the line: 'we was only up one night there was an attack coming off and our section come out without a scratch'.

Corporal Thomas Bashforth, his wife Florence, daughter Ethel and son Thomas, before leaving for France, August 1915. (*Collection of David Bashforth*)

There was time for the human touch. On 31 August, two men from C Company were allowed home on compassionate leave, to visit their dying father. The battalion diary names them as Corporal McLean and Private McLean. A little detective work has helped identify them as Corporal William G. McLean and Private Thomas McLean. Among the battalion's later casualties was Private 16721 Thomas McLean, killed in action on 5 October 1916 and recorded on the Thiepval Memorial. According to official records he was born in Whitby and enlisted in West Hartlepool. In the 1901 Census, there was a family living at 11 Turnbull Street, West Hartlepool. The father was John McLean, a 43-year-old shipyard watchman originally from Whitby. His wife Jane and all but the youngest of his children, two-year-old Isabella, were born in Whitby. There were six sons: John aged seventeen, a rivet heater; James aged fifteen, an apprentice iron moulder; William G. McLean aged thirteen; Thomas aged eleven; Leonard eight and Alfred five. John McLean senior died in late 1915 in Hartlepool aged fifty-seven.[5] William G. McLean was identified from the medal indexes as 18569, Private and later Corporal, DLI.

More casualties were experienced, such as Private 16006 Thomas Stobbart of D Company, who was accidentally shot through the thigh on 10 August. As various sections, particularly newly trained machine-gunners, spent short spells in the trenches at Laventie for experience, some casualties were more serious. On 12 September, Private J. Given was wounded, and four days later Private 17430 Daniel Lister of C Company Machine Gun Section was killed. He was the son of Thomas Lister of 42 East View, Wingate, County Durham, and is buried at the No. 1 Cemetery, Rue du Bacquerot in the village of Laventie. Robert Bennett explained the incident in one of his letters.

> There was a lad killed in No 2 section he belongs to Wingate it was his own fault he was getting pears about 100 yards behind the first line trench a sniper fired 10 rounds at him and he come away. He went back and was hit in the head with the 11th. He is some relation of Catherty they call him Danny Lister. He only lived a few minutes.

Lister's action may have been youthful bravado, though he was actually twenty-eight years old. He was unmarried and, to judge by his conduct record during training, inclined to petty indiscipline. He had been four times awarded periods of confinement to barracks for overstaying his pass and being absent from tattoo. Perhaps the 'scrumping' was just part of his character.

In between bouts in the trenches, which might involve pioneer work or acting as ordinary infantry, the work behind the lines varied. Working

The headstone of Daniel Lister at Rue-du-Bacquerot No. 1 Cemetery. Lister was shot while collecting pears. (*Gaynor Greenwood*)

parties unloaded barges on the canal; Lieutenant Pemberton took No. 1 Platoon for work with 181st Mining Company, returning on 24 September; meanwhile two platoons from D Company were attached to 173rd Tunnelling Company. Most of the work in the line consisted of cleaning, draining and improving both fire and communications trenches, and repairing parapets and wire. Private 18091 Charles Wilson, on mining duties with two platoons from B Company, was accidentally injured at Fauquissart on 28 September.

Robert Bennett was forced to admit to one of the problems of life in the trenches, writing home asking for 'something for the lice, not Keating's Powder it's no use'. He dismissed fears expressed by his mother, based on letters she had read in the local paper about the fighting, saying 'we are safer in the firing line than in the billets'. It is difficult to say whether Robert was unusual in attempting to reassure his mother, or whether this was a common feature of letters and cards home.[6] The men could not go into detail because of the possibility of censorship of their letters, while the very fact that someone else might read what they had written must have had some influence on what they wrote. Robert's main concern this time, apart from how the family dog Spot was coming on, was that parcels got rather battered in the post, mixing cigarettes with grease from cakes. But he was grateful for the cocoa and sugar, which he was saving for the next spell in the line.

All the main infantry units had now gained some direct experience of warfare, with some men being awarded medals for gallantry. In the last week of September 1915, the 20th Division was given its first real taste of action, though not at the centre of events. On 25 September, the French would attack in the Champagne area and the main British assault was around Loos. The 20th Division was sandwiched between the Meerut Division on their right near Neuve Chapelle and the 8th Division on their left near Le Bridoux. The actions were subsidiary to the main events further south, but it was hoped to make some small gains of ground if the opportunity arose. The role of 20th Division was to cause diversions by cutting wire, laying down smoke, providing a wall of covering fire and then to make their own advance, taking advantage of any gains either side. The Pioneers were placed with a battalion from 59th Brigade and the Divisional Mounted Troops in reserve, to be moved forward in the event that any ground was gained.

The plan was a success to the extent that all the troops, including those of the 20th Division, were able to make significant advances into the German front lines. Unfortunately, they were not able to hold their gains due to heavy fire from left and right and had to retreat to their start points by mid-afternoon. The attacks had done their job in pinning down the German troops in the sector, but at considerable cost. The 20th Division, though the least engaged, suffered 19 casualties among its officers and 542 among its ranks. 60th Brigade was so badly depleted that 11th DLI was attached to them as an extra infantry battalion for the next six weeks. On 28 September, just before the battalion left Estaires for its first full spell in the front line, a letter was received from the Chief Engineer III Corps and from Lieutenant General Sir W. Pulteney congratulating them on their efforts during the engagement.

The division was moved a mile to the right. In between normal Pioneer work and service as reserve infantry, 11th DLI experienced more danger, more incidents and more casualties. It was beginning to be more like a real war with every passing day, with the Pioneers assigned to every conceivable task and in constant demand. The adjutant complained during the first week of October about the 'continual drain of the best skilled workers'. There were frequent demands for miners to do tunnelling work, while carpenters, blacksmiths and other skilled tradesmen were continually being requisitioned. The casualties in these few days were the last among 'other ranks' mentioned in the battalion diary by name. On the night of 28–29 September, Private 17478 Hugh McDonald, a miner from Stanley, was killed in action. On the following day Private 20997 W. Jardine and Private 22536 Alfred Turner were both wounded. Turner died later of his wounds and was buried at the Merville Communal Cemetery close to the base hospital. The death of Private 20257 James McSoley, also on 30 September, does not get mentioned in the diary, perhaps because he died from accidental injuries. He was thirty-six years old, the son of Arthur McSoley of Bishop Auckland and husband of Margaret McSoley, who was living after the war at 49 Nelson Street, Otley.

On 1 October 1915, Brevet Colonel Davidson left the battalion in charge of his deputy, Major Collins. On 16 October, Collins was promoted to Lieutenant Colonel and remained in command until well into 1916. In turn, Captain Geoffrey Hayes was promoted to Major as his second-in-command. Captain Dawson remained as Adjutant. More time was spent as infantry in the front line, under shellfire and letting loose 'several hundred rounds a day' in return. On 13 October, 11th DLI were involved in an unusual piece of fighting. They occupied the middle of the divisional line between 6th KSLI on the right and 12th RB on their left. A mock attack was staged. Smoke was laid down and dummies were hoisted on bayonets above the parapets to draw enemy fire, thus identifying their positions for retaliation. It was double-edged in its consequences. Three men were killed by enemy artillery and fourteen wounded, with 36,000 rounds being expended before the Pioneers were relieved by 12th KRRC. It later transpired from captured enemy documents that the Germans believed they had beaten off a major attack.

Gv R1

HE whom this scroll commemorates was numbered among those who, at the call of King and Country, left all that was dear to them, endured hardness, faced danger, and finally passed out of the sight of men by the path of duty and self-sacrifice, giving up their own lives that others might live in freedom. Let those who come after see to it that his name be not forgotten.

Pte. Alfred Turner—
Durham L.I.

D/DU 7/981/1

Memorial scroll sent to the family of Alfred Turner after the war.
(*DLI Trust and Durham CRO, D/DLI 7/981/1*)

Over the following weeks the battalion took turns in the front line. Some men were allowed away on leave (three officers and fourteen men going home to England on 30 October), while the influx of men from 16th and 17th DLI in England continued to fill up the gaps left by miners departing to work as tunnellers. On 20 October, Company Sergeant-Major Bousfield was arrested for being drunk on duty. He became the unlucky first member of the battalion to be court-martialled in the field at Laventie, on 1 November 1915. He was found guilty and reduced to the ranks, though the sentence was commuted to a reduction to Lance Corporal.[7] He did eventually work his way back to the rank of Sergeant, surviving the war in the Labour Corps, regimental number 534551.[8] Two more men found themselves in trouble. Privates W. Hamilton and M. McCormack were each tried by court martial for striking an officer, in the latter case aggravated by being drunk at the time. They were tried at Laventie on 3 and 12 November 1915 respectively, Hamilton being awarded one year imprisonment with hard labour, while McCormack got eighteen months.[9] Drunken behaviour in the reserve areas was not uncommon. As well as any habits brought from civilian life, the men had little else by way of a social outlet.

The Pioneers spent two nights, 31 October to 1 November, involved in repairing trenches and strengthening breastworks, with 320 men engaged in the digging and 20 more providing cover. They took turns in the trenches with 12th KRRC, attempting to maintain the constantly collapsing parapets. On 10 November, the billets at Epinette were hit by shells. Privates John Acomb, William Duffy and Thomas Alfred Isaac were killed, two more dying later of wounds (Privates Alex Coates and Thomas Murray), and seven others were wounded.[10] During this period, Sergeant Frederick Williams of B Company excelled himself with 'good work in the trenches and in front of the parapet' and was awarded the Médaille Militaire. In a sense, this was recognition of the difficult work achieved by the Pioneers in the Laventie front lines. As well as the wet conditions, the distance between the British trenches and the Germans was often close. Work at night in the narrow strip of land was perilous. The French award was provided as a general appreciation and it was left to the British command to decide to whom it should be made.

Robert Bennett's letters home during the last three months of 1915 scarcely mention any aspects of work or military activity. While in some way this was due to the restrictions of censorship, it may also have simply reflected what he was really interested in. His letters are full of references to tobacco and food, and appreciation of parcels with soap and health salts. In one he wrote that 'our lads took a German yesterday he had nothing to eat for 48 hours and we had fried bacon and 1lb of bread for our breakfast that morning so you can see who is the winning side'. Another expressed

The headstones of John Acomb, Thomas Isaac and Hugh McDonald at Aubers Ridge British Cemetery. (*Gaynor Greenwood*)

The headstone of William Duffy at Aubers Ridge British Cemetery. Duffy died alongside Acomb and Isaac. (*Gaynor Greenwood*)

surprise at a novel French treat: 'I got a feed I thought it was tasty it was a plate of chips and a couple of eggs and a slice of bread and butter and cup of coffee. I payed a franc for it I thought it was the tastiest bite I've had for long enough although I'd never heard of eggs with chips before.' He frequently sent requests for spice cake, currant cake, special cigarettes and any little luxury to break the monotony of trench diet. Otherwise his letters were concerned with how relatives were getting on. As well as his younger brother Davy having started work in the pit, his eldest sister Lizzie was now working in a munitions factory in Manchester.[11] He said he had not seen his friend Humphreys in a long time and asked to be remembered to families back home who had lost sons in the war, while constantly reassuring his own family that he was alright himself.

On 14 November, the 20th Division was relieved of frontline duties by the Guards Division, but not for a period of rest. A Company was sent to do tunnelling for 59 Brigade; B Company was split between mining work and cleaning equipment, with C Company at Headquarters. Half of D Company went with 59th Brigade to do drainage work (which indicates that several battalions of the infantry had been commandeered into this particular exercise), while a small troop constructed horse-standings in the transport lines. Within a couple of days they were busy making roads, one corduroy, the other standard, with one party of men employed working a saw bench night and day in six-hour shifts. Corduroy roads were so-called because they used logs laid side by side, making a ridged surface like the textile. Only Sundays provided respite. For once, a batch of thirty-two NCOs and men arriving from 16th Battalion met the approval of the adjutant, describing them as 'strong, well set-up, healthy looking men'.

December was so full of Pioneer work that the diarist ceased to record it on a daily basis and listed everything for the month: drainage, communications trenches, mining, gas drills, deepening and cleaning ditches, revetting the east bank of the River Laies, training, leave, dugouts for Brigade HQ, building head cover for the trenches, carting gas cylinders, making traverses and repairing parapets, some night work, often under shellfire, with rest and baths on Sundays and a rest on Christmas Day. Work like this resumed after the 'holiday', with the addition of laying trench boards and building tramways. The variety of work that Pioneers were called on to perform shows how they contributed to the overall benefit of the division: maintaining and improving conditions in the trenches, providing supplies and creating the infrastructure to move men and supplies in and out of the line.

Corporal Ralph Worfolk of 61st Field Ambulance Unit, 20th Light Division, remembers this first Christmas Day at the front in his notebook. This was the second Christmas of the war, and although not quite so remarkable as the fraternisation that occurred on the first, his memoir provides a glimpse into what Christmas was like in 1915.[12]

> We had a grand dinner (off plates) at 2 o'clock. Roast beef, mashed potatoes and all sorts of good things – each man had two glasses of Worthington's if he wanted it – I wanted it!
>
> The Guards Division were in the trenches and no rifle fire was exchanged between the lines although artillery was active. Three Germans came out of their trenches and started burying their dead. Later more came out to help them. Three or four dead bodies of our men were lying close to the Guards line – the Germans came right over and took away the bodies and buried them along with theirs. An officer of the Scots Guards detailed three of his men to go and help. They did and the Germans gave them wine and cigars. More of our men went over and took a football. There was a lively time for five or ten minutes. There is some trouble over the business and some men are to be court martialled over it, it is said.

Indeed, Sergeant 6406 J. A. L. Oliver, aged thirty, of 2nd Battalion, Scots Guards, was shot and killed on Christmas Day, 1915, and is buried at the Rue-David Military Cemetery, Fleurbaix. According to the writer Stephen Graham, he was shot while fraternizing, potentially by sentries from either side, as they were both under orders to shoot anyone attempting to contact the enemy.[13]

Christmas Day reminded the men of what they were missing and miserable weather was no help. Robert Bennett would not have been alone in assessing his chances of going home on leave. 'One of us goes on leave every week' he wrote, noting himself tenth on the list, later eighth, then 'it will be three months', perhaps February. By the end of January even that date had been put back and he was destined never to make it home. On New Year's Day 1916, he replied to a letter from his parents, acknowledging a parcel with oranges, cakes and Oxo. He sent back his Christmas cards for them to keep and a letter from his Aunt Dolly in Wales, who had broken her leg. A few days later he thanked them for another parcel, commenting that all the lads had had a good time at Christmas with 'tons of bacca and tabs sent out to us and a lot of Xmas pudding'. He commented that the local people closest to the front line were not very friendly and begrudged even a drink of water, but those behind the lines let the soldiers into their houses to write their letters home and gave them coffee.

From 9–13 January, 11th DLI was relieved by the Pioneers from 8th Division and given a week's rest. The route out involved two days' solid marching, which the diary proudly records: 'none fell out'. The first day saw them march from Rue de Bruges via Scully Bridge, Doulieu, Bleu and Vieux-Berquin to Sec-Bois. On the second, they carried on via La Motte, Papote and Morbecque to Min Fontaine in the countryside near the Forest of Nieppe. Each day they marched until 1.30 p.m. and on 14 January they spent the day settling into their billets. Rest for once included more than just training and drill, though these were frequent activities. On 19 January, they spent the afternoon playing football, while at 5.30 p.m. on the 21st the officers gave a two-hour concert party for the men as part of a fond farewell to Lieutenant General Pulteney, the divisional commander. Although 11th DLI had its own concert group under Captain Fillingham, the 20th Division was particularly famous for its concert troupe, The Verey Lights, run by officers from 11th Rifle Brigade.

Fatalities for the battalion by 1916 amounted to thirty. Of these, two had died before embarkation. Most are buried in cemeteries around the area in which they served and died. Ten are in the No. 1 Cemetery, Rue du Bacquerot, in the village of Laventie immediately behind the front line. A further six are at Sailly-sur-la-Lys in a cemetery of about 300 graves started by and mainly including Canadians. Three are among over 1,000 buried at Merville Communal Cemetery where there had been a hospital and casualty clearing station for the wounded. Three more are among the 1,500 burials at Rue-Petillon, Fleurbaix, where many have been concentrated from other burial grounds. The 700 at the Aubers Ridge British Cemetery, situated beyond the Laventie front line in what had been German-held territory, include four men from 11th DLI, probably originally from the former cemetery of Winchester Post, Rue du Bacquerot, at Laventie.[14]

Among these casualties, the service records for Private 21944 Alexander Coates have survived. They tell us little more about his death when the billets were shelled on 10 November 1915, other than that he was with 26th Field Ambulance when he died of the wounds he suffered. He was twenty-four years old when he signed on at Consett on 9 November 1914, almost a year to the day before his death. A miner by trade, born in Crook, he was 5 feet 6½ inches tall, weighed a moderate 129 pounds and was broad-chested at 37 inches. With a typical miner's sallow complexion, he had blue eyes and brown hair. His mother was Mrs Annie Coates of 4 Station Road, Lanchester. She had been receiving 10s 7d a week to make up for Alexander's lost contribution to the family budget. By the time the war ended, both she and his father were dead, so the medals and other commemorative items were sent to his younger brother, Joseph.[15]

Lance Corporal 13797 John Henderson of B Company was of almost identical build to Coates, though a little heavier and broader. He was also a miner when he joined up, older than Coates at thirty-four, and married with two children. His widow, Mrs Julia Henderson lived at 14 Northern

Terrace, Dudley, Annesford, Northumberland, with her two young sons, William and John. There was family around her, with her mother-in-law living at No. 3 and her sister-in-law at No. 50 in the same street. She was awarded a weekly pension of 18s 6d, paid from 10 July 1916 and replacing the previous separation allowance and allotment of pay. Henderson had been a soldier before, serving for three years with 1st DLI during the South African War, and had been discharged at the end of his term of engagement in 1902. He re-enlisted at Newcastle-upon-Tyne on 31 August 1914 and during training with 11th DLI was one of those prone to overstaying his pass. The first time he got off lightly, losing a day's pay. The second time he was three days late back from what was probably his pre-embarkation leave. He was awarded ten days FP2 and forfeited three days' pay. The experience did not prevent him being promoted to Lance Corporal on 14 July 1915. He was wounded, probably a victim of the constant shell fire afflicting the battalion during its heavy month of trench work, dying on 19 December 1915.

On 20 January 1916, the division were ordered north to the Ypres Salient to form part of XIV Corps, Second Army. They completed their rest and recreation before moving on to what was probably the most feared part of the Western Front. In a final piece of fun, the NCOs beat the officers at rugby on 25 January and the men were rewarded for such temerity with a route march a couple of days later, and then again for good measure to impress their new general, Herbert Plumer, at an inspection on the 31st. The battalion had now been in France for five months and were much changed. They were no longer the inexperienced recruits who came out in July 1915, nor were they in fact the same battalion in terms of individual composition. Men in large numbers had been transferred out and replaced by newcomers from the training battalions in England, including new officers and NCOs. Thirty of their number were dead and many more had been wounded. The men had learned something of the realities of frontline conditions and had gained some of the skills for survival while working at night fixing the wire in front of the trenches. They had experienced the boredom, the petty diseases and some of the stupidities that marked out everyday existence in their new conditions. They had grown used to separation from their families in a foreign environment and were learning to manage the means of staying in contact with home. More than ever they appreciated small luxuries such as Oxo cubes, a bath, and egg and chips. They had become soldiers, but remained to their families distinct and loved individuals.

NOTES TO CHAPTER FOUR

1   The National Archives, WO95/2108.
2   Battalion War Diary, WO95/2108, entry for 21 July 1915.
3   Both the British Postal Museum & Archive and the Royal Engineers provide informative websites.
4   The National Archives, British Army First World War Service Records WO 363, James Alexander Bowlt. The witness, William Sheehan, an ironworks labourer from West Hartlepool, was killed in action on 7 October 1916.
5   General Registry Office reference Oct–Dec 1915 Hartlepool 10a 145.
6   See Roper, 2009, for a wider discussion of this issue.
7   The National Archives: WO 213/6.
8   The National Archives: WO 372/3.
9   The register entries bear the note 'S' in red, which suggests the sentence may have been suspended, to avoid escape from frontline service. A minority of entries involving imprisonment for 20th Division have no such note.
10 The names have been deduced from CWGC records. Private 21419 John Acomb, aged twenty-three from Cawood near Selby, Private 25232 W. Duffy and Private 24129 T. A. Isaac were all killed on 10 November 1915 and are buried close to each other and to Private McDonald at Aubers Ridge British Cemetery. Private 21944 A. Coates and Private 25228 T. Murray are buried at the Sailly-sur-la-Lys Canadian Cemetery, having both died on the same day. The full casualty list records ten deaths for this day and Sergeant 18955 William Clennell Siddle, from A Company, should be included as part of this incident. He was formerly a fireman from Blackhill, Co. Durham, aged twenty-three, unmarried and a Wesleyan Methodist.
11 In the 1911 Census, Elizabeth Bennett was aged fourteen and an apprentice dressmaker, following the normal pattern of miner's daughters going into some form of domestic service or related work. By 1915 she was eighteen and used the opportunity created by the war to change her prospects.
12 Papers of Ralph Worfolk, GS 1788, Liddle Collection, University of Leeds.
13 Fussell, 1975, p. 245.
14 Normally fatalities were buried close to where they died, very often adjacent to one of the field ambulance units to which casualties were taken, or in specially allotted areas at the time of major battles. After the war there were so many of these scattered burial grounds, many of which were small, that they were rationalised and the remains moved under close supervision of the War Graves Commission.
15 The National Archives, WO 363, Alexander Coates.

CHAPTER FIVE

A First Taste of Flanders Fields

Soldiers were constantly on the move, from billet to billet, in and out of trenches. Moving to a new front altogether was more unsettling, particularly for a relatively inexperienced unit. The front line at Ypres was a daunting prospect. It was here that the Germans had recently first used gas, a practice condemned, and as ruthlessly adopted, by the Allies. The Germans held the limited high ground, from which their artillery dominated the Allied lines and well beyond. The agricultural drainage system and sea defences had been destroyed, making trench conditions particularly bad and the blue, sticky mud a constant problem. Despite these conditions, both sides were actively attempting to tunnel under their opponents to lay explosive charges.[1]

The 20th Division commenced its march north on 22 January 1916 (11th DLI setting off on 28 January) and spent twelve days around Cassel working with 14th Division learning the ropes for this sector of the front. The Pioneers were based at Zermezeele and, on 1 February, Major Geoffrey Hayes, the battalion second-in-command, went by bus with his officers to inspect the area to be taken over from the 11th King's Liverpool Regiment. On 5 February the battalion moved up to Winnezeele.

For the men of 11th DLI the itch to return home on leave was growing and it shows up in Robert Bennett's letters, expressing concern about and remembrance of people and things back home. From Robert Bennett's letters dated 29 and 30 January, it would appear that the Machine Gun Section arrived at the new base a day or two later than the main battalion. He was beginning to despair of getting home on leave in February. He wished he could help his Dad with the garden and asked specifically for little writing pads that he could slip into his pocket. He seemed anxious for the family back home to keep in touch with each other and frequently

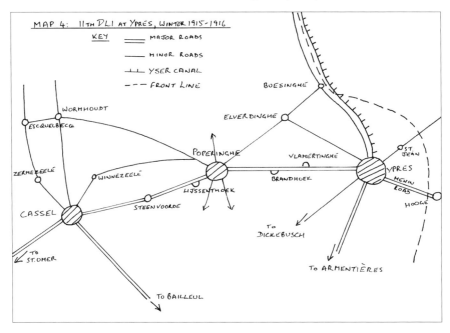

11th DLI at Ypres, winter 1915–1916. (*Martin Bashforth, 2010*)

passed on bits of news from his other letters, especially about Aunt Dolly's progress with her broken leg. Simple things meant a lot, like receiving spare buttons, which the men found difficult to get in such out of the way places, which he said reminded him of Fairburn.[2] He was now being trained in first aid 'as we are always in the trenches with other battalions and we have to shift for our-selves if anything happens'. He wished 'our Leo' was still based where 11th DLI now were, so that they could meet up.[3] Each letter reassured 'we are alright here so you need not worry about me' and concluded with heart shapes encircling kisses for the youngest Bennett children, Peter and Hilda.

On the night of 11/12 February, the division moved closer to the line around Elverdinghe, where the divisional HQ occupied the local chateau. The Germans greeted them with artillery and gas. As Robert Bennett commented in a letter home, 'we dident half get a reception when we got here into our billet they shelled all over the place all night we did not get to sleep till about 5 in the morning'. Every changeover in the Ypres Salient seemed visible to the Germans and was met with their calling card. B and D Companies went into the trenches on the first night, with A and C Companies following the next day. The war diary remarked on the novelty of sighting a Zeppelin at 10.45 p.m. on 13 February. It was probably photographing them.

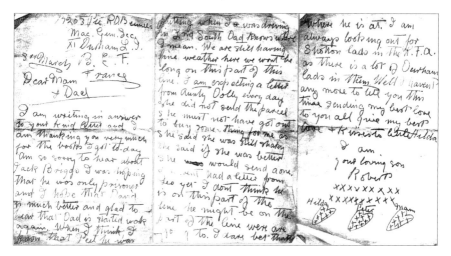

A typical letter from Robert Bennett, dated 3 March 1916, while based at Elverdinghe. (*Collection of Gaynor Greenwood*)

The trenches were much worse than at Laventie. The Royal Engineers field companies and 11th DLI worked together. The writer of the battalion diary took considerable pride in listing every task completed on a weekly basis. Throughout February and March they dug and revetted trenches, cleared fire-bays in communications trenches, buried cables for the Signals Company, put out wire, constructed dugouts and saps for machine-gun emplacements, sank wells and repaired and re-laid tramways. Frost and water damage repeatedly eroded the hard and dangerous labour.

At the end of February, men were still returning from leave and Second Lieutenants Jee and Taylor joined the battalion. Any further leave was cancelled for the time being, as there were continuous alerts. Poor Robert Bennett, writing home on 26 February, clearly had not been told about this: 'the leave is starting again I am standing No. 11 for leave and they send one every 8 days so it is a bit yet'. The weather was bitter cold, with heavy snow and hard frosts, 'but we don't take any harm as we don't go into the trenches'. Robert was grateful for small comforts: 'the shaving brushes will do champion they are good lather brushes'. His letters exchanged news about people and events at home – the local doctor dying, even the death of someone he never knew but the family thought he might.

Letters were received and sent even from the trenches, though parcels might be held back. It was difficult to keep in touch with pals in other units. 'Ive never had a letter from Leo yet. I was thinking of writing another letter to him but you saying that he has come out theres no use writing to him as he would not get my letters.' Eventually Leo sent a letter while stationed in Lydd, Kent, asking Robert to be his best man as he was intending to get married – 'don't tell anyone though', a request Robert ignored. Robert asked for ambulance books from his Dad, as he kept forgetting what he learned from his first aid course. An odd request perhaps, but first aid knowledge was a common part of mining culture and his father was trained. A less peculiar request was for photos of girl friends, pals and growing younger children. Robert often asked for these: 'I will be glad when I get the photos Ive forget how they were and little Hilda will have grown by now.' He had last seen her eight months before. It seemed longer.

Attempts to reassure the family sometimes took the form of bravado: 'don't worry about me I am amongst the best lads in the Battalion and I am alright as regards fighting'. More commonly he wrote: 'I am not in the trenches I have not been in for ever such a long time since, I thought I had told you before we are alright here a home made bed to sleep in and plenty of blankets and plenty to eat so we are like kings to a lot out here.' It had become clear that Robert's chance of home leave had slipped away. On 15 March, he wrote: 'I am very sorry to tell you that I believe the leave is stopped for good theres that many of Kitcheners out here that they cant keep it going so will have to wish the war was over. But don't get downhearted about it we can't make any better of it.'

At the end of March, the battalion set about replacing the tents and huts in the Elverdinghe chateau grounds with dugouts, to provide cover from the frequent, heavy and accurate shelling. The weather, according to Robert, was just like summer and he played down the shelling. 'We are on the grounds of an Austrian Count's estate just like the doctors at Llanberis and there is a lot of hot houses and everything is in bloom, pears and vines and all sorts of fruit. It would be such a nice place but everything is broken now with shells. They always send some over about four in the evening but never hit anybody. They sent some over last night and managed to wound a R.F.A Captain and 3 men.'

News from home included the deaths of people Robert knew. 'I am sorry to hear about Young's lad I knew him well he was in the same class as me at school. His father used to drink a lot.' He was sent copies of the local paper about those who had died, like 'Geordie' Hesp. Private 27459 George Henry Hesp of 2nd DLI was killed on 3 March 1916 and is buried at Poperinghe New Military Cemetery. More happily, Robert occasionally met up with men from home: 'I saw a lad from Shotton here they call him Raine he is in the Royal F.A. he was at Salisbury Plain the same time as me and I did not see him till I came out here.'⁴ Robert's letters often focused on the little things that made life tolerable. He thanked his Dad for a new razor and asked for something for a boil on his leg – 'ask Dad what would do. We get no satisfaction off these doctors they all seem to think we are trying to get off parades.' While grateful for a postal order, he suggested that instead they send 'little parcels and dont put so much cake in just a taste of everything'. Postal orders did not go far because the prices charged by the Belgians were too high 'and theres nothing like a taste of something from home'.

As a change from their usual work, during April, one company was attached to each of the brigades in the front line and they received special notes of praise from brigade commanders on 9 April. Whether the praise included Corporal Thomas Bashforth specifically is doubtful, as he reported sick on 31 March and was sent next day to the care of 62nd Field Ambulance suffering from pyrexia (a fever) and did not get back to his unit until 8 April.[5] On 12 April, the division went for a month's rest near Calais. The Pioneers were stationed at Oodezeele. Among the various delights recorded in the battalion diary Lieutenant Marples contracted German measles, which must have occasioned some ribaldry among his colleagues. There were the usual restful occupations, such as route marches and work parties, to avoid any danger of boredom setting in. Meanwhile officers attended riding school and lectures, such as 'Lessons from the South African War' by Captain Scott and 'Gas preventatives, liquid fire, etc.' by Lieutenant A. I. Ward. Some men were allowed away on leave. Otherwise it was training, PT, bayonets, bombing, and church parades that most approximated 'rest'. It may have been less strenuous for the nine NCOs and men who were sent off to divisional HQ at Esquelbecq to be tested as bandsmen. The simple delights of baths at Wormhoudt on 28 April would have been an occasion of relief. The irregular bathing and living conditions took their toll in the form of skin diseases. On 13 May, the diary recorded the unpleasant experience of '17 men with scabies sent from detachment at H5b and isolated'.

On 20 May, the 11th DLI was ordered back into the line to relieve the 4th Battalion Coldstream Guards, between 6th Division and the Canadians. They were based at Brandhoek and 300 men were sent by train to Ypres every evening around eight, returning around two in the morning. Mostly it was trench work, reclaiming, draining, wiring, repairing and building up parapets. The battalion war diary systematically lists the trenches they worked on during June: Strand, Haymarket, Garden Street, X8 Extension, Kaaie Salient, West Lane, White Chateau, Muddy Lane, Congreve Walk. This regime continued until mid-July, with the occasional dangerous variation. They provided wire-cutting in advance of trench raids as part of divisional fighting against German attacks around the Hooge, Hill 62 and Sanctuary Wood. On 13 June, there was a memorial service for Lord Kitchener at Poperinghe, and the next day the battalion war diary recorded that 'the Daylight Saving Bill was adopted here at 11 pm'.

After a short hiatus in hospital for treatment for her broken leg, Aunt Dolly resumed her exchange of letters with Robert Bennett. For all her troubles she was sprightly enough to wish she was a soldier so she could do her bit and particularly wanted to go up in a flying machine. Lizzie sent Robert a copy of the evening paper 'when they were shouting about Kitchener being drowned so I got it in good time but we knew a bit before but we got the details'. A parcel arrived but the top was damaged and Robert's supplies of clay pipes were broken, though fortunately a cousin Katie from Bangor had sent some cigarettes. Once again on 18 June he reported that all leave had been stopped. In early July, amid wet and thundery weather, Robert received another parcel and this time the clay pipes survived the journey, along with some much-needed shaving soap. He sent a silk postcard to his Aunt Dolly's mistress, expecting a reply. He was keen to reassure the family that the battalion was not in the thick of fighting. Many miles to the south, the Pals battalions had been receiving their baptismal slaughter on the Somme. On the Ypres front 'every day is just the same out here sometimes we lose count of the days'. Robert was adamant in his reassurance: 'I am miles away and you need not fret I am alright you need not be frightened of that.' At home, his younger brother Davy, aged about thirteen and already earning more in the mines than Robert had done before the war, had his confirmation ceremony at the local parish church. All was peaceful at home.

Meanwhile, 60th Brigade moved on 13–14 July from Poperinghe to Steenwerck to support II Anzac Corps, taking 150 men from 11th DLI with them. HRH the Prince of Wales visited the battalion headquarters at Brandhoek on 14 July. A couple of days later the battalion (less the 150 on detachment) went to rest billets in Winnezeele for training. It was the prelude to a change of scenery. After the march Robert Bennett wrote home, still anxious to reassure and expressing interest that 'the Boch has been sending some whiss bangs at Seaham Harbour they do no damage they have to nearly hit you before they hurt you'.

Casualties during the battalion's time in the Ypres sector, in 1916, were comparatively light. The summary for the period between 20 May and 16 July gave one officer and one ranker killed, while forty-five were wounded. By comparison, with these casualties from enemy fire, an officer and forty-three other ranks were evacuated sick in the same period. The rough equality of these statistics illustrates well the steady, low-level, attritional nature of casualties for a Pioneer battalion at one remove from the main fighting.

The officer killed was Second Lieutenant Ernest Rowan Butler Clough, aged twenty-two and from Bristol, originally from the Devonshire Regiment. Born 11 June 1894, Clough was the son of Lieutenant Colonel

Alfred Herrick Butler Clough of the Royal Munster Fusiliers. Solidly built and standing almost 5 feet 10 inches tall; when he applied for a temporary commission his first choice was for a Pioneer battalion. He had matriculated Second Class from London University in July 1912 in English, Mathematics, Chemistry, French and Modern History. He suffered a bad bout of dyspepsia, with jaundice and catarrh in December 1915 and had to be shipped back to England to recover at 1st Southern General Hospital in Birmingham, returning to his unit on 21 April 1916 after some active convalescence with 16th DLI at Penkridge Camp, Rugeley. On 27 June 1916, while supervising trench improvement works in the Brandhoek sector on St Jean Road, he was killed by shrapnel. The telegram to his father at The Grange, Alvestone, Gloucestershire, stated baldly: 'Deeply Regret to Inform that 2 Lieut ERB Clough Durham Light Infantry Died of Wounds June 27th the Army Council Express their Sympathy.' His estate amounted to £154 14s 3d, for which his father received letters of administration. On 4 February 1919, his father, then living in Bristol, received the customary scroll and plaque presented to those families who had lost relatives in the war.[6] Clough is buried at Brandhoek.

On the same day and perhaps in the same incident, the death of Private 12870 Henry Leonard of D Company, who was the same age as Clough, is not mentioned by name in the war diary. He is buried at Lijssenthoek, near Poperinghe, probably the site of 3rd Canadian Casualty Clearing Station, where he died of his wounds. Before the war, Leonard worked for the North Eastern Railway Company as a platelayer maintaining the lines around West Hartlepool.

The death of Private 21547 John Brady, earlier in the year and prior to this incident, became the source of a long correspondence between the Army authorities and his very articulate and determined mother. Although from Renfrew in Scotland, John Brady attested in London on 1 September

H. Leonard,
Durham Light Inf.

Portrait of Henry Leonard from *North Eastern Railway* Magazine, 1916. (*Courtesy of the British Rail Board (Residuary) Ltd*)

The headstone of Henry Leonard at Lijssenthoek Military Cemetery, Poperinghe. (*Gaynor Greenwood*)

1914, was assigned originally to 7th DCLI before being transferred to 11th DLI when the latter became a Pioneer battalion. He gave his father's name as James Farrell Brady, but, in fact, the family name was Farrell and 'Brady' was his mother's maiden name. The deception was occasioned by a previous attempt to enlist in the Scots Guards in the first week of the war. As his mother, Catherine Farrell, later explained, 'he was discharged for having a badly shaped toe (they were very particular then) and instead of coming home he went on to London'. John Brady was clearly of a high-spirited nature. He was constantly in trouble during basic training, being disciplined on several occasions for being absent without leave, sometimes for days at a time. On 3 December 1914, he was accused of refusing to obey an order and 'making an improper reply to an NCO', for which he was fined fifteen days' pay. During a later occasion when he was undergoing FP2 for one of his repeated absences he was 'found in canteen when a defaulter'. Perhaps he got this spirit from his mother or at least her example. She pestered the paymaster's office for further information about her son's death. The following letter dated 6 April 1916 is a typical example.

> Dear Sir, I received your letter this morning and am very grateful to you for your kindness in replying to mine. While my son 21546 John Brady was home on leave he's spoken of the Brothers O'Neil, one a Sergeant, also one Gibson who were in his Company. He had a photo of the group 8th Platoon 'B' Company and they were in it. Would it be too much to ask from you if you could give me the number of any one of these so that I might write and see if I could get any further news, failing them could I get the name of the Sergeant Major of his Company. I am sorry to give you any trouble but surely you won't blame a poor mother, Yours respectfully Kate Farrell. I enclose 2 stamps that will pay for the last letter.

It would not be the last that the Army was to hear from Kate Farrell.[7]

Coincidentally, two of those who lost their lives during this spell in the Ypres sector were both called Hewitt, but they do not appear to be closely related. Private 13306 John Cousins Hewitt of C Company was killed on 11 February 1916, at Zermezeele, aged twenty-five, though the battalion diary records nothing in the way of action that day. His service records reveal a somewhat unusual figure at 6 feet tall, weighing 155 pounds with a chest of 38 inches unexpanded. He was a labourer from Blaydon-on-Tyne. The most prevalent characteristic that appears in his records is a lack of attention to appearance and hygiene. His height made him a useful choice as an NCO, but he could not live up to the demands,

The headstones of John (Brady) Farrell, John Hewitt and Stephen Ferry at Ferme-Olivier Cemetery, Elverdinghe. (*Gaynor Greenwood*)

constantly admonished during training for being absent from bathing parade, not washing before breakfast and neglecting his duty. He reverted to the rank of Private after a short spell as Acting Corporal. His namesake, Private 16000 James Hewitt, a miner from the Crook area, served with No. 5 Platoon 'B' Company. At 5 feet 3½ inches tall, he was of a more stocky build and perhaps his Wesleyan persuasion kept him out of too much trouble, other than the common overstaying of pass. He died, 21 March 1916, of wounds to the shoulder and face, after being shipped back to Boulogne for treatment.

As Keith Mitchinson has commented, Pioneer battalions generally suffered fewer casualties than ordinary infantry battalions.[8] Inevitably this was true to a certain degree, but the number of dead is no guide to the contribution made by a group of men. The problem for Pioneer battalions was less the occasional catastrophic losses suffered by infantry battalions engaged in assaults (though the Pioneers shared these dangers at times), but the steady attrition of men as a result of the particular dangers they faced. Working at night and in front of the lines, they were particularly exposed to snipers and machine-gunners, periodic trench raids and the constant harassment of speculative shelling. It was a pattern with which the men of 11th DLI were becoming all too familiar by the summer of 1916.

NOTES TO CHAPTER FIVE

1 Barton, Doyle and Vandewalle, 2004. Although 11th DLI were rarely directly involved in this work, several former miners from the battalion transferred to mining companies.

2 It is not entirely clear where the place referred to is located. There was a mining community at Fairburn in Yorkshire, just west of Selby, where the miners could only reach the pit by assembling together at the commencement of their shift, to be ferried across the Aire and Calder Navigation, as there was no bridge.

3 'Our Leo' has not been positively identified by the present-day family, but was probably a cousin of Robert Bennett.

4 Gunner 96585 J. Raine, A Battery, 50th Brigade Royal Field Artillery, died on Thursday 19 October 1916 and is buried at Flatiron Copse Cemetery, Mametz.

5 The National Archives, WO 363, Service Records, Thomas Bashforth, Form B103L, Casualty Form – Active Service.

6 The National Archives, WO339/19682. Collection of papers relating to Ernest Rowan Butler Clough.

7 See chapter 13, p. 227.

8 Mitchinson, 1997, p. 41.

CHAPTER SIX

The Quick and the Dead: The Somme, 1916

Robert's letters seem to suggest that the men from 11th DLI had heard something about the losses on the Somme, where they were now headed. By the time they arrived and saw the physical conditions, they would have quickly gathered what experiences they might expect in their new assignment. Their families back home became more anxious as the casualty reports attained catastrophic levels. There had been large and bloody battles the year before at Gallipoli, Neuve Chapelle and Loos, but the attrition on the Somme was on a different scale. Communication between men at the front and their families at home was even more important in keeping everyone reassured. The pace and volume of losses would disrupt the efficiency of mail deliveries and would begin to overwhelm the official channels for advising families of the men being wounded or killed. Families at home did not know where their men were located.

From 20 July, the 11th DLI was at Bailleul, from where they marched to St-Sylvestre-Cappel. On the 25th, they entrained at Balinchove station for Doullens. Arriving too late for billets, they had to make do with a temporary bivouac. Next day they marched on to Couin, where the billets were so filthy that they had to spend the whole of the following day cleaning them. It was to little avail. On the 28th, they moved to the Dell, to take over what was described as 'the dirtiest camp we have ever struck', formerly occupied by their Pioneer counterparts, the 19th Welsh Fusiliers. They barely had time to clean up before they were involved in trenching work. On 29 July 1916, the division was moved into a line between Beaumont Hamel and Hébuterne. The Pioneers began to restore the trench system and communications, to clear the battlefield and bury the dead, and to generally reclaim the defences. Conditions were atrocious. The area had been targeted ruthlessly by the German artillery in order to hold up

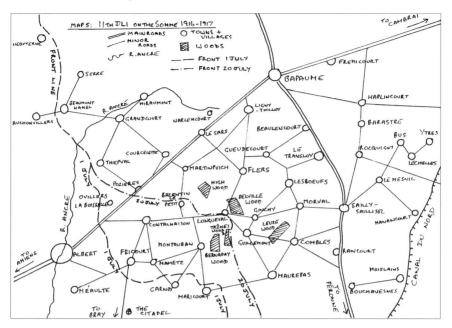

11th DLI on the Somme, 1916-1917. (*Martin Bashforth, 2010*)

the British advance. The trenches were totally wrecked and together with the area around were strewn with dead bodies. Some trenches were so badly damaged that, to begin with, the area was held only by advance parties. Working parties moved in and out from camps behind until the area was cleared and stabilised. Many trenches were simply filled in as makeshift graves, and new trenches made in front of them up to 200 yards from the enemy. Communications trenches were made, dugouts created and the battlefield cleared as far as possible. So much work had to be done that units from the 3rd Battalion Grenadier Guards and field companies of Royal Engineers reinforced 11th DLI.[1] This appalling work continued for the first two weeks of August, during which several officers reported sick, including Captain Pemberton, Lieutenant Cunningham and Lieutenant Floyd. The August battalion war diary was sent to division late, with an accompanying apology, because both the CO and his adjutant went sick. It would be delayed again in September. Conditions were then so poor that they were constantly on the move and had no settled 'office accommodation in the trench'.[2]

The battalion remained here throughout August, with occasional relief cleaning equipment and enjoyable baths (at Orville on the 17th), and PT and bayonet practice (at Berneuil on the 19th). Robert Bennett reported fine weather at the beginning of August: 'we are have it red hot sweating like anything'. Unfortunately, there was a long delay to mail, with parcels not getting through. There is a two-week gap in Robert's letter writing that reflected the extent to which the battalion had been on the move during the last two weeks of July, as well as the tiring work. He asked to be excused for not writing as 'we have been very busy'. He did manage to meet a neighbour's son, Lonsdale of the Coldstream Guards, and had a long chat with him in the trenches. He was also able to exchange letters with 'Lizzie's young chap', who was a sergeant 'not far from here'.[3]

On 22 August, after a short rest, the 20th Division moved further south to relieve the 24th Division at Guillemont. Access to this part of the Somme battlefield was via the staging post that became famous to many units as The Citadel. Today, a narrow road runs across the area past a British military cemetery of the same name, lying just below a rise in the typically rolling chalk landscape of Picardy. Nothing remains to suggest the conditions experienced in September 1916. Then the slopes were filled with bivouacs, cut through by roads that were constantly in use by battalions moving in and out of the line around Bernafay Wood, Lesboeufs and Combles.

During the first week in the area, Robert reported a gradual change in the weather from fine to wet. His letters continued their role as the conduit for family information, as everybody seemed to write to him and he could pass around the news from aunts, uncles and grandparents as well as his own snippets of information. It seems possible that soldiers at the front had the effect of bringing dispersed families closer together in this way. Robert hoped that by the winter he would get the chance to come home on leave, particularly to see his sister Lizzie. One of his Shotton neighbours, Bill Jones, had been sent to Ireland (this was a few months after the Easter Rising) and Robert commented that it was 'a long better than being out here I wish I had my choice I know which I would pick'.

Parcels had now caught up with the battalion and Robert appreciated some nice moist bread, a great improvement on 'biscuits as hard as iron'. In a letter dated 27 August, he reported the work as very hard, not helped by heavy rain. The Pioneers were digging assembly trenches for a forthcoming attack, though Robert could not give details. There was constant shelling, which Robert described in matter-of-fact style as 'the Boche only puts over a shell now and then'. He mentioned the resultant death of Sergeant Henry Andrew Clasper, a Gateshead man from D Company, with whom he had shared a tent at Woking. Clasper had been a former regular soldier, but was a fireman in civilian life, now aged thirty and promoted to full sergeant just two months before.

The overall aim of the attacks, for which 11th DLI was doing the preparatory work, was to straighten the line by capturing Leuze Wood and the village of Guillemont, thus securing a foothold on a ridge of high

ground. Guillemont had already cost thousands of casualties and seemed
almost impregnable. Even before the attack was launched, 20th Division,
especially 60th Brigade, had lost so many men that the date of the assault
was postponed until 3 September 1916. The village itself was well fortified;
the German trenches around the village were deep and heavily reinforced,
while a quarry in front of the main fortifications acted like a medieval
moat. Following an initial reconnaissance by battalion officers on 23
August, three companies of 11th DLI constructed the assembly trenches.
Rain made work impossible from 29 August, with roads impassable and
dugouts falling in on themselves. Once the rain ceased, the German artillery
opened up with continuous barrages, throughout which the Pioneers had
to keep working. They lost seven men killed and thirty-six wounded over
a period of three days. But their contribution would extend beyond these
preparations into the battle itself.

On 2 September, the day before the attacks began, Robert wrote what
was to be his final letter.

I am writing to you in answer to your kind and welcome letter I got the
other day and I am thanking you for the tongue it was alright I can tell
you and the bread was nice and moist. Who do you think was here to see
me yesterday Leo he is only about 20 minutes walk off here. We had a

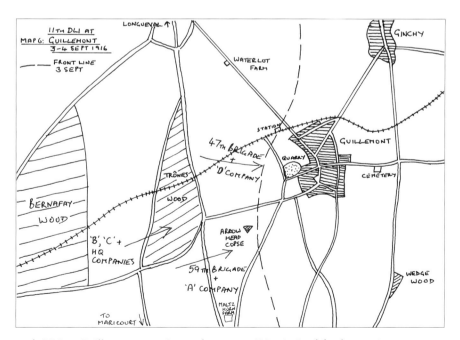

11th DLI at Guillemont, 3–4 September 1916. (*Martin Bashforth, 2010*)

good talk to him I was so pleased to see him. I am so sorry to hear about
Jack Briggs tell Mrs Briggs I sympathise with her. I havent very much
to tell you only I have had a letter from Maggie she is at Nains for her
holidays and she says that Nain and Taid are going on alright and that
Uncle Morris father has died and he was buried yesterday that was the
27 August. Well I havent any more to tell you this time am sending my
best love to all at home and to you and Dad.

He signed off with his usual set of hearts encircling kisses for Mam, Hilda
and Peter, and a P.S.: 'Tell Dad that I was praised on my stretcher bearer
work so the St John's has not been in vain.'

The battalion was split up on 3 September, with A and D Companies
supporting, respectively, the 59th and 47th Brigades, who formed the
main attack to the south and west of Trônes Wood, to the left of the road
between Longueval and Maricourt. The remainder of the battalion (B,
C and HQ Companies) was in reserve at Bernafay Wood to the east of
Montauban. Moving out of their base in craters at Carnoy, the division
went through the assembly trenches on 3 September. The 59th Brigade,
including A Company 11th DLI, fought on the right with the aim of taking
Arrow Head Copse while the group on the left, including D Company
11th DLI, supported the 6th Connaught Rangers in taking and holding
the village of Guillemont itself. The remaining companies were to follow
the second line of the attack, passing through the first group. In order not
to fail in the capture of Guillemont as previous attempts had done, the
advance units went in ahead of and close to the creeping barrage, in order
to fall on the German trenches the moment the barrage was lifted. It was
a costly risk, but it worked. Previous attempts to take the village had been
so bloodily repulsed that the ground in front of the village was full of
dead and decaying bodies, making progress both difficult and gruesome.
Nevertheless, all the objectives were achieved; the village was captured
and the Germans driven out completely. It is not surprising that the 20th
Light Division would choose Guillemont to erect one of its two memorials
after the war.

On 4 September, the day following the successful attack, the two advance
companies of 11th DLI continued to consolidate the hold on Guillemont
under heavy fire from machine-guns and artillery, with no water and no
stretchers. The other companies hastily dug communication trenches
and brought up wire for the new front line. At 10.50 a.m. Major Lloyd
advanced B and C Companies to relieve the exhausted 59th Brigade.
Losses for the day included several wounded lieutenants, and three other
ranked dead, fifty-two wounded and one man missing. Until 7 September,
11th DLI remained in the line with 60th Brigade and 6th KSLI, ensuring

The remnants of the 20th Division Memorial at Guillemont, 1999. The original obelisk was unveiled 4 June 1922, but was damaged by war and erosion. (*Martin Bashforth*)

the line was properly consolidated, although they were allowed a short break 'resting in the craters at Carnoy' on 5 September. These particularly insalubrious quarters were literally as described – deep shell holes with makeshift canvas shelters covering them. Casualties for the division continued to be high and 11th DLI lost four officers and eighty-seven other ranks.[4] These included the wounded, but there were at least twenty-one dead or missing, including Lance Corporal 22506 Charles Robert Potter from A Company, who is buried at Bronfay Farm Cemetery, adjacent to the former field hospital not far from the village of Bray-sur-Somme.

The 20th Division commanders noted the quality of the work that had recently been done by 11th DLI. In the 'Narrative Report of Actions 3–5 September 1916', paragraph eleven reads: 'The successful consolidation of the positions won and the construction of various strong points was very largely due to the assistance rendered by the R.E's and 11th DLI (Pioneers). These troops worked gallantly and strenuously without rest for some 48 hours and during part of that time two companies of the 11th DLI took over and held part of the front line of the 59th Brigade.' The rather bland report glosses over the bravery of the infantrymen, Pioneers and engineers in the first assault.[5]

On 7 September, the battalion went via Bois de Tailles, arriving at Méricourt on the 9th for a rest and clean-up. On 13 September, they

Left: The headstone of
Charles Potter at Bronfay
Farm Military Cemetery,
who died of wounds
sustained during the
capture of Guillemont.
(*Martin Bashforth*)

Below: View of German
trenches destroyed
by British artillery at
Guillemont, September
1916. (*Imperial War
Museum, Q 1165*)

were in reserve at The Sandpits, with the mixed pleasures of two days of road-making and drill. On the morning of the 15th, they were back at The Citadel, and at 12.55 p.m. they marched out 'as strong as possible in Battle orders for Talus Boisé'. They carried two days' rations and, when they reached their destination, found they had neither shelters nor dugouts. During the period of rest, on 10 September, Ginchy had been taken, completing the capture of the ridge of high ground. A further advance was made on 15 September, with 20th Division in reserve. The infantry was put into action on the 16th, though its ranks were severely depleted. The strongest brigade was not much more than a full battalion in numbers, about one third of its normal complement. Accounts of battles during the Somme campaign sometimes do not recognise the way in which units continued to be thrown forward, despite being severely depleted in numbers and physically worn down.

From 17 to 21 September, 11th DLI was employed consolidating the trenches for the new front line around Bernafay Wood in spite of bad weather and under hostile fire. Three men of C Company were badly wounded on 17 September when one of them struck an unexploded shell. Among them was Private 16984 John George Cummins, a coke worker from Stockton-on-Tees. The Admission and Discharge Book for 34th Casualty Clearing Station describes wounds to the face, right hand and back.[6] The other men listed were Private 20731 John Ivison, with wounds to the head and hand, a fractured leg and two fingers amputated, and Lance Corporal 16026 John Little (or Liddle), aged thirty-one, with wounds to the left foot and left arm, with the arm being amputated. Ivison and Cummins died on 20 and 21 September respectively and are buried at Grove Town Cemetery, Méaulte. Private Little was shipped out via 6th Ambulance Train. He died on 19 September at St Sever Hospital, Rouen, and was buried in the cemetery nearby. Despite the casualties and the conditions, the men worked night and day to make the assembly trenches west of Lesboeufs for yet another planned assault. The battalion worked on in poor shape, with the diary recording the strength of the four main companies as about 440 men, less than half the normal complement.

On 20 September 1916, during this work, Robert Bennett was killed. The battalion war diary was typically sparse for the day:

8 AM   Roads in Vicinity of Wood shelled. C & D Companies
        had to move out of their lines. 150 men only working at night.
6 PM   Battalion less 150 men marched out to Sand Pits
        and arrived 12 PM. Officers arrived 2/Lieuts P. Kemp,
        J. Liddell, R. Bushell, W. Inglis & J. Fillingham. Casualties
        OR Killed 2. Wounded 13.

Portrait of John George Cummins,
killed in an accident near Guillemont,
21 September 1916.
(*Collection of Sean Gregory*)

The original grave marker for
Cummins.
(*Collection of Sean Gregory*)

The modern headstone for Cummins at Grove Cemetery, Méaulte. (*Sean Gregory*)

The headstone of John Iveson, killed in the same incident as Cummins, also at Grove Cemetery. (*Sean Gregory*)

Alongside Private 12291 James Martin Thompson from Consett, Robert was the victim of shelling. Neither man has an identified grave and both are recorded on the Thiepval Memorial. The next day, the remaining 150 men referred to in the diary rejoined the battalion and everyone moved from The Sandpits into billets at Méaulte, just south of Albert. There was some rest, but only in between cleaning up the mess they found at the billets and sending work parties back towards Carnoy to make roads ready for the next advance.

Sergeant E. J. Lambert of 13 Platoon took time out to write a heartfelt letter to the Bennett family and was able to explain a little more about Robert's death:

> It is with the greatest regret that I sit down to pen these few lines. In response to the pleadings of the men in my Platoon & to my own hearts desire. You will have heard, I have no doubt, by the time you receive this, of the unfortunate death, in action of your son Bob. Of his death, there is little to say, he was killed instantly by a shell, while on very dangerous, although very important work. He died as he lived, doing his duty, faithfully & well & was buried by his comrades near by where he fell. I have had the privilege of soldiering with him since the time of his enlistment & can truly say that man could not want a better pal in any place at all. He was a friend to every man in his Platoon & among

Unidentified troops road-building near Bernafay Wood, September 1916. (*Imperial War Museum, Q 1157*)

the Machine Gun Section where he earned the good wishes of all. Let me on behalf of myself & all the N.C.O's & men of 13 Platoon express to you our deepest sympathy with you in what must be a very sad loss. Words almost fail one when trying to say all one would like to say when talking about so good a comrade. Again sending our best respects, & deepest sympathy with yourself & all his relations, I remain, on behalf of N.C.O's & men of 13 Platoon, Yours sincerely, E. J. Lambert, Sergeant.

Tragically, a number of letters from home, including some from Mrs Bennett and sister Lizzie, were returned in December 1916 with 'Killed in action' written across the front. Among the news that never reached Robert was the death of Tom Lonsdale, with whom he had not long since had such a pleasant conversation.[7] A parcel was on its way containing special razor blades Robert had requested. No doubt the pears and tongue that accompanied them were shared among the men in the platoon. Just as Robert had wanted, Lizzie had looked forward to having a spree with him when he got home on leave – so many disappointed hopes.

There would be many more reminders to come at 135 Victoria Street, Shotton Colliery. On 19 October, in response to a letter from Mr Bennett, one of the officers from D Company, 'the only officer left in the Coy who was with the Coy at Woking Depot', gave more kind words and some further information about the circumstances of Robert's death. They were

The cover of one of the family's letters to Robert Bennett, returned December 1916, marked 'Killed in Action'. (*Collection of Gaynor Greenwood*)

involved in the 'not inglorious work of this campaign – namely digging a trench from which to kick off an attack. We got the work done and were going away when we were spotted – it was a bright moonlight night – and shelled. We had two killed. Your son was one and one of my officers stayed and buried him.' Unfortunately the letter is damaged and the name of the officer missing. On 16 May 1917, Catherine Bennett signed a receipt for the few surviving personal articles: a testament, pocket book, postcard and five photos (one of them a picture of his Dad received just a few weeks before he was killed). His campaign medals arrived in May 1920, along with a printed scroll and a bronze plaque. On 3 September 1921, a memorial was unveiled on Station Road with Robert's name among 152 others from the village who died in the war.

From the arrival of the battalion on the Somme in late July 1916 to the end of September, thirty-eight men of 11th DLI lost their lives. One of the first was Private 12204 John Atkinson, who died alongside three other comrades on 2 August in an incident that is not even recorded in the battalion war diary. Like Robert, they were probably doing their normal work when they were hit by a shell. John Atkinson was a former employee of the North Eastern Railway Company, a shunter at Tyne Dock, South Shields. With several hundred other railwaymen his photograph appeared in the company magazine and his name is recorded on the fading tablets of the impressive company war memorial at Station Rise in York.[8]

Approximately twenty men lost their lives in the work during and immediately after the Battle of Guillemont. Private 14966 Francis Brown died of wounds on 4 September. Born in Darlington, he was a boiler

Portrait of John Atkinson, from the North Eastern Railway Magazine, 1916. (*Courtesy of British Rail Board (Residuary) Ltd*)

fireman, living in West Hartlepool at the outbreak of war. Francis had been single and aged just twenty-one. He had not been long back with the battalion after forty-seven days in hospital at Wincanton recovering from myalgia – a form of rheumatic muscle pain and exhaustion more commonly associated nowadays with chronic fatigue syndrome and repetitive strain injury.

The death of Private 20879 Stephen Davies on the same day resulted in considerable anguish for his family. He was a much-tattooed ironworker from Stockton, though originally from Bilston in Staffordshire. Earlier in the year, SSAFA at Stockton had sent a telegram on behalf of the family asking that he might be allowed home following the sudden death from tuberculosis of his twelve-year-old daughter Dorothy May. There is no sign in his records that leave was granted. After the report of his death SSAFA wrote again to the Territorial Office at Durham because his mother, Mrs Sarah Ann Davies, 'had received a field postcard postmarked 24 September. It is one of the usual postcards sent by soldiers and Mrs Davies states that it is her son's handwriting. Naturally she is anxious to know whether there is any possibility that he is still alive. Can you give any help?' There was no such hope however. His widow clearly found the bureaucracy of the War Office distressing, writing on 26 October 1916:

> Dear Sir or Madam, Anxious Wife of Stephen Davies killed in action Sep 4th 1916 I received the official news of my husbands death on the 22 of Sep and I sent to you my marriage lines and my 4 childrens certificates and I have not heard of them sense [sic] it is all I have left know after my dear husband as been took away from us Wife and Childern of Stephen Davies anxious for News of all this left of the Dear husband and Father marriage lines children certificats send away on 22 of Sep 1916 and as not been heard of sense. Mrs S Davies.[9]

Phoebe Ann Davies and her four surviving children, Sarah Ellen, Violet, Horace and Lilian were granted a pension of 25s a week from 26 March 1917. After the war, a further note was sent from the War Office to say that Stephen's body had been moved to Guillemont Road British Cemetery.

The War Office was unable to trace the family of Private 16202 Patrick Connolly, who died of his wounds on 5 September 1916. He was an Irish labourer, a Kilkenny man by birth, who signed up in Newcastle on 30 August 1914. His conduct during training was described in chapter 3. The whole conduct record, which runs to several pages, shows him to have been the worst disciplined soldier in the battalion, albeit in petty ways. No amount of punishment had any effect. As late as 27 August 1916, he was awarded seven days FP2, though the conduct sheet does not state

Headstones of Stephen Davies and William Laws at Guillemont Road British Cemetery. Both men died in the capture of Guillemont. (*Jon Miller*)

what for and nothing appears in the official Field General Courts Martial registers. The work the battalion was involved in will have spared him the punishment before he lost his life. The War Office sent letters to his recorded family address, but these were all returned 'no trace'. Eventually his 'small book' turned up containing a will, which left his personal effects to the wife of Private 23317 W. J. Redler of Whymple, near Exeter. She signed a receipt for his belongings: two identity discs. By contrast, the father of Connolly's comrade from A Company, Private 20993 Ralph Gray, who died on the same day, had to write from the Bute Arms public house where he lived in Rowlands Gill, to say: 'I have had one of his companions here and he told me that he had been at headquarters in France and was told that all the above soldiers' belongings had been sent to me but I have not received anything if they have come to head quarters you might let me know and oblige, Yours truly, R. Gray.'

Sometimes the War Office can be forgiven for their seemingly clumsy bureaucracy. It was immensely difficult dealing with bereaved families who were not used to dealing with figures in authority, especially in writing. When names were common, extra care had to be taken. The service papers for Private 18420 Joseph Brown, a miner from Houghton-le-Spring, include

a typed memo dated 28 January 1916 to notify the officer commanding
11th DLI that he had two men of the same name serving under the same
number – the other should have been regimental number 17222. It would
have been extremely distressing for both families had the error been
compounded in September and the wrong people notified, especially as
Private 17222 Joseph Brown had married Mary Edith Smith at Durham
Registry Office, just before the battalion was sent overseas in 1915.

Given the high casualty rate throughout the late summer months, it is
worth describing the process of reporting casualties and how the authorities
set out to inform a next of kin, setting the examples among 11th DLI
casualties in context. As the first step in the procedure, the soldier's identity
disc was taken from round his neck and his paybook from his pocket. Until
1916, each soldier had one disc, but from 24 August 1916 he had two:
one to remain with the body, one to be returned. The identity disc showed
name, number, unit and religion. The paybook generally contained the same
details, plus next of kin and a short form will. Whoever removed these
would note any other identification and the location of the body where
buried. The disc, paybook and information would be passed up through
the chain of adjutants from battalion, to division and eventually to GHQ.
The details and material would then be sent to the appropriate regional
Record Office in the UK (York in the case of the Durham Light Infantry). It
was from here that the family was officially notified. Officers' families were
informed by telegram and other ranks on Army Form B 104-82 (if dead) or
B 104-83 (if reported missing).

A few days after the event, depending on circumstances, the company
or section commander would write to the family offering consolation
with minimal, and usually reassuring, information about how the soldier
died. Such letters might prompt either a thank-you letter from the family
or further questions. Occasionally the family would be told by the Army
Record Office where the soldier was buried, though this was often much
later and in many cases not until after the war. In the case of Robert Bennett
one of the officers described how he had been buried, though the grave was
later lost. Many months after the report of death the family would receive
from the Record Office any personal effects, often pitifully few where a
soldier was killed in action, usually more if he died of wounds at a Casualty
Clearing Station or Base Hospital. While the process was fairly efficient
and staff at the Record Office were patient and courteous in handling
repeat enquiries, there was no welfare department, only a constant stream
of forms to be filled in for widow's pensions and receipts to be signed
and returned. Families depended on neighbours, friends, relatives and,
when difficulties arose, local officials or the Soldiers and Sailors Families
Association if there was one nearby. The armed forces were not geared up

The Thiepval Memorial to the Missing of the Somme, 1916, includes the names of twenty-two men from 11th DLI, such as Robert Bennett, Patrick Connolly and William Sheehan. (*Martin Bashforth*)

to provide family support, especially of the emotional kind and on such an enormous scale. Relatives of the deceased had to manage as well as they could. When problems arose in any of these processes, one can only imagine the personal anguish and confusion of the relatives, often with only a very basic education and no confidence in dealing with figures of authority. When this shows up in the surviving records, it illuminates the wider human cost of war.

NOTES TO CHAPTER SIX

1   Inglefield, 1921, p. 62.

2   Notes attached to the Battalion War Diary (WO95/2108) volumes for August and September 1916.

3   Sergeant William Davison of 10th DLI married Lizzie Bennett after the war. He was badly wounded at Third Ypres, losing part of his skull. A Canadian doctor saved his life and Bill kept in touch with him after the war. As a party trick he would take off his hat, cough and cause a bulge through the gap in his skull. He appears to have adapted well following his experiences. He ran a timber business and owned properties in the Shotton Colliery area after the war. (Information from Gaynor Greenwood.)

4   These casualties include twenty-one dead identified from the CWGC database for the period from 31 August to 7 September, plus any dying of wounds at hospital sites in the few days following.

5   The National Archives, WO 95/2096, 20th Division War Diary September 1916 and accompanying reports.

6   The National Archives, WO 95/415, records of 34 Casualty Clearing Station (Third Army), November 1915–June 1918.

7   Private 13960 Thomas Lonsdale, 4th Coldstream Guards, aged twenty-four, was killed in action on 27 September 1916 and is buried at Dantzig Alley British Cemetery, Mametz.

8   Funding was announced in 2010 to supplement the stone inscriptions with new, bronze tablets to be erected on the adjacent supporting walls of the memorial.

9   The National Archives, WO 363, Stephen Davies.

CHAPTER SEVEN

Changing Seasons on the Somme

The successful attack on Guillemont was not the last time that 11th DLI was used in close support to an infantry assault on the Somme. The British forces carried on beyond Guillemont to try to gain the higher ground of Le Transloy Ridges. With periods of rest and opportunities for home leave, the battalion was to remain in the Somme battlefield area until July the following year, experiencing both the worst and the best that the weather conditions and the state of the terrain could provide. Although most of the time was spent on labouring duties, there were occasional spells as infantry.

On 26 September, 11th DLI passed through The Citadel to carry out work in the Maltz Horn Valley cleaning and repairing tracks between Ginchy and Morval. The following day they arrived at Talus Boisé. It was pouring with rain and there were no shelters, so the next day was spent making something like a decent camp. As usual, the work would be of more benefit for the men who followed. On 29 September, 11th DLI marched on to Carnoy, where the camp consisted of trenches and shell craters covered in whatever materials were to hand. On 30 September, the battalion was in the third-line trenches at Waterlot Farm, echoing to the sound of artillery coming from both sides. Corporal Thomas Bashforth was made up to Sergeant that day. The service records show him promoted 'vice Hodges', which suggests the latter had been wounded or had moved on.

The infantry battalions were stationed close to the front. 61st Brigade was in the line, 60th Brigade in support at Trônes Wood and 59th Brigade in reserve at Carnoy. From 1 October, 20th Division attacked in an area between Gueudecourt and Lesboeufs, moving forward in short intervals of 200 yards at a time until 7 October. The Pioneers provided frontline

Temporary shelter in a shell-hole near Guillemont, 1916. Rough accommodation like this was common on the Somme battlefield. (*Imperial War Museum, Q 1166*)

support, assisting in keeping the trenches linked and in line, bringing up supplies and digging assembly trenches. They worked under constant heavy fire, including gas shells, and each day brought more casualties. Seven were killed and twenty-one wounded in the first four days. On 5 October, while A Company was separated from the rest of the battalion and sent to Montauban, casualties were one killed and ten wounded. On 6 October, there was an inspection by the CO, while two more were killed and buried at Bernafay Wood, and another two wounded. In total there were nineteen dead between 1 and 7 October, with another six dying of wounds in the following few days.

There is a noticeable characteristic of many reports from 20th Division HQ in relation to the Pioneer battalion's operations, compared with accounts in the battalion's own war diary. Divisional reports describe the work in the passive tense, without specific mention of 11th DLI. Accompanying the October 1916 diary is a 'Report on Operations 6–8 October 1916'. For 4 October it is written: 'During the day the new track from Brigade Headquarters towards the front line was staked, and all trenches crossed by it bridged, to admit of pack animals being used as forward as N.33.b.' There is no mention of who actually did the work. By contrast, the following day states: 'Steps for egress from the departure trenches were cut by a company of 11th Durham L.I., 3 sections of R.E. and a working party of 200 men found by the 12th KRR and 6th KSLI.'

General support work behind the lines 'just happened', but anything directly related to an immediate military action merited a mention for those who did the work, especially if it involved drawing manpower from infantry units. It is a pattern of description that is repeated in divisional histories and accounts of particular battles and campaigns that constantly undervalues and under-records the work of Pioneer battalions.[1]

On 7 October, the division attacked the German lines to capture strongpoints known as Rainbow Trench and Cloudy Trench. A company from 11th DLI, alongside 84th Field Company Royal Engineers, was designated to follow the infantry directly from Leek and Rose Trenches to secure the line as soon as the objective had been taken. The attack was successful and the remainder of 11th DLI was involved in consolidation work: building new communications trenches, dugouts and aid posts. The picturesque names for the trenches reflect the sense of irony used by the Army in designating their new 'streets'.

The Pioneers were not yet finished with the Somme battlefields and still faced some of the worst conditions they had ever experienced as the seasons changed through winter to spring. On 8–9 October, the division was sent to the neighbourhood of Treux for a rest. Officially everyone was out of the line for two months until 9 December, to rest, retrain and recover their strength with new recruits. The Pioneers were not so lucky. They spent a few days at camp in Méaulte for a rest and clean-up. On 13 October, the Corps Commander visited them for an inspection, to offer a speech of thanks and watch them march past, a day to take pride in what they had achieved. They joined the division at Treux on 15 October, where they were rejoined by Lieutenant Colonel Collins returning to command after sick leave. Within a couple of days they were back at work, based with the Royal Engineers at The Citadel, providing working parties in the forward area with XIV Corps. Amid very changeable weather, with frost, rain, cold and strong winds on successive days, the men spent a miserable two weeks repairing roads, setting up huts and laying railways. They were constantly wet through, coming back from work each day to a camp thick with mud. A small unit of twenty men were sent up to Ginchy for mining work. The battalion would have been glad of the eighty reinforcements that arrived on 31 October, even happier when they marched out the next day for a well-earned period of rest.

At 5.30 p.m. on 1 November, they entrained at 'Edge Hill' railhead and arrived at Saleux by 9 p.m. As so often in their experience, there were no billets for the tired Pioneers and they had to bivouac as best they could for the night. The diary blames this on the French, as it was in their area. The diary reports Second Lieutenant Hopkins going sick and he was probably not alone. The next day brought a 16-mile march in pouring rain and along bad roads to Bourdon, where they stayed for a few days, cleaning billets, entertaining a visit from the GOC, and enjoying drills, church parade, P.T. and lectures. Private 36618 Thomas Henry Dunn wrote home from Bourdon to his family in Evenwood on 4 November, but gave absolutely no indication of what the battalion had just been through.[2]

> Dear brother and sister
> I am writing to tell you that I am in the Pink. I hope you are both the same. I am sorry that I have not been able to get hold of anything for the bairns yet, but I will look out for something for them without fail. I am at a very pleasant place here, within sound of the big guns, but I can still sleep alright. I was sorry that our Nelson and Matty could not get with us. I am enclosing a photograph which you can give to Mother. It is of a pal of mine from Etherley. You can send a few Woodbines if you like. We cannot get them here, that is the only drawback here. I think that is all at present, promising to write again soon. I will close with Best Love and hoping to see you all again soon.
> From your loving brother Tommy

Tommy Dunn had not long joined the battalion, a conscripted miner who landed in France on 27 October 1916, one of the eighty reinforcements previously mentioned.

On 8 November, the battalion marched to Picquigny, north-west of Amiens, arriving mercifully early for once, as they had the pleasure of cleaning up some very dirty billets left by departing Australians. The issue of taking over filthy billets crops up so many times in the diary that one is inclined to think that either the adjutant was obsessively touchy on the subject, or the battalion was being used as a mobile cleaning squad. Nevertheless, Picquigny turned out to be more of a rest than usual. There was drill of course, and P.T., but there were baths and, on Sunday 12 November, apart from church parade delivered by the newly arrived Reverend Walton, they had a day's holiday. As Picquigny was safe from enemy artillery, the men were able to wander along the village streets in search of local pleasures, such as an estaminet with some wine and beer. For two days, 14–15 November, there were battalion sports to be enjoyed and the men were entertained by the battalion concert party, captured in a contemporary photograph.[3] Sadly the members are shown in uniform rather than costume, so we get no flavour of what kind of entertainment they provided. 11th DLI did not shine in the sporting competitions, the football challenge being won 1–0 by 7th SomLI against 11th KRRC, in a replay following a 1–1 draw.

On 16 November, the battalion headed back to the Somme at Corbie by foot and bus, arriving at 1 p.m. to find yet more very dirty billets to clean.

Rest continued here until 24 November, with more drill and training. By 3 p.m. on the 25th, they were back at The Citadel, drenched and cold from heavy rain, to find the huts wet and leaking and the camp inches thick in mud. Another rain-soaked march followed in the morning, when they took over from the 18th Middlesex Regiment at Montauban. After some work constructing a light railway and drainage work, and loading wagons and improving the accommodation, they quickly moved on to yet another filthy camp in the area, with the roads practically impassable to transport. Much the same work continued for the first week in December, but gradually men were being sent home on leave, with twenty going on 9 December. Robert Bennett would not be among them as he had hoped.

The realisation that Pioneer battalions, Royal Engineer field companies, infantry working parties, Labour Corps and other similar units could not keep up with the demand for labour, became evident from a new army venture. A divisional order was issued on 26 November 1916 to form a road battalion. Each brigade of infantry was instructed to provide officers and men with road-making experience, specified according to a table of requirements, including the necessary support team of clerks, cooks and orderlies. The new battalion was to be organised in three companies of 204 men, with 8 lance corporals, 4 corporals, 4 sergeants and a selection of officers drawn from across each brigade. This was a substantial drain on the infantry battalions and illustrates the false impression that diary references to rest and recreation can provide. It also suggests that the continuing forward movement of the infantry against the Germans, which went on unabated, was being carried out by much-reduced units.

From 9 December, 20th Division moved forward to relieve 29th Division beyond Lesboeufs, overlooking the village of Le Transloy. Advanced parties from B, C and D companies of 11th DLI went up to sort out the new accommodation. Conditions were miserable with rain and sleet turning the ground into a quagmire and causing trenches to collapse and bury the men. Throughout the winter period, 11th DLI were very much acting in their primary role as a labour force for the division. Much of the work involved improvements to the trenches, with the diary naming some of the trenches worked in: Hogsback Trench, Morval Road, Flank Avenue and Ozone Trench. But the battalion also brought up bulk rations including tins of water, provided carrying parties for ammunition, cut wood, improved their own bivouacs and renovated the Combles Extension Railway near Guillemont.

On 23 December, the rest of the division had gone out of the line to recuperate from the miserable conditions, but the Pioneers were kept hard at work. Drafts of additional men arrived, but the diary notes that of fifty-two arriving on 22 December only three were suitable for the work, the rest comprising 'grocers, agents, musicians, etcetera'. Conscription was not

The German Cemetery at Fricourt. The tablet records a mass grave containing more than 17,000 burials. (*Martin Bashforth*)

providing many tradesmen and tough labourers. On Christmas Day 1916, Second Lieutenant Bushell and eleven men went off on leave, while the rest worked on the railway and others were 'removing putrid German corpses'. The latter task continued into Boxing Day with 'men still removing piles of decaying corpses'.[4] As if to add insult to injury a message arrived from the Army commander wishing them all a Happy Christmas, and as an afterthought 'also best wishes from C-in-C'.

On Boxing Day, Private Tommy Dunn died from the effects of a wound to the thigh at 6th General Hospital, Rouen. Not able to fulfil the promise of his recent letter, to see his brother and sister soon, all he was able to leave were the effects sent to his mother, which arrived on 24 May 1917: twopence halfpenny in coins, disc, four letters, cards, wallet, mirror, upper denture, religious book, cigarette case, hairbrush, watch, nailbrush and purse. He was possibly the first conscripted man to die in 11th DLI, having enlisted only in February and been called up 26 June 1916. He had had barely three months training and three months overseas.

On 28 December, Major Hayes made representation to divisional HQ about the state of the men. The diary for the next three days illustrates why he took this unusual step and that it was successful:

29 December: The men are thoroughly weary on arrival in bivouacs after work. They parade daily at 7.15 a.m., carry haversack rations, and return at 4.30 p.m. They take both breakfast and dinner in the dark. Some are too tired to eat dinner – others too weary to turn out for the rum ration. The CO and 2nd Lt Rees proceeded to Corbie to attend a court martial on the 30th. News to move out on 30th for rest at Trones Wood. Rain fell heavily during the night, flooding many of the dugouts. Men slept little, having to continually bale out the dugouts.

30 December: Work as above continued to mid-day. Two parties working on dugouts at Ginchy recalled. Transport proceeded at 12 noon to Ville. Owing to appalling conditions of camp two hours were occupied in getting transport clear of camp on to the road. GOC Guards Division and OC 4th Coldstream Guards visited this camp during the morning. They were astonished at men being quartered in such a place and are not likely to take over the camp. Battalion quitted the camp by 3.15 p.m. and entrained for Grovetown. Detrained and marched to Ville arriving at 9.15 p.m. The men have only once in their 18 months in France been so thoroughly done up. 2nd Lts Liddell and Fillingham and 15 men proceeded on leave.

31 December: The brief period at Ville is being spent in cleaning clothing, equipment etc., refitting, bathing and resting, before proceeding to Combles and Wedge Wood on 3rd January. The billets in Ville are not clean.

The camp the Guards refused to occupy consisted of little more than shell holes covered with tarpaulins in the Montauban area. The working parties had to trudge long distances through the mud to and from their place of work in the dark. The strain was telling on the officers, including the adjutant writing the diary, who was taken to hospital on New Year's Day 1917. His duties were taken over by Second Lieutenant Dennis until the latter went on leave, later in January.

Respite for the Pioneers was short. The rest of the division returned from Corbie on 4 January and took over the line at Sailly-Saillisel, with their HQ at Arrow Head Copse, near Guillemont. Although bad weather rendered January comparatively quiet, there were occasional surprise attacks even in the snow. On 28 January, the division was relieved and despatched behind the lines to Heilly. The Pioneer battalion was taken by bus to Trônes Wood, from where B Company was driven on to Combles, while A, C and D Companies marched up to Wedge Wood, three Lewis gun handcarts breaking down on the road. The work during January was averagely uneventful: trenches, dumps, tunnelling, drainage, lifting and carrying, revetting trenches, cutting and stacking wood for fuel and erecting huts at Maricourt Siding being some of the tasks listed. There were complaints about replacement clothing not being clean, a report of ten cases of scabies in C Company on 10 January and a note about snow falling on 17 January – all reports indicating very little going on. The major excitement was on 25 January, when an enemy aeroplane was brought down near the battalion HQ and the pilot captured.

The diarist enthused over a new batch of recruits arriving on 23 January. Among the draft of eighty-two men, the NCOs were picked out as 'a good set; they are men of over 12 months Home Service and have attended a month's course at NCO School, Eastern Command'. Men were also going off on leave at very regular intervals. The representation by Major Hayes had been attended to and a plan put in place to give the men a real chance to get away for a while, including pulling the whole battalion out to rest at Méaulte at the end of the month. Nineteen men under the supervision of Second Lieutenant Kemp were sent home on leave on 4 January, with Second Lieutenant Dennis and nineteen other ranks on 10 January, and Second Lieutenants Devey and Philip with seventeen men on 20 January. In this last group was Sergeant Thomas Bashforth on his way home to Darlington, on 'Leave to England' from 21 to 31 January 1917. It was no short journey from the Western Front to the north-east of England, but a delight to be home. The former plasterer, now with three stripes on his sleeve, would have been well received by family and friends. He was a very different man from the one his wife last saw in the summer of 1915. Nine months later on 5 November 1917 his youngest son, John Raymond, was born.[5]

The men went on leave in groups, often initially in the charge of an officer or NCO. They would go on foot until they could get motorised or horse-drawn transport to the nearest railhead. From here they would go by train to a Channel port and embark on a ferry to England. Transport from there was by train. Their leave pass entitled them to free travel. Men heading back to County Durham would have to change at one of the London stations, such as Victoria, terminus of the South Eastern & Chatham Railway. Here they would find warning notices about the danger of thefts, special arrangements for exchange of foreign currency, a hot cup of tea and a sandwich at one of the free buffets staffed by volunteers. If they had a long wait for a connecting train, there was advice on where they could find a safe place to wash and rest. Depending on how far the men had to travel and how fortunate they were with their connections, it could take anything up to three days to get home and three days to return – losing six out of ten days leave. Trains were crowded and journeys could be long and tedious. But many of these men in January 1917 had not seen home for eighteen months and more. The chance to experience home again was something they longed for, as Robert Bennett's letters showed. In practice, it may have been something of a strain for both the returning soldier and his immediate family, if only because of the short time allowed and the gulf between life at home and life at the front.[6]

At the end of January, Sergeant Bashforth rejoined his unit, still at rest in Méaulte, and was quickly back to the usual routines of P.T., drill, bayonet practice and baths. The battalion remained here for the first week in February and led the division back into the line on the 8th and 9th of that month. Guillemont was the destination for A Company, while the remainder were based at Montauban before being split up. The Hogsback Trench was the first destination for B Company, while C went to Sunken Road and D company was split between the two places. All leave was cancelled and an officer and eighty-nine other ranks joined as reinforcements from 35th Infantry Base Depot at Étaples. On 13 February, there was a Court of Inquiry into the accidental burning of Private Tombling of C Company at Méaulte, led by Captain C. Palmer and two subalterns from A Company. Company Sergeant Major McEvoy replaced Sergeant Major Cox as acting RSM when the latter went to England.[7]

By 10 February, the whole of the 20th Division was back in the line between Le Transloy and Sailly, with the reserve at Carnoy, where battalions on relief took their rest. For 11th DLI there was the normal round of trench work. The diary systematically records all the dugouts, saps, duck walks, camouflage screens, shelters, wiring and knife rests they worked on over the first two weeks, and then their work on repairing roads and track laying between Sailly-Saillisel and Le Mesnil; Le Mesnil and Manancourt; Bus and Ytres; Bus and Lechelle. So it continued well into March, much of the trench work at night and with a small but steady stream of casualties. Two privates from C Company were killed in a train accident on 14 February: Private 25211 James Connfey from Sunderland and Private 16241 John Salkeld Long from Gateshead.[8] Three more were wounded in the lines. One man was reported, on 4 March, to have died of pneumonia in hospital (possibly news of Private 55591 Walter Smart, died in Leicester, 16 January 1917). The nineteen-year-old Second Lieutenant Noel William Scott Fletcher was killed on a working party on 7 March and another man slightly wounded. Fletcher is buried at the Guards' Cemetery, Lesboeufs. In the next grave to him is Private 24736 J. Carr of A Company who fell victim to a shell burst on 10 March, blowing in a signal dugout, an event in which two more men were wounded and one left suffering from shock.

During February and March, the Germans began a steady and destructive retreat eastwards, towards newly built defences. Fourth Army, including 20th Division, followed in pursuit from 17 March. Any objectives gained were hard-won, such as the shattered villages of Neuville, Metz-en-Couture, Trescault and Bilhem. Meanwhile, 11th DLI shifted camp between Le Transloy, Le Mesnil and Rocquigny, still engaged on the roads at Bus, Ytres and Lechelle, and improving drainage, filling in craters and removing mines. During the last weeks of March, 11th DLI, along with 96th Field Company, 10th RB and 7th KOYLI, were detached for work on roads and railways to support the advance, catching up with the rest of the division progressively from 24 to 29 March. More reinforcements arrived, with the complete approval of the diarist, who described them as

Territorial soldiers fixing barbed wire to knife rests, near Arras, May 1918. Pioneers commonly did this kind of work. (*Imperial War Museum, Q 8798*)

'one of the best drafts received – good, strong, hardy-looking men – all from Durham'.

Captain Palmer, assisted by Second Lieutenants Lascelles and Rees chaired a Court of Inquiry at Bus on 4 April, into the circumstances of injury to Private 14964 George Brown.[9] Brown was a coal miner, born at Monk Hesledon near Castle Eden, County Durham. He enlisted on 31 August 1914, at West Hartlepool, aged nineteen. His family lived at Spennymoor. Initially, he was one of those sent to 16th DLI for training, before transfer to D Company, 11th DLI. He was one of several brothers serving, according to a letter from his father: 'Dear Sir, I wish to explain to you that I have three sons serving the colours. Pte Joseph Brown is the oldest and as got married a fortnight before he went to the front and the second is Pte George Brown Reg No 19464 [*sic*] 16th Batt DLI France, third Pte Thomas Brown Reg No 25073 17th Batt DLI Penkridge Camp near Stafford No 8 Hut. Yours truly, Thomas Brown, No 6 Armstrong St, Hesledon, near Castle Eden.' Brown's record contained the usual short spells of absence, but nothing serious. Health-wise, he suffered an attack of scabies and had some trouble with his knee for which he received treatment at Étaples during September–October 1916. Nothing in his record suggested he was inclined to 'swinging the lead'.

The Court of Inquiry examined the possibility of a self-inflicted wound. Private 11591 Michael Hennessey was one of the witnesses, though only part of his statement survives. On 26 February, the men were working next to each other in a new trench near Le Transloy at night. As Brown brought his shovel back, Hennesey was bringing his pick up and accidentally struck the back of Brown's hand. The wound was serious, but not regarded as likely to affect his 'future efficiency as a soldier', according to the doctor. The court and the CO were content to conclude that it was merely an accident, though the inquiry shows how seriously the possibility of self-inflicted wounds was taken. Brown was lucky, in the circumstances, not to have suffered a more serious infection, such as tetanus or septicaemia. He was treated at 14th Camp Reception Station[10] for several weeks before being sent to Infantry Base Depot at Étaples, finally returning to his unit on 11 May. He enjoyed some home leave in July 1917. The leave was his last, but the wound was not, for he was fatally injured during the German Offensive and died on 25 March 1918, being buried at St Sever Cemetery, Rouen.

On 5 April, the battalion was ordered forward to establish a new main line of resistance. The work details for 13 April 1917 specifically record: 'Ruyaulcourt-Neuville Road and Neuville-Fins Road. Clearing villages. Filling in craters and shell holes and draining road. Road cleared of wreckage from P.22.d.0.7 to P.22.d.2.5. Road now passable for wheeled traffic from Ruyaulcourt to P.35.central. Working on corduroy road at P.29. c.25.45 – this road now being used by vehicles.' The description belies the difficulty and danger involved in the work. The Germans set booby traps in the abandoned villages and along the roads and tracks between them.

Meanwhile, on 13 April 1917, Private T. H. Myers survived a Field General Court Martial, being acquitted of self-inflicted wounding.[11] His case appeared more serious than that of George Brown, hence the court proceedings. Company Sergeant-Major Williams and Sergeant Dawson were interviewed as candidates for commissions on 4 April and were sent back to England for training a few days later. Between training courses for machine-guns, stretcher-bearing and signalling, the battalion continued with road works and the picketing and wiring of the reserve trench lines. The diary proudly records them wiring 2,350 yards overnight on 2 May. A couple of young officers get a mention, with Acting Captain R. L. S. Pemberton being made Temporary with effect from 22 June, and Second Lieutenant Adams going to Péronne to be interviewed for the Royal Flying Corps.

We get some idea of the numbers of men around at the time. On 5 May the battalion strength was recorded as:

	Officers	Other Ranks	Total
	36	903	939
On details away from battalion	6	112	118
Remaining with battalion	30	791	821

The working strength was, however, recorded as being only 540 men, the rest presumably on leave or sick but still considered as part of the nominal strength. Figures were reported in this format every month.

On 23 May, divisional HQ was set up just north of Bapaume and the infantry brigades went into the line facing Quéant. The division was now part of the Fifth Army, IV Corps, and had been very highly praised by Sir Henry Rawlinson of the Fourth Army for the work they had performed under his command. On 22 May, the Pioneers moved from Ytres to Bancourt to relieve the 5th Australians in the line, where they were engaged in a mixture of tunnelling, mining, trench repairs, dugout building and laying of Decauville railways.[12] Companies and platoons were allocated around the lines as necessary. On 27 May, several men were mentioned in despatches: Acting Lieutenant G. Hayes, Temporary Captain C. Palmer, Temporary Second Lieutenant A. Philip, Sergeant 13308 J. Dawson (who had just gone to England for a commission), Corporal 21508 J. A. Boyne, Corporal 16814 H. Seggar and Lance Sergeant W. Johnston. The last two men were killed during the German Spring Offensive on 28 and 30 March 1918. Johnston is buried at the Namps-au-val British Cemetery just to the south-west of Amiens and Seggar is recorded on the Pozières Memorial.

On 31 May, the battalion HQ was moved to a dangerous spot at Vaulx-Vraucourt. A shell hit an ammunition dump on 3 June, wounding thirteen men. As the diary described:

> Battalion HQ is situated in a large garden, but position anything but comfortable. Our battalion being in fairly close proximity, the battalion HQ billets come in for more than a fair share of splinters from hostile shells bursting NE and SE of us, although the shells drop fully 500 to 600 yards away. The Companies are equally uncomfortable excepting perhaps D Company in Vraucourt.

There was occasional fighting during June, but mostly it was a period of consolidation. Acting Captain Philip took ten other ranks to St-Valery-sur-Somme for some rest and recreation at the seaside. Another small group travelled to Bapaume for a lecture on wiring by the Chief Engineer from IV Corps. From 27 June, the men spruced up billets and clothes, had something of a rest and paraded for inspection. When the division was moved on the 30th June, without mentioning 11th DLI specifically, the divisional commander drew attention to 'the work done in digging the elements of an excellent trench system in the line near Havrincourt Wood, and in greatly improving the defences in front of Noreuil and Lagnicourt'. This was primarily the work of the Pioneers, though working parties from infantry battalions were often used to supplement the labour required for bigger tasks.

By 1 July, the division, including 11th DLI, were at rest at Domart, south-east of Amiens on the road to Roye, an area to which they would return in less relaxing circumstances the following year. Here they stayed until 19 July for a round of church parades, drill, training, sports and lectures. One group helped a local farmer with his haymaking on 9 July, which would have been a fairly pleasant change. Leave allotments went up from twenty-three men to forty-six men per week to give as many as possible a chance to get away on leave, though the arrangement was almost immediately countermanded from 13 July when the next assignment for the 20th Light Division was notified.

The battalion had been on the Somme now for almost exactly a year. Given the length of time and the experiences they had been through, it is not surprising that this extended tour of duty produced a long list of fatalities. The CWGC database lists ninety-one killed during the Somme Campaign, of whom eighty were privates. There were ten NCOs and only one officer. Of the forty-seven for whom we have sufficient recorded details the majority were in their twenties, Lieutenant Fletcher at nineteen was the youngest while the oldest was Private J. Murphy at forty-seven. Several were married. Twenty-one have no recorded grave and their names are inscribed on the Memorial to the Missing of the Somme at Thiepval.

In the period from 1 October 1916 to the end of June 1917, there were fifty-two recorded fatalities, of whom exactly half lost their lives in the actions to take Rainbow and Cloudy Trenches in the first month. Private 33026 William Barker had only been with the battalion for three weeks. He was not an early volunteer, having not enlisted until December 1915 and not been called up for active service until the end of May 1916. A quarryman aged almost twenty-nine from Tow Law, County Durham, he was married with no children. After initial training with 21st DLI, he was sent abroad on 13 September and, on arrival at Boulogne the next day, was assigned to 11th DLI. He lost his life on 5 October. Several requests for information from comrades produced only confusing answers. Private Shuttleworth said he saw him wounded, while Lance Corporal Hamilton 'had heard that he was killed'. He has no known grave. His widow, Margaret Jane (née Maddison), was awarded a pension of 13s 9d a week. By September 1919, she had remarried to become Mrs Margaret Dodd.

Private 32862 Richard Nicholson Bond was a similar age, a fish curer from South Shields, married and with a young son. Like William Barker he enlisted in December 1915 and was called up in May 1916. He trained alongside Barker and joined 11th DLI on the same day. Both served with A Company, died on the same day, and were probably friends. Bond was treated at 34th Casualty Clearing Station for wounds and compound fractures to his left arm and both legs. He will almost certainly have died in appalling pain. His wife Annie got 18s 9d a week for herself and her son, Richard Hinman Bond, whose third birthday on 23 October 1916 was clouded by the news of his father's death three weeks before.

Both of these men enlisted under what came to be known as the Derby Scheme. The government had become concerned that large numbers of men were holding back from volunteering, but was reluctant to introduce conscription. Lord Derby, who had been successful as Director of Recruiting for the volunteer New Armies raised in 1914, was appointed to oversee a scheme whereby men could, by December 1915, register for the forces and be called up in batches according to age and marital status. Many married men did so, expecting that it would be a long time until they were called to the colours. Although almost another quarter of a million men registered, it was not long before these numbers were used up. The Derby men were not well regarded by those already serving, in some ways less than the conscripts who followed. Training was rudimentary in comparison with the Kitchener volunteers, and large numbers were of dubious fitness.[13]

It was A Company that seems to have borne the brunt of the deaths on 5 October. Private 16046 Joseph William Davison, a miner from Willington, was another from the same unit. How he arrived at this turning point also has its twists. Initially assigned to 13th DLI, he went overseas but was hospitalised at Étaples, suffering from a hernia, and returned home. After recovery he was briefly allocated to 16th DLI, before being sent back to France on 13 January 1916, and found to be still insufficiently fit. Before returning to 11th DLI he was sent to an Entrenching Battalion until improved. These units worked behind the lines doing 'lighter' duties. He rejoined the battalion on 5 April 1916, dying six months later. His young wife Dorothy was awarded 18s 9d for herself and their baby daughter Mary, but remarried by the end of the war, to become Mrs Sands. Joseph never saw his daughter, who was born only a month before he was killed.

Private 45832 James Henry Ellis had already suffered twice serving with other units before he was transferred to A Company, 11th DLI. A railway signal fitter from Bardney, Lincolnshire, he enlisted in Sheffield on 12 September 1914. He served originally with the Yorkshire and Lancashire Regiment. On 1 October 1915, while serving with their 10th Battalion, he was shot in the chest and returned to England for treatment. He joined the 7th Battalion on 31 January 1916, but by 27 March was back in hospital suffering from neurasthenia and spent some time at the Convalescent Camp at Étaples; while there he was fit enough to be awarded fourteen days FP1 for an improper reply to an NCO. On 2 June

1916, he was temporarily attached to 11th DLI, but was soon in hospital again suffering from myalgia. Only on 11 September 1916 was he finally assigned to 11th DLI with a new regimental number. In less than a month, on 7 October 1916, he was shot in the chest again, but this time fatally. He was just twenty-two years of age. His grave can now be found at the Guards Cemetery, Lesboeufs.

Though several officers were wounded, only one lost his life in this period on the Somme: Second Lieutenant Noel William Scott Fletcher. Unlike the majority of his men, he was not from the north-east, but from Ipswich. He was the son of the Reverend William Edward Fletcher of St Matthew's Rectory, Ipswich. From the age of ten he was a pupil of King's College Choir School. When his voice broke, he moved to Rossall School, Fleetwood, Lancashire, where he joined the OTC. He was still a schoolboy, barely seventeen years of age, when he applied to join the Army on 11 January 1915. He was unlikely to have been of particularly imposing appearance for an officer. He was youthful, not especially tall at 5 feet 7 inches, quite slight at 130 pounds and with a normal chest measurement of only 32 inches. He also had imperfect eyesight and wore glasses. The surviving papers for Fletcher provide little detail about his military service. He was picked out as suitable for work with a Pioneer battalion, and sent to the Pioneer School at Reading before being assigned to 11th DLI. He left for France in January 1917, though his arrival is not mentioned in the battalion war diary. By then he would have been much more ready to assume command of a bunch of former miners, much fitter and more strongly built, trained to give orders and perhaps, like many young officers, sporting a moustache. But his career as an officer was cut short by a burst of shrapnel while instructing a night-time working party on 7 March 1917. He died before he reached medical treatment at 60th Field Ambulance Advanced Dressing Station at Ginchy. He was initially buried there, but moved after the war to the Guards' Cemetery at Lesboeufs.

Fletcher is remembered in memorials at Rossall School, less for his academic prowess or other accomplishments, all unremarkable, than for his singing. 'A chorister and soloist of King's – which he dearly loved, he carried away with him the artistic touch and refinement of part-singing, and he will be remembered as one of a house quartette, stated at the time by those best able to judge as the best heard for many years from a school platform. Of a naturally happy disposition, and full of the joie-de-vivre, Fletcher quickly made friends and among his men developed unsuspected and hitherto untried qualities of leadership.'[14] His death proved a double blow for his mother, only recently widowed. She sent many letters to the War Office, all bordered in black, trying to find out more about his death and what had happened to his belongings. On 12 April 1917, she enquired about the whereabouts of his sword, apparently left in the DLI Depot at South Shields, and a cheque for £30 from when he had sold his motorcycle. Otherwise his effects amounted to £3 11s 10d in cash along with a silver cigarette case, identity disc, wristwatch, leather strap, leather note case and correspondence. While materially different from the effects of Private Dunn listed above, the emotional significance they carried for a grieving mother were the same.[15]

   The service records of soldiers who died during the long period on the Somme show how the constitution of the battalion was changing. While still at its core were hundreds of miners from County Durham, men who had volunteered in the autumn of 1914, gradually this somewhat homogeneous body was changing. Men with different accents, different origins, and different civilian experiences were coming into the battalion. The only evidence of how they were viewed by the 'veterans' are comments in the war diary, which tended to value strong men from Durham, rather than the mixture arriving from elsewhere. On the one hand it demonstrates a sense of *esprit-de-corps* from the early days of the battalion, but on the other it may suggest a degree of prejudice, and we have no way of knowing how widespread such attitudes were among the ranks. Were the tightly knit groups of miners with their shared culture welcoming of these outsiders? Or were non-miner NCOs able to cut across any such prejudice, if it existed? Sadly, we lack the personal stories that would inform us.

NOTES TO CHAPTER SEVEN

1   National Archives, WO 95/2096, 20th Division War Diary and reports for October 1916.
2   Durham County Records Office, D/DLI/7/871/1 letter from Private T. H. Dunn
3   See Mitchinson, 1997, facing page 113.
4   No location is given for this work, but it may involve the mass grave in the present day German cemetery at Fricourt, near the area in which 11th DLI was working.
5   The author's father.
6   There are several examples from memoirs quoted in Brown, 1999, pp.156–9.
7   RSM Patrick McEvoy, 15084, died of wounds, aged twenty-eight, on 20 April 1918, following the German Spring Offensive. He was awarded the Military Cross. He left a wife, Evelyn May, of 10 Dagnan Road, Balham, London.
8   The service papers for neither of these men have survived, so nothing more can be discovered about the nature of the accident. Connfey

actually served under the name Carthy, but, in the absence of records, the reason remains a mystery.

9   Private Brown from Spennymoor appears to have survived this injury, but died of wounds, aged twenty-four, on 25 March 1918 and is buried at the St Sever Cemetery Extension at Rouen. Lieutenant Rees was well suited to the role in the inquiry as he was a barrister at law, from Swansea. Not as young as many of his rank, he died aged thirty-seven in England on 7 July 1919 and is buried at Wandsworth (Putney Vale) Cemetery, London.

10 A Camp Reception Station was a small hospital unit close to the front line, normally used for short term treatments. As Brown appears to have remained here for somewhat longer, he may have suffered an infection.

11 Charges in the registers of Field General Courts Martial were frequently denoted by abbreviations, in this instance the note 'S.40'. The suspicion of possible self-wounding may have been prevalent around any accident, given the frequency with which S.40 appears in the registers.

12 These were light, narrow-gauge railways, 60 cm between tracks, made from prefabricated sections that could be quickly and easily laid. They were extremely useful between supply depots and the areas immediately behind the lines.

13 Messenger, 2005, pp. 130–5. Although the perceived benefit to the Derby volunteer was deferred actual call-up, conscripts also generally experienced a gap between enlistment and being assigned for training.

14 Quotation from 'The Rossallian', 30 May 1917, p. 6, brought to the author's attention by Kate Wills.

15 The National Archives, WO 339/57644, papers of Second Lieutenant Noel William Scott Fletcher.

CHAPTER EIGHT

The Capture of Langemarck

It would be a particularly bloody late summer and autumn. General Gough's Reserve Army, to which 20th Divison was attached, was reorganised as the Fifth Army. Having acquitted itself well during the later stages of the Somme Campaign, the new army would now be used more frequently as the formation of first choice for difficult tasks. For 20th Division and their Pioneers, there would be a second military honour to that earned at Guillemont. At Third Ypres they would be responsible for driving beyond Pilckem Ridge to take the strategic village of Langemarck.

There is a much-reproduced photograph of hundreds of men from 11th DLI riding in narrow-gauge wagons, packed in tightly, laughing, smiling, waving and cheering to the cameraman, Lieutenant Ernest Brooks. The photograph was taken on 31 July 1917, somewhere near Elverdinghe, when the men were going forward to help out behind the lines, road-making and laying railway tracks. As this image was taken, thousands more men had gone over the top on the first day of the Third Ypres campaign. The day was characterised by bright sunshine and equivalent expectation at headquarters level, only to be followed by four solid days of torrential rain. Third Ypres became a series of battles, in some ways a repeat of what had happened a year previously on the Somme, with mud and rain an even greater characteristic. The series of battles is popularly known by the name of the village that formed one of its main objectives. 'Passchendaele' has become synonymous with the depths of horror to which the First World War could sink, though other names could be added. The late veteran, Harry Patch, who fought as a very young man with a Lewis gun team from 7th DCLI, in the 20th Division, remembered 'Pilckem Ridge' and 'Langemarck', but was confused as to which was which.[1] Both 11th DLI and the 20th Light Division would have the name 'Langemarck' inscribed

Pioneers of 11th DLI waving to the camera of Lt Ernest Brooks, near Elverdinghe, 31 July 1916. This was the first day of the Battle of Third Ypres. (*Imperial War Museum, Q 2641*)

in their battle honours and a commemorative monument was built near the village of that name, complementing the one at Guillemont.

As the last men returned from leave on 19 July, the division left Domart for Doullens, north of Amiens, where they entrained for the Ypres front. The 11th DLI arrived at Hôpoutre late on 20 July and marched overnight to Proven, just north of Poperinghe. The next day was devoted to training, drill and inspection before 11th DLI moved on to headquarters at 'G Camp', near Elverdinghe. From the day the assault on Pilckem Ridge began on 31 July, 11th DLI was involved in constructing artillery tracks, roadways and railways under heavy shellfire. Communications for both supplies and men would be absolutely critical to the success of the battle. The rain that blighted the whole campaign gave less quarter than the gas and shells of the enemy guns. A fairly typical day was 2 August 1917, the diary describing how the 'men now have a march of 14 miles daily and in addition have six hours work to do. C Company continued work on the railway from 11 am to 7 pm'. By 5 August, despite the heavy rain and appalling conditions, Pilckem Ridge had been taken, though the hold on the Steenbeek, a flooded stream beyond the eastern slopes of the ridge, was tenuous.

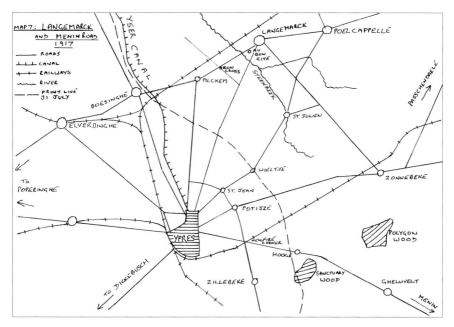

Langemarck and Menin Road, 1917. (*Martin Bashforth, 2010*)

The Pioneers continued improving communications until 16 August. The work served to support those troops already committed in the new front line and was part of longer-term plans to push forward. Pioneers, engineers and infantry work parties were all involved. They were protected by continous barrages targeted on the German lines from Divisional and Heavy Artillery. Meanwhile other preliminaries for the attack were assembled: supply dumps, ammunition dumps, Field Ambulance facilities. Engineers from 84th Field Company were given the more specialised task of constructing sixteen canvas-covered bridges that would be hauled forward at the last moment to span the Steenbeek and let the attacking troops from 20th Division pass on their way to Langemarck.

An attack was launched on 5 August to secure the crossing points on the Steenbeek, against fierce opposition. On the eastern bank of the Steenbeek, the rising ground towards Langemarck was defended by a network of concrete outposts, centred on a massive emplacement known ironically as 'Au Bon Gîte'. Any attempt to take Langemarck and the ridge beyond was dependent on suppressing these strong points. Though some of the preliminary objectives were achieved by 14 August, at heavy cost, this amounted mainly to a secure position on the eastern bank of the Steenbeek. Au Bon Gîte was battered but not yet finally subdued. Several of the German outposts remained, little more than 80 yards beyond the stream. The final assault on 16 August included special measures to isolate

The Steenbeek in 1917; it had to be crossed on the way to Langemarck. (*Imperial War Museum, Q 17654*)

The Steenbeek in 2009, looking south from the road to Langemarck. (*Gaynor Greenwood*)

and suppress these German strongholds. It was achieved in appalling conditions and in the face of fierce counter-attacks, occasioning many individual acts of bravery and the award of two Victoria Crosses to men in the infantry brigades involved.

At this stage in the battle, 11th DLI was held back. They were not used in the early waves of the attack, as they had been at Guillemont, in order to provide the labour to secure objectives taken by the infantry. Instead, their orders for 16 August were: 'To open up a track for wheels from about C.8.a.80.80 on the Pilckem-Cinq Chemins-Est Road to C.3.c.15.85 on the track from Stray Farm to the Pilckem-Iron Cross Road.' Essentially, this involved a consolidation of the network of tracks and duckboards on the western bank of the Steenbeek, along the central line of the divisional assault. By this means, any gains could be consolidated and support ensured for the continuing assaults on the ridge beyond the Steenbeek. While the troops attacking the village of Guillemont had had the cover of trenches and woods, the swampy ground around both sides of the Steenbeck was almost impossible to occupy and resulted in long and exposed supply lines. It was vital to keep those lines open, despite the conditions and the constant targetting of the stream crossings by the German artillery. Langemarck was taken.

On 18 August, the 20th Division was relieved by the 38th Division and retired to Proven for three weeks' rest. The 11th DLI joined them

Unidentified soldiers preparing salvaged trees for use in road-making and strengthening dugouts, near Zillebeke, 18 September 1917. (*Imperial War Museum, Q 2888*)

at a place called Seaton Camp. As usual, rest did not imply relaxation, the best part being bathing. There was the ubiquitous drill, more training, working on railway tracks and sidings, and anti-aircraft work. Despite losses during August, the battalion had a nominal strength of around 1,000 men, significantly reinforced since the Somme campaign. At the end of the month, the war diary entry showed a net loss of twenty-five men, forty having joined and sixty-five having been struck off, reported killed, wounded, or sick.

These losses were dwarfed by those infantry battalions directly involved in the capture of Langemarck, summarised in a divisional report on the action.[2] The Pioneers lost 7 men killed and 3 officers and 22 men wounded – roughly comparable to the losses of the divisional engineers, the 217th Machine Gun Company and the Field Ambulance Units. 62nd Field Ambulance came under particularly heavy fire and the dressing station was destroyed. Captain Adam of the RAMC was awarded the MC for continuing to work in the open until the position became untenable. The divisional artillery lost 2 officers and 18 men killed, while 5 officers and 90 men were wounded. The worst affected infantry battalion was 12th KRRC, losing 4 officers and 43 men killed, 5 officers and 152 men wounded and 2 officers and 51 men missing. Each of the other infantry battalions was almost as badly affected. The single heaviest loss for 11th DLI was the 7 fatalities, all from 16 August 1917, the day of the capture of Langemarck. They lie buried in relatively close proximity to one another at Bard Cottage Cemetery, Boesinghe. Their service records reveal an odd mixture of individuals and backgrounds.

Private 45678 Charles Hildreth enlisted on 13 August 1915, aged nineteen, in a Territorial Battalion, 6th DLI. A miner from Tow Law, he was keen to go overseas, signing form E 624 to agree to serve outside the United Kingdom. As part of this agreement he was supposed to remain with 6th DLI, but in fact he served with three different battalions of the regiment. On 10 September 1916, he was transferred to the 15th Battalion, but was shot in the left hand a few days later and returned to England to recover. On arrival in France on 6 March 1917, he was attached to 11th DLI. Hildreth's mother had died and most of the family lived with the eldest sister, Mrs Dora Armstrong, who was classed as his guardian (his father was still alive). Unusually, Hildreth made his younger sister Elizabeth Jane, then in her early teens, the recipient of 8s 6d separation allowance and 3s 6d allotment of pay. He made out his will to her on 9 March 1917, and after his death she received his effects and later his medals, scroll and bronze plaque.

Two of the other fatalities had been deserters. Private 20757 Nathan Donkin served six years as a regular before the war, with 4th DLI. When he

The headstone of Joseph Tansey (second left) at Bard Cottage Cemetery, Boesinghe, close to those of Robert Taylor, Nathan Donkin and Henry Hodgson (together on the right). All died in the capture of Langemarck. (*Gaynor Greenwood*)

joined up again on 20 August 1914 he was a labourer, living in Gateshead with a wife and three children. He was originally assigned to 10th DLI, went to France with them and was appointed Corporal in August 1915. He gave up his rank on 17 January 1916, after a dispute over his leave, when he was refused a one-day extension after a particularly difficult journey home from Flanders. On 7 January 1916, he had written asking for what he clearly regarded as a fairly small concession:

> Please Sir, I write these few lines to let you no if I could get my 1 day extra account of the Boat been delayed. We left Poperinghe 3 o'clock on Sunday morning landed in Bullong ½ past 10 on Sunday we had to stop their all night got into Folkestone ½ past nine left their by the train to Victoria Station ¼ twelfth at night and we had to stop their allnight and I did not get home till Monday night.[3]

The letter has 'not approved' scrawled across it, but Donkin not only took his extra day, he was five days late back. Given a severe reprimand and a loss of five days' pay, he asked to revert to the ranks. A few weeks later, on 12 March 1916, he was badly wounded, fragments of shell lodging in his right thigh. While convalescing in England his discipline deteriorated. On 2 May 1916, he deserted, not rejoining until 28 July. He was awarded twenty-eight days' detention, which he served in the Detention Barrack at York Castle. He was released with four days' remission and handed over to 3rd DLI on 25 August. On 6 September, he was struck off, having gone missing again. This time he was absent for almost six months, handing himself in on 19 March 1917. He was tried at District Court Martial and found guilty of desertion and losing his regimental clothing and equipment. He was sentenced to eighteen months' detention, plus stoppage of 18s 6d from his pay, which would have been a severe blow to his family, though the amount in the circumstances was nominal (about one week's allowance). However, on 16 April 1917 the sentence was remitted, providing he embarked immediately for France. The Infantry Base Depot at Étaples handed him first to 12th DLI, but they transferred him a month later to 11th DLI. His wife suffered the double blow of losing her husband on 16 August and his namesake child on 2 September, from an epidemic of enteritis. At least she got a full pension of 22s 11d for herself and her two remaining children, Richardson and Catherine.

Private 15047 Arthur William Hunt went absent without leave at almost the same time as Donkin, but there does not seem to have been any direct connection between the men. Donkin served with A Company and Hunt with 6 Platoon, B Company. Hunt was born in Durham City, though when he enlisted in West Hartlepool on 31 August 1914, he was working as a miner at Castle Eden Colliery, where he lived with an aunt. His parents lived in Sunderland and his mother, Mary E. Lynn, received ten shillings in pay and allowances. Hunt was assigned to 11th DLI from the beginning. During training, the only blot on his record was a short absence at Pirbright on 6 December 1914, for which he was confined to barracks for two days. His later bad conduct seems to have followed a severe illness, much as Donkin's followed a serious wounding. On 17 November 1915, while serving in France, he was diagnosed with albuminuria. Protein in his urine indicated kidney damage, diabetes or hypertension, or a combination of the same. He was hospitalised at Étaples until 16 December and then attached for working convalescence to No. 10 Entrenching Battalion. He was back in hospital at Étaples on 17 March 1916 with influenza. There was a problem with his lungs and, on 6 June 1916, he was sent to England and attached to 3rd DLI at South Shields for convalescence. It was here that the conduct problems emerged. He overstayed his pass on 3 September 1916 and lost five days' pay. He was absent from tattoo on 22 September and confined to barracks for seven days. On 1 October, he went absent and was apprehended in town by the civil police three days later. He was charged with failing to salute an officer and being improperly dressed in town, docked four days' pay and confined to barracks for another seven days. He went absent overnight on 2 November 1916 and was confined for four days. He did it again on 8 November and, despite being confined to barracks for seven days, broke out of camp the next night and got another ten days confinement to follow the first. Finally on 30 November, he disappeared and did not rejoin 3rd DLI until 5 March 1917. Hunt was tried and convicted of being absent without leave and given seventeen months' imprisonment. Like Donkin this was largely remitted and, on 16 April 1917, he embarked for Étaples, spent a short period with 12th DLI and on 11 May joined 11th DLI. Hunt was one of the seven who died on 16 August 1917. His mother later received his few effects: photos, pocket book, religious book, paper, wallet and two discs. It seems strange that so ordinary a man could have produced such a bizarre spell of behaviour. One can only speculate, but the illness does seem to have been a contributory factor to his attack of 'madness', just as Donkin's close shave with an exploding shell seems to have triggered his own unruly response. Whatever the truth, both men returned to the front, returned to action and died alongside their comrades, any personal shame expiated.

The headstones of Charles Buckle, Arthur Hunt and Charles Hildreth, together at Bard Cottage Cemetery, Boesinghe. All died in the capture of Langemarck. (*Jon Miller*)

After the capture of Langemarck, 20th Division had a spell of rest. For 11th DLI this meant continuous work on tramlines, dumps, cables and other chores. There was a parade on 5 September 1917 for the presentation of medal ribbons and on the 8th there was time for sports competitions. The Pioneers went back into frontline action ahead of the Division, travelling via Elverdinghe back to the Yser Canal Bank on 9 September and were straight into their usual work. Lieutenant F. Atley went with six Lewis gun teams up to the forward area around Langemarck and the Steenbeek, to operate as anti-aircraft defence. The support lines came under frequent attack from the air.

The main divisional force returned to the line on 11 September to prepare for an attack scheduled for 20 September, though by now the average effective infantry battalion strength was only 350 men, which contrasts with the figures for the Pioneers and reflects the losses sustained during the earlier attack on Langemarck. The aim was to capture some strong and complex defences known as Eagle Trench and it took three days of desperate hand-to-hand fighting and even more heavy losses. The Pioneers worked overnight before the morning of the attack, building strongpoints in the new front line. Four were built by A Company, but D Company got lost in the dark and only managed one. It was easy to get lost in the featureless, muddy and primeval landscape.

Lieutenant Atley's Lewis gun teams joined the infantry attack, with four teams covering anti-aircraft work and another four providing fire in the front line. Not all of the objectives were achieved on the first day, Eagle Trench proving exceptionally difficult. Until the German line was finally subdued, 11th DLI continued with their consolidation work amid constant battery from artillery, including gas. The transport of materials to the front still involved crossing the Steenbeek, an easy target for German artillery who laid down frequent barrages along its length. In recognition of the work achieved, Captain W. G. L. Sear was awarded the Military Cross.[4] Seven men died during these days and many more were wounded, including Second Lieutenant Fleming. Among the more minor casualties was Sergeant Thomas Bashforth. He was slightly wounded on 25 September 1917, but remained on duty.

At the end of September, the 20th Division was relieved by the 14th Division and on 1 October sent by train for a rest at Bapaume. There they received the warmest commendations from the Fifth Army commander, Sir Hubert Gough.

The Army Commander wishes to thank all ranks 20th Division for the part they have played in the third battle of Ypres. The Division may well be proud of the capture of Langemarck on August 16th and the taking

The Memorial to the 20th Division at Langemarck, 2009. (*Gaynor Greenwood*)

of Eagle Trench on September the 23rd. While holding the line of the Steenbeck during a prolonged spell of bad weather the Division showed a good soldierly spirit under difficult conditions. The Army Commander is sorry to lose such a good fighting Division.[5]

The reference to losing the division relates to their transfer out of Fifth Army for the time being, in order to take part in a new and innovative enterprise further south. However, the artillery brigades remained behind until 18 October, when they were moved out to Péronne. By then they had been in continuous action for three months and had suffered heavy losses, working in the most appalling conditions, and were thoroughly exhausted. The Germans had adopted an unusual practice during the attacks of Third Ypres. Instead of manning the front line in strength, they had done so lightly, relying on fast and heavy counter-attacks. The artillery was extremely effective in making sure that these attempts were only done at great expense. However, the conditions in which they had to work were almost beyond human endurance.

NOTES TO CHAPTER EIGHT

1   Harry Patch died in 2009, the last surviving First World War veteran in the UK. See Patch and Van Emden, 2007, chapter 5, for his firsthand account of the events of 16 August 1917.
2   The National Archives, WO 95/2096: Sub-Appendix C, 'Casualty Reports' to the 20th Division Report on the actions at Langemarck.
3   The National Archives, WO 363, Nathan Donkin.
4   *London Gazette*, 27 October 1917.
5   The National Archives, WO 95/2096, letter to CO 20th Division.

CHAPTER NINE

Advance and Retreat at Cambrai

Preparations for the enterprise that culminated in the British Army's campaigns for 1917 were enveloped in secrecy. With little opportunity for rest, 20th Division was detached from Fifth Army in Flanders and sent south; leaving others to finish what had been started in Belgium. On 10 October 1917, 20th Division set up headquarters at Sorel, all three infantry brigades were in the line, and the division became part of III Corps, Third Army. They were joined on 25 October by the divisional artillery, following their extended duty in Flanders. The Pioneer battalion left the Ypres sector on 1 October to Bapaume, travelling by stages via Barastre (4 October) and Ytres (6 October) to a camp that was known in the diary only by a map reference number (Camp W3C.57). They spent October improving trenches. They cleaned them up; dug them to a depth of at least 6 feet, widening them where necessary; lay trench boards; completed communication trenches; improved fire-bays, drainage and revetments; and completed double apron wiring in front. Generally, three companies worked on the trenches while one established and improved the camps and supply yards. By 29 October, the line had been reinforced and reorganised, leaving 20th Division on an extended and incomplete front defending the villages of Metz-en-Couture and Gouzeaucourt. It was not intended that they should passively occupy these lines.

There followed several weeks of secret preparation for what was to be the first full-scale tank battle of the war. Among the jobs allocated to 11th DLI was the construction of camouflaged camps to assemble troops just before the attack. They worked in the vicinity of Villers-Plouich developing shelters, communication trenches, filling in craters and preparing roads. One party of fifty men under Second Lieutenant Atley constructed a railway (incidentally illustrating that officers also switched

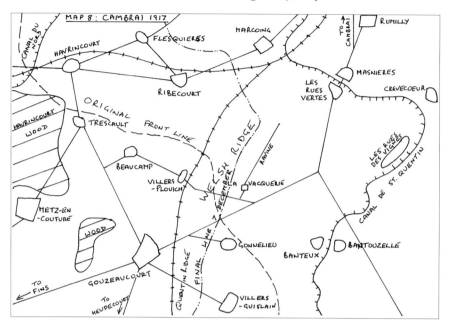

Cambrai, 1917. (*Martin Bashforth, 2010*)

between infantry and pioneer roles, he being previously in charge of the Lewis gun teams). During 9 October, one company built a scale model of the coming operation, used for the training of the various units involved. On a more personal note, Captain Palmer was transferred to the Tank Corps, to be replaced in charge of A Company by Captain W. G. L. Sear. On 17 October, the battalion headquarters was moved to a new base, still known only by its map reference, W5b.

The attack on 20 November was designed as a surprise, with no preliminary artillery bombardment preceding the advance by hundreds of tanks and supporting infantry. The 20th Division infantry went into attack at 6.20 a.m. Initial advances were spectacularly successful, but began to falter around the line of the St Quentin Canal. Meanwhile A and B Companies of 11th DLI followed to prepare roads and tracks for the cavalry and tanks. Within twenty minutes of the divisional attack, C and D Companies were digging a new communications trench from the British front line towards the enemy front line. These two companies transferred to work on the road between Villers-Plouich and La Vacquérie in the afternoon, and two platoons remained on this job all night. Lieutenant D. Ellwood took charge of the eight Lewis gun teams to provide anti-aircraft support during the operations, before they joined the main infantry brigades in the forward area. All Pioneer companies transferred onto road works after the first day.

Pioneers building a light railway near Arras, June 1917. 11th DLI did similar work at various times. (*Imperial War Museum, Q 2475*)

Instructions were issued on 27 November, contained in divisional order No. G116.[1] The Pioneers had to create a strong defensive line behind a reinforced main line under the control of 12th Division. The orders demanded that the line 'be constructed from the outset as a continuous, well traversed trench 7 feet deep and 7½ feet wide, 20 foot traverses, and firestepped as required'. In front was a double-apron fence covered with 'an irregular line of entanglement so sited that every portion of it can be flanked by machine gun fire'. In front of the defensive line they constructed an outpost line of strongpoints, wired all round to defend them against bomb-throwers, and within sufficient distance of each other to offer mutual support. The new defences included an elaborate system of communications trenches and, thanks to the loan of a Tunnelling Company, a dugout for the headquarters of each of the three infantry brigades. The speed and design of the construction illustrated the intention to hold the area permanently. However, by 29 November, after several days of bitter fighting, the Allies were in an exposed salient, surrounded by Germans on high ground.

On 30 November, the Germans launched a powerful counter-attack with air support, quickly outflanking and overrunning exposed units. Shelling began at 7 a.m. on 12th Division and 55th Division fronts, and half an hour later on 20th Division. The other two divisions took the brunt of the early infantry charges, but 20th Division's outpost line was quickly overwhelmed, followed by machine-gun attacks from the air. The right of the division was outflanked and fell back. At the time, the various companies from 11th DLI were scattered throughout the area on working parties, helping with roads, tracks and railways. They instantly converted into regular infantry in an attempt to stem the German attacks, especially on the right flank around Welsh Ridge and Gouzeaucourt, though not all the men were carrying arms. It was the machine-gunners that provided the core of the defence in the first instance. B Company was the first to notice the German counter-attack. They had been digging trenches overnight under the command of Captain Jee and were on their way back, tired and ready for a good rest. At about 6.45 a.m. large bodies of men were seen straggling back in some disorder. Jee set his men up in defensive order in a sunken road, with two platoons up ahead, intending to prevent any attacks up the Marcoing Valley. He also established contact with 61st Infantry Brigade and Brigadier General Banbury ordered him to hold their positions, which was done until 5.30 p.m. B Company opened fire on the enemy several times during the day and they were constantly harassed by aircraft. They were finally reunited with D Company, having lost one officer seriously wounded, three men killed and six more wounded.

D Company, under command of Captain R. L. S. Pemberton, had been working in trenches in the former Hindenburg Line. Like Captain Jee, Pemberton also quickly established contact with the infantry battalions. A message had been sent by Major Owen of 11th RB to 7th DCLI. The message came into Pemberton's hands and he moved his men forward to link up with the Rifles. Brigadier General Banbury asked him to link up with 7th KOYLI in front, drawing the latter into contact with 11th RB and then withdraw D Company into a support position. By early evening, Pemberton was joined by Captain Jee and B Company.

Captain Sear and A Company had been out all night, working on road construction between divisional HQ at Villers-Plouich and Marcoing. He brought his men back into HQ for instructions and was sent forward onto Borderer Ridge, which lay between HQ and the village of Gouzeaucourt, which was under heavy attack. They dug in under light shell and machine-gun fire and remained in position overnight, suffering only two men wounded.

It was HQ and C Company, in Gouzeaucourt, that were most exposed. At first the situation was confused. Shelling, at around 8 a.m., seemed not heavy enough to warrant concern. By 9.15 a.m. the artillery units began to dash about and Lieutenant Colonel Hayes, the battalion commander, enquired what was going on. The Germans were rumoured to have broken through from the direction of Villers-Guislain. Hayes led his men towards Hill 135, from where he had a vantage point to see what was happening for his own eyes. The Germans were advancing in perfect order completely unopposed. At the same time the top of Hill 135 came under machine-gun fire from Quentin Ridge. Hayes sent one platoon to defend his left in a line stretching from the houses at the southern end of Gouzeaucourt village. Two platoons were ordered to line up in the centre to act as the main line of defence along the Heudicourt–Gouzeaucourt road. The fourth platoon, led by Lieutenant Bushell, was sent to protect the right flank, though they were themselves somewhat exposed in the process. Fortunately, three sections of Royal Engineers came up to provide reinforcements and were spread around to help maintain contact between the DLI platoons. Major Robinson in charge of the Engineers was commended for his coolness and courage in keeping his men up to scratch, when they were inexperienced in conditions of open warfare and all around seemed to be confusion and panic. Heavy machine-gun fire was becoming a serious threat, enfilading from the south of Hill 135. By the time the platoon on the left had got into the south of Gouzeaucourt, the Germans were already infiltrating the village and they found themselves involved in house-to-house fighting against great odds.

Hayes ordered Sergeant Major McEvoy and twenty men to get back to the support trenches south of the Gouzeacourt–Fins road, to hold it at all costs and provide covering fire for the rest of the company to fall back. Here they all rallied astride the main road. They were joined by Captain Symons of the 27th Siege Battery, Royal Garrison Artillery, and his men. The artillerymen had kept firing their howitzers until the last possible moment before rendering the guns useless and falling back themselves. The effect of forming this defensive line seemed to steady the German attack, which now became more cautious, giving time to send back for reinforcements, machine-guns and ammunition. Major Lloyd, who had sprained his ankle, was left in charge while Hayes and Symons explored the situation along the support trench line. Stragglers were rounded up and set astride the Metz–Gouzeaucourt road. By now the 20th Hussars had come forward and occupied the lines to the south of 11th DLI, shortly followed by the well-disciplined 2nd Coldstream Guards, who immediately launched a counter-attack. Hayes judged that his thinly stretched and poorly experienced band would be more help remaining behind, though a section from C Company and some Hussars joined the Guards' attack.

The HQ and C Companies lost between them one officer and six men killed, one officer slightly wounded and thirty-four men wounded. Hayes' own report paid particular tribute to the Engineers who, he believed, had suffered proportionately more casualties due to their lack of experience. He wished that they had had Lewis guns with them, as they would have proved very effective against the advancing Germans. He praised the gallantry and coolness of several of his officers: Lieutenant Bushell in charge of C Company; the Reverend H. P. Walton for his help with the wounded and gathering stragglers and the Adjutant Captain Tollit, who had escaped with the battalion papers, gathered machine-guns and reinforcements, and returned to the fight. Lieutenant William Winters Freeman was singled out for showing great gallantry, though he had been killed early on.

Fighting continued, backwards and forwards, for several days. On 1 December, B Company held the support trench on Borderer Ridge behind 7th KOYLI and provided them with ration details. The following day, Lieutenant H. S. Parkin led a bombing party from A Company on a counter-attack to clear an enemy trench. During the first couple of days, B and C Companies of 11th DLI were used to reinforce the exhausted and decimated 11th KRRC. They established and held a new line on the slopes of the Welsh Ridge to the north-west overlooking La Vacquerie. On 3 December, the battalion was taken out of the line and into huts at Sorel to regroup for a few days. Meanwhile, the mixed pattern of gains and losses was resolved into a somewhat smaller salient around Flesquières, rationalised along the higher ground and stronger points of defence. Territorially, the Battle of Cambrai had turned out to be a costly stalemate, though a great many lessons were learned about the use of tanks and how to coordinate them with other troops.

From the point of view of 11th DLI, these events would be an uncanny precedent for the retreat during March the following year, in the course of which many of the same officers and NCOs would again play a leading part. Meanwhile, at Cambrai the Pioneers had, through quick and independent thinking by company commanders and by their colonel, been instrumental in defining the point at which the German advance was held in their sector. They had done so through establishing close links with their comrades in the infantry battalions, supported by units from the divisional artillery, cavalry and the engineers. The division as a whole had proved its worth.

Casualties for 11th DLI were remarkably light in the circumstances. On 31 October, the nominal roll consisted of thirty-two officers and 949 other ranks. At the end of November they had twenty-nine officers and 916 other ranks, making a net loss of three officers and thirty-three men. Nineteen men from the battalion had been killed, fourteen of them on the first day of the German counter-attack on 30 November. A further six men died in the first few days of December, possibly from wounds incurred during the same battles. Lieutenant William Wiley Inglis had died on 20 November, during the original Allied attack, but the only officer to lose his life in the German counter-attack was Second Lieutenant William Winters Freeman, who is buried at Gouzeaucourt British Cemetery along with five privates killed on the same day.

Freeman was twenty-four when he signed up at Felling on 7 September 1914. Originally he was attached as a private to 13th DLI and went overseas with them on 25 August 1915. Before leaving, he married Ethel Ridley at St Albans church, Heworth. He retained a strong affiliation to his parental family, as witnessed by the will he wrote on 22 August 1915 at Bramshott.

In the event of my death I, 19106 Sergeant William Winters Freeman of the 13th (Service) Battalion Durham Light Infantry, do hereby leave the sum of £31.0.0 to my mother Sarah Ellen Freeman to be used at her discretion for her own personal use or for the education of my brother Horace Kimberley Freeman. I also leave to my mother all my personal effects at present at home, Musgrove House, Windy Nook in the County of Durham. I leave to my wife (Ethel Freeman) any Club Money which may be due to her from either of my two Clubs, and also any of my personal effects which she may have at the present time at her home at Felling on Tyne.[2]

The headstone of 2nd Lt W. W. Freeman at Gouzeaucourt New British Cemetery. He died in the German counter-attack at Cambrai. (*Jon Miller*)

Before going overseas he had distinguished himself enough to reach the rank of Sergeant in 13th DLI and was further promoted to Colour Sergeant-Major on 4 September 1916. After receiving his commission he was attached to 11th DLI from 2 April 1917. His few remaining effects reached his widow on 3 January 1918: an advance book, a cheque book, photos and papers. He left a balance at Messrs Holt & Co of £9 8s 0d. There were no children.

The family held a memorial service in his honour at 3 p.m. on 23 December 1917 at St Alban's church, Windy Nook. The traditional Anglican service spoke much of resurrection. There were excerpts from the gospel of St John, from Job and the letters of Paul to Timothy. The psalm was 27, 'The Lord is my light and salvation', and the lesson from 1 Corinthians XV, 'The Resurrection of the Dead'. The final hymn was the DLI hymn, 'Abide with me: fast falls the eventide', which became a staple of all Remembrance events in later years. As the congregation left they were invited to contribute towards a collection 'for the erection of a Memorial in the Church of all Parishioners who have fallen in the War'. It was an interesting precedent for what many families would seek after the war, in memory of their loved ones and in the absence of a funeral and personal grave.[3]

Also gathered in from the battlefield of Cambrai at Gouzeaucourt New British Cemetery are the graves of Privates 181443 Robert Barrasford, 12531 Robert Cain, 22193 W. A. Kipling, 16467 Anthony McFarlane and 25673 J. Neale. The eight other men killed the same day have no known grave and are commemorated on the Cambrai Memorial at Louverval.

Barrasford was a miner, aged almost thirty-one, when he enlisted in Durham on 1 October 1914. He served with several units, including 18th DLI in both Egypt and France. After a series of accidents, illnesses and being wounded, he convalesced in England before returning to France in September 1917 and being assigned to 11th DLI. Mrs Martha Barrasford originally lived at 56 Smokey Row, Framwellgate Moor, and they had no children of their own. However, Barrasford's friend, Robert Hayes, died leaving his wife with six children, including six-month-old Thomas. Arrangements were made through solicitors for the Barrasfords to take care of the boy, with a view to adoption. Enormous complications followed as Mrs Barrasford moved back to her mother's home in Northumberland. It took several police enquiries to track down her whereabouts and check the circumstances of the adoption. Her original pension of 13s 9d from 24 June 1918 was increased to 20s 5d to include the adopted son, even though he had not been part of the family when Robert Barrasford had enlisted. Further problems arose over entitlement to the medals, scroll and plaque after the war, as Mrs Barrasford had by then died, leaving poor Thomas

The four headstones at the front are of Robert Barrasford, Anthony McFarlane, William Kipling and Robert Cain, at Gouzeaucourt New British Cemetery. All died in the German counter-attack at Cambrai. (*Gaynor Greenwood*)

Hayes Barrasford in the charge of his adoptive grandmother. Fortunately, as in many instances of confusion, common sense prevailed and they were passed to the care of the grandmother for the adopted son.

Robert Cain was a DLI regular for twelve years before re-enlisting in Sunderland on 11 August 1914. He was transferred from 10th DLI to 11th DLI in September having been made up to Lance Corporal. He struggled with the idea of being in charge of other men. Despite several misdemeanours, a sentence of twenty-eight days' detention, and being charged with neglect of duty, there were better hopes of Cain and he was confirmed as Corporal before going overseas. He reverted to Private at his own request on 22 July 1916. Throughout his career with 11th DLI there were health problems: dental caries, emphysema, a fall causing back problems and a severe attack of diarrhoea. A letter in his service papers indicates that, like the others who share his last resting place, his remains were exhumed for proper burial at Gouzeacourt.

Private 53552 Rowland Charles Barrow has no known grave and is commemorated on the Cambrai Memorial. He was an unusual recruit in many respects. Far from being the usual Durham miner, he had been born in Wolverhampton and had enlisted under the Derby scheme in November 1915, while living in Barnet. He was almost forty years old and employed as a works manager. Tall and slim, he volunteered for training prior to call-up and distinguished himself at musketry, training others in the same. He was ideal material for NCO rank. Although originally placed with the King's Royal Rifle Corps, when he arrived in France at Étaples on 27 December 1916 he was posted to 11th DLI with the rank of Corporal. He was 'deprived of his appointment' on 26 September 1917, reason not recorded, and two months later he was dead. His widow was left with a pension of only 13s 9d, a huge drop in income from what Barrow must have previously earned.

Private 76898 Frederick Charles Bradley originally signed up in Kent with the Royal Engineers, getting extra pay for his skills as a bricklayer. He kept this rate of pay when he was transferred to 11th DLI in April 1916. He was with Captain Sear's A Company on 30 November 1917, which was the least heavily involved of the 11th DLI companies. Only two men were recorded as wounded. Bradley was reported wounded and missing, and finally assumed to have died in German hands. Information came back to the War Office via the Red Cross, including his disc on 25 January 1918. He left a widow and two daughters, aged one and three, to survive on 25s 5d pension, a severe reduction at the time from his pay allotment of 31s 6d.

One who died later of wounds received at Cambrai was Private 76788 James Sidney Cole. Like Bradley he had enlisted in the Royal Engineers. He travelled from Gateshead to Chatham on 22 November 1916 at barely nineteen years of age, using his trade as a plumber to help him get into the regiment. He was trained at the RE Depot in Newark before embarking at Folkestone on 17 September 1917. On landing in France, instead of being allocated to a Royal Engineers unit, he was assigned to 11th DLI, joining them on 1 October. When he died on 1 December 1917, he had survived merely seventy-six days in France. His mother, the recently widowed Mrs Ellen Cole, received his effects the following April, including a testament, mirror in case, cigarette case, pipe, knife, cap badge, small wallet, pocket wallet, letters, photos, numeral, jug purse and strap, a button and two celluloid discs.

Following the Battle of Cambrai, the 20th Light Division was in reserve, before returning north to the Ypres Salient. After two successive major actions they were in great need of a period of recovery. On 8 December, the Pioneers went by train from Sorel to Hesdin, and marched to billets at Écquemicourt, arriving on 10 December. By 12 December, the division was concentrated 20–25 miles south-west of Ypres, with headquarters at Blaringhem (apart from the artillery, who rejoined them on Christmas

The entrance to Louverval Military Cemetery, 2009. The memorial plaques to the missing of Cambrai are on the curved wall at the rear. (*Gaynor Greenwood*)

Eve). The Pioneers went by bus to Wardrecques on 11 December for drill, training and baths, and were joined there by an influx of newly commissioned officers. On 15 December, the battalion was transported to Dickebusch, where they set about their usual first task of cleaning and improving the billets. After a day or so of drill and inspections, they began wiring details in the Menin Road sector and kept at it right through Christmas, apart from Christmas Day itself. Despite the influx of new officers and over a hundred men, the battalion strength was slightly depleted, recorded nominally at 35 officers and 767 men at the end of December. The number of officers was fairly substantial, though in practice several were away on training. Almost 300 men were struck off (many being transferred to 2nd and 14th DLI to replenish their depleted ranks), had been killed or wounded, or had reported sick.

On 7 January, 20th Division, less artillery, relieved 30th Division in the left sector of IX Corps' front, on a line 2,700 yards long, crossing the Menin Road north-west of Gheluvelt. This was later extended 600 yards further left towards Polygon Wood, illustrating how stretched the British units were. The line was extremely important to the overall defences, but had not quite been completed and it fell to the 20th Division to make it impregnable. Fortunately, the weather was so cold that for six weeks the line remained quiet. Apart from a couple of reciprocal trench raid actions on 9 and 10 January, infantry activity was reduced to patrols. Early January's snow and frost gave way to torrential rain, a thaw and the inevitable mud and water. Some trenches had to be evacuated into defensive posts behind. The Pioneers continued improving defences throughout January without let up, apart from one small party engaged on railway works at Voormezeele. For those working in the front line near Polygon Wood, reliefs were frequent, sometimes every 24 hours, but were dangerously exposed to enemy shelling. There was shelter along the ridge in the Tor Top Tunnels – underground bivouacs big enough to accommodate a whole brigade – providing they lit no matches and didn't smoke!

The nominal roll remained at 41 officers and 767 men, with some going off sick and others obtaining leave. Sergeant Thomas Bashforth was away on leave from 23 January until 6 February. It was his second opportunity to go home to Darlington and a chance to spend a little time with his new son, John Raymond, born on 5 November 1917, as well as his three-year-old namesake son, Tom, and five-year-old daughter, Ethel. For those who had already been home once and had to suffer the pain of another family parting, the emotional pressure could be great. The story that has passed down through the Bashforth family is that on his way back to Bank Top Station, not a hundred yards from his front door, Thomas confided to a next-door neighbour, Mrs Ingledew, who was working for the railway as a porter, that 'he was going to take his hook'. She persuaded him otherwise. Family tales such as this tend to be embroidered in the re-telling over the years and it is likely that he had not seriously intended to desert, but was expressing his feelings about going back to the front. His eventual fate gave the story the emotional significance that it retains for the family today.

During the early months of 1918, the British Expeditionary Force was reorganised. Infantry brigades were reduced to three battalions each, necessitating the break-up of some units, amalgamations and re-designations. Within the 20th Division, 6th OBLI was disbanded, while 10th KRRC and 10th RB were broken up, some amalgamating with the respective 11th Battalion and the rest being transferred. The 7th KOYLI left the division and became the 14th Entrenching Battalion. The 2nd Scottish Rifles (Cameronians) joined as part of the 59th Brigade. Meanwhile Lloyd-George was allegedly holding back thousands of new recruits. There was no change to the role of 11th DLI, although the number of companies was reduced to three and their sizes changed (A, B and D companies were those retained). Reinforcements came from the disbandment of other units. On 11 February, 118 other ranks from 14th DLI arrived to join the Pioneers. These (apart from some former 11th DLI men who had only recently been sent to the 14th to bolster their numbers) had been ordinary infantrymen in the 18th Division and would become very useful in days to come. Accompanying officers included several who would play a major part in future events, such as Captain Endean and Second Lieutenants Banks and Duckett. By the end of February 1918, the battalion had a nominal strength of 830 men and 48 officers.

On 17 February 1918, the Pioneers were relieved from frontline duty and taken back to Racquinghem, where there was drill and musketry practice for a couple of days. On 19 February, the 37th Division took over from the 20th Division and the next day the latter were sent to rejoin Gough's Fifth Army south of the Somme. The Pioneers went by train via Steenbecque Station to Nesle, where they arrived on 21 February. Within a month of arriving, the division, including 11th DLI, would be put to its strongest test: not in attack, but in a fighting retreat.

NOTES TO CHAPTER NINE

1   A copy is with the divisional war diary papers at the National Archives.
2   The National Archives, WO 339/101504, papers of Lt Freeman.
3   Durham CRO, D/DLI/7 231/1 Order of Memorial service for Lieutenant Freeman.

CHAPTER TEN

The Fighting Retreat

Early 1918 represented a window of opportunity for the Germans to launch their own offensive rather than continuing the policy of defending the Hindenburg Line. The Americans had entered the war on the side of the Allies and would soon be able to put significant numbers of freshly trained forces into the field. A peace treaty had been signed at Brest-Litovsk with the newly established Russian Soviet Republic, ending the war on the Eastern Front. The Germans could dedicate more forces to the Western Front and the Austrians could focus on the Italian Front. The Allied commanders knew that the Germans would launch a major offensive at the earliest opportunity. It remained a matter of dispute as to where the main force of this assault would fall, though the early consensus was an area further north to that which actually occurred.

The area around St Quentin was a relatively quiet sector manned by French forces in between the Somme battlefield area and that around Verdun. From January 1918, the French relinquished control of this area to British forces, principally the Fifth Army under Sir Hubert Gough, who took control of the line south of the Flesquières Salient. Gough found that, while the front line was fairly well established, there was little defensive preparation behind, making the sector vulnerable to an all-out attack by the Germans. With little time to rectify the light defences, Gough took the precaution of ensuring that a former defensive line in front of Amiens near Villers-Bretoneux was preserved. He prevented local farmers from filling in the trenches to return the land to harvest for the coming season. Gough argued that the long front his forces were expected to cover needed massive labour support in order to build the hundreds of miles of communication trenches, support trenches and dugouts that would provide defence in depth. While he won the argument, these men did not arrive until well into

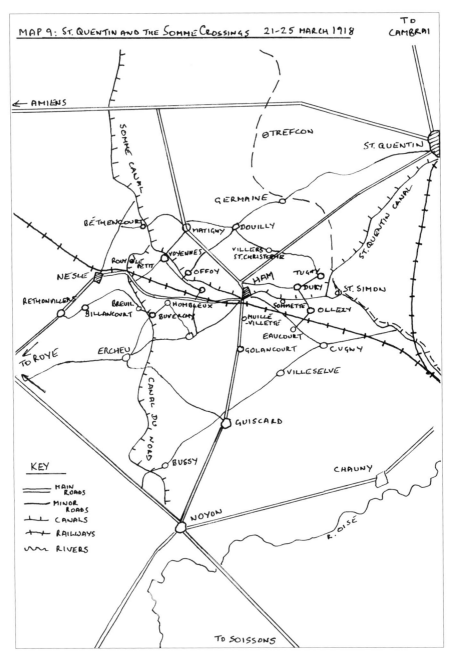

St Quentin and the Somme Crossings, 21–25 March 1918. (*Martin Bashforth, 2010*)

March, by which time the gathering intelligence was that German forces were massing in the area of St Quentin, directly in front of the Fifth Army and an attack was even more imminent.

On 23 February 1918, the 20th Division (attached to the Fifth Army as a reserve division) set up its headquarters at Ercheu. The 60th Brigade was located around Ham, the 59th at Beaulieu, three miles south of Ercheu, and the 61st near Fréniches, three miles south-east of Ercheu. The 91st Field Artillery was at Esmery Hallon and the 92nd at Rouy-le-Grand, 2½ miles north-east of Nesle. The 11th DLI was initially billeted between Muille-Villette and Golancourt. They built a railway between Ham and Noyens, which occupied them more or less completely for the following weeks. In the early part of March, there was additional training in musketry and the Lewis gun teams were brought up to full capability. All of this helped to integrate the influx of new recruits and weld the battalion back together after the reorganisation. The combination of infantry training with railway plate-laying and ballasting would have emphasised to those recently joined from infantry battalions that Pioneers had to be equally good in both spheres.

The division was placed at the disposal of Lieutenant General Maxse's XVIII Corps. Approximately a month was spent retraining, reconnoitring the area and constructing the defences behind the main battle zone. The various companies of machine-gunners from the infantry battalions were reorganised into A, B, C and D Companies of the 20th Battalion, Machine Gun Corps. All units were placed on twenty-four hours' standby, but this was to be reduced to twelve hours on 10 March and one hour on 20 March, as intelligence began to be gathered about the planned German offensive.[1] There was still time for recreation. On St Patrick's Day, Sunday 17 March, the 20th Division organised sports and General Gough took part in an Officers' Jumping Competition.[2] On Tuesday, 19 March, the weather worsened with the first of several days of rain, but 11th DLI continued to work on the railway both then and the next day. The 20th Division was held in reserve, ready to cover the right of the Fifth Army at a moment's notice.

The diary for 11th DLI during the coming days was written up after the event and was heavily reliant on memory. Each company commander assembled their own account. These would frequently not be the original company commanders. The account that follows is based on the diary, with additional information from Captain Wilfrid Miles[3] and Captain V. E. Inglefield.[4] The events of the next few days were so intense and dramatic, only a day-to-day account can help to make sense of it.

21 March, Thursday

According to General Gough: 'At 10 minutes past 5, I was awakened by the roar of a bombardment, which, though it sounded dully in my room in Nesle, was so sustained and steady that it at once gave me the impression of some crushing, smashing power.'[5] The experience was rather more rude and personal for those directly on the receiving end of the barrage, especially as it was reported to have commenced at 4.40 a.m., some thirty minutes before it disturbed the general's sleep.[6]

Maxse's XVIII Corps was put to battle stations. The 20th Division was directed to cover the rear zone defences between the Somme and the Omignon rivers, from St Simon to Trefcon. By 1 p.m. they were helping to cover threatened breaks in the forward lines. The various elements of the division were broken up, with 61st Brigade detached to support 36th Division, covering the Somme crossings.

At 6.20 a.m., all companies of 11th DLI were brought to battle stations and ordered to assemble at Golancourt. In the afternoon, A and B companies were ordered forward to Villers-St-Christophe. Captain Jee, in charge of a separate detachment of 6 officers and 133 men[7], was ordered to the Divisional Reinforcement Battalion at Matigny, under the command of Major Storr, detached from 12th KRRC for the purpose. Lieutenant M. Cooper and D Company were sent to join 61st Brigade at 8 o'clock in the evening and spent the night digging in between Tugny-et-Pont and Dury, covering the road with the 12th Kings. The first fatalities for 11th DLI were Privates George Berry and James Oakley.

22 March, Friday

By the morning of the second day, the 20th Division had been pushed further back, but was holding a strong line, covering the withdrawal of other divisions and dealing with units of the enemy that had broken through. The various units of 11th DLI were in three separate groups. The largest was comprised of HQ Company, plus A and B Companies, under the overall charge of Lieutenant Colonel Hayes. His HQ Company was officered by Lieutenant Cooke (Acting Adjutant), Second Lieutenant Ellwood, Lieutenant Bushell (Scouting and Intelligence), with Captain Turnbull RAMC as Medical Officer. Captain Endean was in charge of A Company, supported by Second Lieutenants Craig, Galley, Rutherford and Alexander. Captain Kemp commanded B Company, supported by Second Lieutenants Martin, Morris, Naylor and English. Lieutenant Cooper led D Company. The fourth and smallest unit was the reserve group equivalent to about half a company, in command of Captain Jee.

Early in the day, D Company was seconded under the orders of Major Norman, Royal Engineers. He sent them forward to Tugny to report to Lieutenant Colonel Vince of 12th Kings prepared to do some rapid and heavy trench digging. They had finished their trenches by 3 p.m., and took up positions in old German trenches astride the Tugny–Dury road with 12th Kings. During the late evening, they were ordered south of the Canal de la Somme and made a bivouac by the road around Ollezy-Sommette-Eaucourt. They continued in support of 12th Kings, covering and defending the canal crossings. During the evening, Captain Jee and his men had dug in to form a rearguard north of the Matigny–Douilly road, facing north-east. Coming under attack, they were forced to retire to Voyennes.

Lieutenant Colonel Hayes established touch with 59th Infantry Brigade and dispersed his troops at their disposal, including the battalion transport. In the afternoon, A and B Companies were sent forward to occupy a trench system protecting the village of Germaine. As soon as they arrived there, they were ordered by divisional HQ to join up with 60th Brigade to plug a gap between 60th and 61st Brigades at Tugny-L'Avesne. This was supposed to be a reserve line, but by the time the DLI men arrived the KRRC had retired from Tugny and this was now the front line. Although trench lines had been marked out, no digging had been done. Apart from Jee's half company, this brought the battalion temporarily into one consolidated line, though not under unified command. They covered the gap with 6th KSLI to the left adjoining B Company, while A Company formed the right, adjacent to D Company. Lieutenant Cooper with D Company remained technically under the orders of 12th Kings just ahead, which may have caused some communications difficulties. At 8.30 p.m. Captain Endean reported that A Company was exposed on their right, the 12th Kings having had to pull back, taking D Company with them. In order to protect the right flank, two outposts were quickly dug at an angle, facing right.

Thick fog had descended. Up ahead, the Germans were moving around in Tugny, shouting in English and generally making a lot of noise. Patrols were sent forward to investigate. In the fog and darkness, Germans (following the retreat of 12th Kings) had outflanked the DLI and worked round into their rear. Suddenly, around midnight, B Company came under attack from behind, as did 6th KSLI to their left. The whole formation had been surrounded and confusion quickly ensued. It was hard to know which way to fire in case it was aimed at comrades. Urgent efforts were made to regroup, gathering everyone together, including the Machine Gun Corps, regardless of which battalion or unit they belonged to. About a hundred men in this party were brought together. A counter-attack in the conditions was hopeless, so Hayes decided to pull them back down the main road towards Ham, while Second Lieutenant English with twenty men and a pair of Vickers machine-guns formed a rearguard. Despite being almost completely surrounded, Captain Endean and A Company managed to hold out long enough to help the others and then, down to about forty men, fought a way back through Dury and to Ham.[8] Company Sergeant-Major Craggs and a section of B Company linked up with some men from 12th RB and fought their way back in parallel. The shape of the battalion was being rapidly broken up under the pressure of events.

Casualties included twelve men killed. Second Lieutenant Ralph Galley of A Company was one of these, and is buried in the north part of Eppeville Old Churchyard, south-west of Ham. He was twenty-seven years of age, from Monkwearmouth. Private George Beilry is buried a long way north at Serre Road No. 2 Cemetery, presumably as a result of a post-war concentration of graves. Private W. Hurst is buried at Mézières Communal Cemetery Extension, another concentration. Similarly Private John Kennedy's remains have been moved to Bouchoir New British Cemetery. His death is incorrectly recorded in the Book of Remembrance at Durham Cathedral as 27 March rather than the 22nd. The other eight are all recorded as 'missing' and are commemorated on the Pozières Memorial; all privates, these were Ernest Clover, Frank Donoghue, William Hughes, William Leadley, Joseph Sadler, George Shephard, Tommy Smith and Sam Thompson.

Four officers were taken prisoner: Second Lieutenants Rutherford, Alexander, Morris and Craig. Craig of A Company was to die in captivity of influenza, on 5 November 1918 in Germany, where he is buried in the Poznan Old Garrison Cemetery.[9] It is not known exactly how many men from the other ranks were captured. Confusion was the norm during the next few days, and any attempts to keep track of numbers involved creative mathematics rather than controlled counting. Many were wounded and taken back to dressing stations. Scores of men became detached and mixed up with other units, perhaps managing to regroup with their own days later. Scores more fell into the hands of the Germans, either wounded or forced to surrender. Unfortunately, records of prisoners among the other ranks are virtually non-existent.

Using the admittedly suspect information contained in the battalion war diary, we can make a rough calculation that perhaps 100 men of B Company, 40 men from A Company, 200 men from D Company and a further 100 men with Captain Jee's detachment, led by about 20 remaining officers, had survived the first two days. This was less than half the battalion. The experience they had been through, the confusion caused by a mixture of fog, darkness and the speed and guile of the German strategy, illustrates well the problems faced by the British forces in the face of the onslaught.

23 March, Saturday

In the early hours of the third day, A and B Company, now combined as one, covered Offoy, while the remnants of Jee's detachment were with 12th RB. The rest of 20th Division had successfully withdrawn across the canal, blown the bridges and formed a new defensive line. Divisional HQ had regrouped at Nesle.

Overnight, D Company had been on the far right of the line covering the canal bank near Ollezy with the 12th Kings. Early in the morning, the Germans crossed the canal nearby and D Company was obliged to form a defensive line facing east towards Canizy, to the right of 12th Kings. Beyond them, further right, there was no contact with other British troops. Three platoons led respectively by Lieutenant Cooper, Second Lieutenant Banks and Second Lieutenant Gibson held a strong point in front just west of Annois, with a fourth platoon about a mile behind led by Second Lieutenant Duckett and CSM Robson. By 2 p.m. the three forward platoons were in action in support of 12th Kings. Since the attacks appeared to be fairly light, 12th Kings moved forward to engage the enemy. However, sections of the German units had skirted round the main 12th Kings formation and were attacking their second line company. Second Lieutenant Duckett's platoon advanced in support of the other three 11th DLI platoons but was never seen again, having walked straight into the ambush.

At about 6 p.m. the main units from D Company remained linked to 12th Kings, and were joined by about twenty men, remnants from 7th SomLI. The latter reported that there were no troops to their left, a fact soon confirmed by scouts. Almost at the same time it was reported that troops to the right had pulled back towards Cugny. D Company retired in good order to Cugny Railway Cutting where they came across a party from an Irish regiment of the 36th Division. Information from their officer was confusing. He stated that they were in touch with men on both flanks, but Lieutenant Cooper checked and found no-one to their left. Meanwhile two Irish sergeants reported that the troops to their right had fallen back on Cugny village. D Company did the same only to find it completely deserted. The officers discussed the situation and decided to continue retreating towards Guiscard. Second Lieutenant William Banks and a small group of men were detached to help the Irish officer, described as 'in a highly excited condition', to get his men out. When Banks failed to return, Lieutenant Cooper and Second Lieutenant Gibson took a small group of men back through the village but found no trace of Banks or the Irish. Banks was reported missing the next day, but had been badly wounded, dying a few days later in a German field hospital. Finally, D Company managed to link up with units of 61st Brigade, digging in north-east of

Villeselve. Cooper was only able to obtain three boxes of ammunition. There were no decent rations to be had, only biscuits and tinned meat. Here they rested overnight, their numbers badly depleted but lucky to have made it this far. By now most of the British forces were fragmented into relatively small groups, desperately trying to keep in some kind of contact with other units. Much depended on luck and on the native wits of often quite junior officers with comparatively little battle experience.

At about 4 a.m., 12th KRRC arrived, led by Lieutenant Colonel Moore, and took over the Offoy defences from 11th DLI. Lieutenant Bushell was given charge of a joint company made up mainly from B Company, with a few stragglers from A Company, assisted by Second Lieutenants Martin, Naylor and English, and CSM Craggs. They extended the line to the right from 12th KRRC as far as Canizy, assisted by twenty-six men from 6th KSLI. The combined strength was about 120 men. On their right they linked up with the 30th Entrenching Battalion, an illustration that semi-fit men were being drafted into the line to help make up the rapidly dwindling numbers. Battalion HQ was dug in about 200 yards behind this trench line, from where telephone communication was re-established with 60th Brigade HQ. There followed a comparatively quiet day, broken by intermittent sniping from the other side of the canal. The firing increased towards evening and, as darkness fell, there were bursts of machine-gun fire and trench mortars. The Entrenching Battalion was having difficulty holding their position and Lieutenant Colonel Moore secured the assistance of men from a neighbouring division to help reinforce them.

Captain Jee's detachment remained fairly intact. They covered the withdrawal of 2nd Scottish Rifles across the canal and at 9 a.m. marched back to dig a defensive line facing north-east near Languevoisin. Until midday, Lieutenant King and about twenty men held a forward position to the left of the Scottish Rifles. By 5 p.m. Captain Jee's detachment was supporting 59th Brigade, facing north and about a mile north of Rouy-le-Petit.

The rest of 61st Brigade was faring badly and forced to retire, fighting all the way. Overnight the remnants of the brigade were withdrawn to Neuvilly to rejoin the rest of 20th Division, where they were reorganised into a composite battalion of four companies, with a total strength of 9 junior officers and about 440 other ranks. A brigade of three battalions had been reduced to less than half a normal battalion. The relentless pace of the German attack, in conditions that made communications difficult, was taking a heavy toll.

All but two of those who died on this day are commemorated on the memorial to the missing at Pozières: George Arthurs, Jonathan Bainbridge, Arthur Bell, Frank Crofts, Henry Curd, Tom Dobson, Second Lieutenant

Vincent Duckett, Mark Farn, George Longstaff, Sergeant Llewellyn Monger, Robert Morrill, CSM David Robson, Fred Toll, Corporal Lawrence Uttley, George Watson and George Wray. The exceptions are Private G. N. Cook who is buried at Grand-Seraucourt British Cemetery south-west of St Quentin (which suggests he died of wounds having been captured previously), and Private H. Kitchen, who is buried at St Souplet British Cemetery, which was close to a hospital on the coast (indicating that he was one of those lucky enough to be shipped out by the battalion medics). Second Lieutenant Naylor was taken prisoner,[10] as probably were many other ranks.

24 March, Sunday

At dawn the combined DLI Company were joined by Captain Endean's section of A Company, having escaped from Ham. According to the war diary, they included Second Lieutenant Galley, though other records are clear that he had died on 22 March.[11] The diary also states that Galley and about thirty men were sent forward to take shelter in a railway cutting and, with the assistance of a Vickers and a Lewis gun, helped cover the area on the British side of the canal, both to left and right. Here they were joined by a small detachment from the Bedfordshire Regiment under Captain Parker, who assumed control. Meanwhile Captain Jee's detachment were dug in one mile north of Rouy-le-Petit, while D Company, under the command of Lieutenant Cooper, were at 61st Brigade HQ at Villeselve.

At 5 a.m., under the cover of thick fog, the enemy crossed the canal at Pargny, forcing a gap between the 20th and 8th Divisions. Patrols sent out to make touch with the Warwickshire Regiment to the right failed to return. The Germans gradually wore down the defences and began to turn the division's left flank held by 11th RB, succeeding by early afternoon and forcing terrible losses on the riflemen. Similar pressure was being exerted on the right flank, where the 11th KRRC was forced to retreat at about 3.30 p.m.

At 6 a.m., A and B Companies of 11th DLI came under artillery and mortar fire at Canizy. At 8 a.m., the B Company section retired under heavy rifle and machine-gun fire, but joined with A Company to launch a joint counter-attack. They successfully, if temporarily, checked the German advance and regained their trenches. However, units to the right were simultaneously retiring and trying to set up a defensive flank. Reinforced with men from 12th KRRC, the DLI men moved forward to the railway line, occupying some partially dug strongpoints at Calvary Farm. Captain Endean discovered that a complete gap had opened up on the right as far as Esmery-Hallon. The combined DLI and KRRC forces on the left flank were holding their own.

Finally, at about 2.30 p.m., the Durhams were outflanked on their right, lost control of Calvary Farm and were forced to retreat to Breuil, passing through Hombleux. Such was the precipitate nature of their retreat that it was only the action of some Canadian motorised machine-guns that prevented greater disorder. By nightfall they were under the command of 60th Brigade and holding the bank of the Canal-du-Nord on its western side, between Buverchy and Breuil. One unit under Captain Endean and Lieutenant Bushell held the bridge at Breuil (under the command of 12th KRRC), while Lieutenant Cooke placed another unit under CSM Lambert, mixed with KSLI men, which dug in near Buverchy under the command of the KSLI. About 100 yards behind, Lieutenant Colonel Hayes, Lieutenant Cooke, Second Lieutenant Ellwood and a small number of signallers and runners formed the HQ. Once established, the units experienced a relatively quiet night. By now all the British forces were severely mixed up, with troops from four divisions jumbled together. They were joined by several sections of French troops to help hold the line of the canal. The French disturbed the quiet by firing periodic bursts of machine-gun fire towards the opposite bank.

Captain Jee's position, north of Rouy le Petit, came under attack at dawn on the same day and by 9 a.m. they were the front line of defence. At 10 a.m., his men gave covering fire for a counter attack by 61st Brigade from Mesnil-St-Nicaise towards Béthencourt-sur-Somme. The attack failed and by afternoon Jee's men had been outflanked, losing the village of Rouy in their rear. A defensive flank was dug overlooking the village. Lieutenant Dodds was wounded during this action. By evening they had managed to retreat by stages to a defensive position in front of Nesle, on the road between there and Ham.

On Sunday morning, about 6 a.m., D Company moved forward from Villeselve in thick fog. They were unable to make contact with any of 61st Brigade, and dug in about one mile to the north. To their left was a company of Irish troops and a section from the Machine Gun Corps, while on their right were men from 14th Division. Around noon the fog cleared and they came under fire from artillery to the east and south. Along with the accompanying units, they retreated to a sunken road near Villeselve at 3.30 p.m., where they were able to link up with some men of 7th DCLI from their own division. They covered the retreat of French *mitrailleurs* (machine-gunners) and British cavalry men. Although the Germans continued to slowly advance towards them, the officer in charge of the DCLI, desperate to conserve the dwindling supply of ammunition, would only let them fire at a hostile aircraft.

At 6 p.m., D Company came under well-targeted shrapnel fire from the German artillery and their line broke. The only line of retreat was through the village of Villeselve and they pulled back under constant machine-gun fire. Reaching the village of Guiscard at 7.45 p.m., they were scattered by a barrage of gas shells. Lieutenant Cooper and four men found they had become separated from the rest of the company. They reached Muirancourt at about 10 p.m. and, with assistance from the Military Police, managed to get back to Bussy at about midnight. Here Cooper found the medical officer and another officer from 7th DCLI and gathered together a group of about twenty-five stragglers from other 20th Division units.

The afternoon of 24 March had seen a general retreat across the 20th Division front, in order to maintain the line and close any gaps where flanks had been threatened or turned. A new defensive line was established on the Libermont Canal. At the end of the day, most of 11th DLI were with 60th Brigade, holding its right flank near Buverchy with support from 83rd Field Company Royal Engineers and 6th KSLI. The 59th Brigade, having been outflanked on the left, was reinforced with whatever could be mustered from the confusion, but despite every effort could not re-establish touch with the 8th Division to their north. Any other surviving remnants of the 20th Division were scattered.

Ten men were killed during the day, all privates and all, except one, are commemorated among the missing at Pozières. These were John Angel, Alfred Collingwood, William Douglass, Thomas Fenton, John Fieldhouse, John Lincoln, James Logan, John Rundle and Matthew Youll. Norman Meek from Seaham is buried at Hangard Communal Cemetery Extension, one of the concentration cemeteries, and may have died in captivity of wounds.

25 March, Monday

By dawn, the remnants of A and B Companies were still in position between Buverchy and Breuil on the canal bank, Captain Jee's detachment was dug in on the road north of Nesle, while the handful of survivors from D Company were at Bussy, along with other stragglers from a variety of regiments. Lieutenant Colonel Hayes and Lieutenant Cooke were sent to the rear to Languevoisin to direct operations strengthening the line. The combined remnants of A and B Companies fought a retreat during the evening from Breuil, through Cressy to Roye. Hayes was now suffering badly from the effects of gas and was evacuated to Rouen. Captain Sear took charge of the battalion. Early on 25 March, a mixed force, made up of remnants from the 20th, 61st and 8th Divisions, managed to form a defensive line, but found its left continuously outflanked by the pressure of the German advance and were constantly pressed back. During the afternoon there was a further general retreat around Nesle and by 9.45 p.m. the divisional HQ had retired to Roye.

For about three hours from 7.30 a.m., Captain Jee's men, along with other units from 20th Division, remained under the overall command of Major Storr. They were forced to retire after the Royal Berkshire Regiment were driven back on their left, and made their way from Nesle towards Roye. The DLI split into two parties, with Captain Jee on the left and Second Lieutenant R. H. King on the right, either side of the road. French reinforcements arrived about 11 a.m. and, with the DLI men, jointly manned an outpost line 200 yards south-west of the Herly–Billancourt road. At 5 p.m. the Germans attacked again and the DLI provided covering fire to allow the French to retire, before falling back and joining them at Réthonvillers.

Before dawn, at 3 a.m. on the 25th, Lieutenant Cooper was advised that the retreat was in full swing in the sector. He and the four survivors from D Company set off and reached Roye in the afternoon. The situation late on 25 March saw the 20th Division holding the line Cressy–Billancourt–Réthonvillers, with 60th Brigade on the right, 59th Brigade on the left and HQ at Roye. The 61st Brigade rejoined at Gruny late in the evening and took up a position on the left towards Liancourt. The 20th Division was

Pipers at the head of a mixed body of troops from 20th Division, retiring to a line Réthonvillers–Billancourt–Orsay, 25 March 1918. (*Imperial War Museum, Q 10816*)

British wounded passing through the joint British and French outpost line near Roye, 25 March 1918. (*Imperial War Museum, Q 10824*)

now being reinforced by French forces and was placed under the GOC, 133rd French Division, who had taken command of the line south of the Somme. The plan was for 20th Division to retreat to Le Quesnel to establish new lines of defence, while the French held the line to the south.

Four men were killed during this day. Of these Francis Boynton, Thomas Kear and Sergeant James Pickering are commemorated at Pozières. Private J. McGill from West Hartlepool is buried at Bouchoir New British Cemetery. Private George Brown and Sergeant J. Hopkinson (D Company), who had been wounded previously and evacuated, died of their wounds at the hospital in Rouen and are buried at St Sever Cemetery Extension. Sergeant T. H. Packard also died, probably as a prisoner of the Germans, as he is buried at Grand-Seraucourt British Cemetery behind what had been their lines.

26 March, Tuesday

At dawn on 26 March, the remnants of A and B Companies were at Roye, where Captain Jee's men joined them at one in the morning. The handful of survivors from D Company had been in the vicinity since the previous day, but had not yet made contact with their other comrades. The planned retreat, organised with the French reinforcements, took effect but was to prove very difficult because of the speed of the German advance. Flanking cover provided by the 61st Brigade allowed the division only just enough time to make its march along the road from Royes to Le Quesnel. In the process, 7th DCLI virtually sacrificed itself, holding the German advance at Le Quesnoy. By the time the division reached Le Quesnel at noon, the Germans had already got patrols onto the main Amiens road near Damery. Communication with the French towards Roye was now broken, and the gap had to be plugged by the 36th and 30th Divisions, who had been brought back into the line after a brief respite.

On arrival at Le Quesnel, everyone from 20th Division was directed to creating new defences just to the east of the village, in order to make a supporting line for the 30th Division, who were now holding the line between Bouchoir and Rouvroy. The exhausted 11th DLI were the backbone of the diggers, though any trenches were fairly rudimentary in the circumstances. During the day, Captain Jee carried out reconnaissance between Erches and Bouchoir, just behind Le Quesnoy. At 6.30 p.m., the 20th Division was replaced by the 61st Division and ordered forward to provide an immediate line of defence behind the 30th Division. The Pioneers of 11th DLI dug defences at Arvillers, just to the rear of the 30th Division, in the area previously surveyed by Captain Jee. At 7.30 p.m. in

Men of the British 20th Division and the French 22nd Division in hastily dug rifle pits covering a road in the Nesle sector, 25 March 1918. The exposed landscape is typical of the area. (*Imperial War Museum, Q 10810*)

the evening they were finally joined by Lieutenant Cooper and the four survivors of D Company.

The separate company accounts in the battalion diary cease from this time on, indicating that the battalion was operating as one unit. By this time any distinction between companies, battalions, divisions and regiments was academic. Their numerical strength bore no resemblance to normality. Contemporary photographs of the 20th Division during this period show them forming lines mixed up completely with French units.

There were four privates killed on this day, all commemorated on the memorial to the missing at Pozières. These were Ernest Brydon, Henry Fox (aged twenty, from Sherburn), Ernest Hope (aged nineteen, from Wakefield) and Robert Lomas. But there was much more yet to come.

NOTES TO CHAPTER TEN

1   The Germans referred to their offensive as 'Operation Michael', preceding the later 'Operation Mars'.
2   Gough, 1934, p. 63.
3   Miles, 1920.
4   Inglefield, 1921.
5   Gough, p. 73.
6   Middlebrook, 1983.
7   The officers were Second Lieutenants Whitfield, R. H. King, F. G. McGreehin, F. Arnott, T. Applegarth and J. H. Dodds.
8   According to the battalion war diary, he was accompanied by Second Lieutenants Galley and Craig. This has to be inaccurate as both these men were listed missing on 22 March 1918. Craig was taken prisoner, while Galley was killed. See note 10 below.
9   Cox and Co. Ltd, 1919, reprinted 1988.
10 There may be some confusion, as the one listed as wounded has the initial F while the one listed as captured has the initial P.
11 The other records include both the Commonwealth War Graves Commission and his surviving service papers, which include two independent accounts of his death. The confusion may be with another captured officer, whose name was Gallie.

CHAPTER ELEVEN

To the Last Man

As the remnants of 11th DLI reorganised around Arvillers on the night of 26 March, they had been under sustained attack for six days without respite. They had advanced, fought, retreated, counter-attacked, tried to hold onto strongpoints, held the line to protect other retreating troops and had found strength to repeatedly dig new defences on demand. They had dug trenches twice that very day. Their numbers were severely depleted, their CO had been pulled out of the line, and they were headed by a much-diminished number of junior officers. They had regrouped into something resembling a unified battalion, which in the preceding few days had several times seemed beyond possibility. Their officers and NCOs had been a steadying influence at critical junctures. They were hungry, exhausted and in desperate need of a rest. That was not to be.

Events had been happening above their heads, about which they were probably oblivious. The idea of a retreat on this scale, accompanied by terrible losses of men and equipment, would have seemed unthinkable to an army that had fought valiantly on the Somme, at Third Ypres and at Cambrai. Yet great swathes of territory had been lost and a near catastrophic collapse had been avoided by the French transferring several divisions as reinforcements. Despite this, although the line of the Fifth Army was fragile, not least because of a gap of 1½ miles between them and Third Army to the north of the Somme, the Germans had not broken through and the British forces had not collapsed into total disarray.

The politicians found their scapegoat in General Gough, commander of the Fifth Army, who was dismissed from his post and relegated to the task of preparing a Reserve Army to hold the line from Amiens to the sea. The Fifth Army was so fragmented it existed in name only, nominally under the command of General Rawlinson and his staff. Much of one corps was

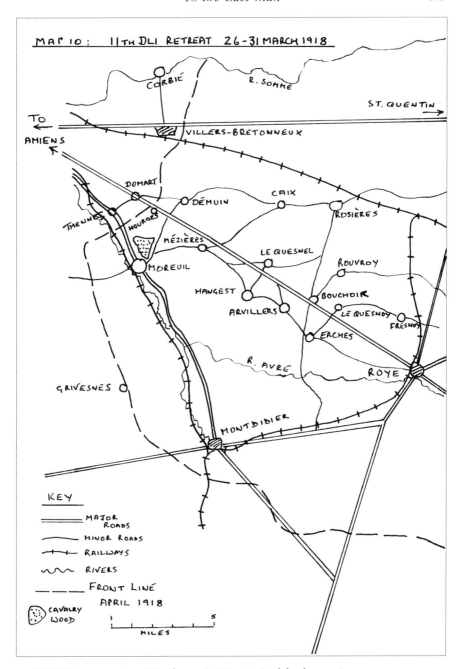

11th DLI Retreat, 26–31 March 1918. (*Martin Bashforth, 2010*)

already detached to the north, under the command of Third Army, while the most southerly units, including the remnants of 20th Division, were under the command of the French. Strategic planning was now effectively under the control of the French commander-in-chief, with Haig reduced to his second.

27 March, Wednesday

By early morning, 60th Brigade held the right at Arvillers, 59th Brigade held the centre at Folies and the 61st were on the left at Beaufort. The Divisional Reinforcement Battalion remained at Le Quesnel. Now effectively part of 60th Brigade, 11th DLI held a line of trenches south and east of Arvillers, which they had dug the previous day, and formed the extreme right of the British forces' second line. To their left were 12th KRRC, then 6th KSLI, with 12th Rifle Brigade holding the village behind, assisted by 60th Trench Mortar Battalion, now equipped with rifles. A long way to the right and out of sight was the main French force, covering the valley of the River Avre.

A few miles ahead of the 20th Division, the Germans launched artillery attacks on Erches to the front and Bouchoir to the left. Erches was captured

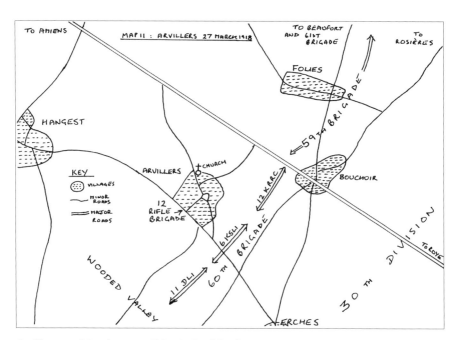

Arvillers, 27 March 1918. (*Martin Bashforth, 2010*)

by 10.40 a.m. and Bouchoir by 12.30 p.m. The 20th Division helped pull together the groups of men streaming back along the main Amiens road and reorganised the defences across it to hold the German advance. By 6.30 p.m., the 60th Brigade held the right of the front line in advance of Arvillers. To the right of 11th DLI there were virtually no troops for 1,200 yards. The Germans were advancing to right, left and in front, and the 11th DLI was in danger of being overrun. Men from 12th RB were sent out from the village to extend the line to the right of the DLI and plug the gap between them and the French, though the distance involved rendered the task hopeless.

During these actions, an advanced post of 11th DLI came under intense fire. The entries in the battalion war diary for 27–28 March overlap and are rather confused. More clarity can be obtained from the war diary of 12th RB, who had a clear view from the village. As the DLI came under fire, there was commotion around their positions and it appeared that they were about to abandon their posts. Men of 12th RB were about to be sent to reinforce them, but before they did so the problem was resolved and the DLI settled again. At some point during this day my grandfather, Sergeant

The ruined church at Arvillers from a French photograph of 1916. Church towers were used by signallers as look-out posts during the March Retreat. (*Imperial War Museum, T 1203*)

Thomas Bashforth, was killed, most probably in this incident. Many years after the war, my father was decorating a house in Darlington occupied by a former DLI soldier called Towers. Towers recognised his name and recounted how my grandfather had been wounded and he had tried to carry him back to the village over his shoulders. However, a second bullet killed my grandfather, passing through and becoming lodged in Towers' back, where it remained for the rest of his life. This chance encounter seems to fit the incident described by the 12th RB diary. Sergeant Bashforth's body was not identified after the war, probably one of many roughly tumbled into trenches and ditches used as makeshift graves. He is commemorated on the memorial at Pozières. Close by, at Bouchoir, there is a British concentration cemetery, which could conceivably contain his remains.

By the end of the day, chances of survival were running out. The battalion as a whole did not amount to much more than a full company strength, around 200 men. There was yet more action and courageous effort still to come before 11th DLI was finally pulled from the line. Of the deaths that day, five are commemorated at Pozières: Frederick Atkinson, Sergeant Thomas Bashforth, Lance Corporal James Brown (C Company), Fred Schofield and Robert Snowball. Private Snowball had, ironically, been charged with absence earlier in the month and sentenced to 84 days FP1, a sentence he never served. Private Bertie Handisides from West Hartlepool is buried at Caix. Private George Redpath died in the rear at Namps-au-Val, from wounds received on an earlier day.

28 March, Thursday

Wednesday had witnessed a dogged attempt to keep the remnants of the battalion together in an exposed position, under heavy fire from ahead and with their flanks exposed. The Durhams were exhausted, but not defeated. As the following days would prove, they remained able to play their part in finally bringing the German advance to a grinding halt and deny them their objective, the city of Amiens only a few miles away.

On Thursday, the division was due to be relieved by French forces. Before dawn, the 59th and 61st Brigades marched out along the Amiens road to a wood south-east of Démuin, which they reached at midday. However, at 8 a.m., before the 60th Brigade, including 11th DLI, could be replaced, they came under a heavy barrage, followed by a fierce attack on their whole line. The advanced platoon of the 11th DLI was heavily shelled and its Lewis guns put out of action. The enemy were massing in woods on the right flank and the Durhams turned their defences to meet the threat. In danger of being surrounded, the brigade was ordered to retire, which they did under heavy shell and machine-gun fire. The mixed unit of 12th Rifle Brigade and Trench Mortar men were pushed to the right to plug any gap and help cover the retirement. The brigadier general commended the courage of the Durhams in their efforts to hold back the German attack.

By 3 p.m., the DLI were at Fresnoy, from where they marched further to the rear to occupy a wood north-west of Mézières. They stayed there all night, sheltering from the rain. Captain Sear had been hit by machine-gun fire, a bullet perforating the left lung close to the heart and coming out through his left shoulder blade. Coughing up blood, he was moved back to hospital at Rouen. Coincidentally, Captain R. L. S. Pemberton returned to the battalion at the same time and took command. Pemberton had been on extended leave since 19 February and had missed the terrors of the previous days. He was fresh and ready for action and had already experienced leadership in the conditions of a defensive retreat, winning the MC at Cambrai.

Five deaths from this day are commemorated at Pozières: Arthur Busby, Thomas Hall, Reuben Harland, Allan Hill and John Lowerson. Private W. Amour died in hospital at Rouen from wounds received earlier in the retreat and is buried in the St Sever Cemetery Extension.

29 March, Good Friday

The 20th Division was transferred to the command of Lieutenant General Watts and XIX Corps to reinforce their right flank. They occupied a defensive line in between the villages of Mézières and Démuin, with 59th Brigade on the right up to the main Amiens road, the 61st on the left and the 60th (including 11th DLI) in reserve west of the road from Démuin to Moreuil. The French held Mézières itself. The reserve positions came under heavy artillery fire, which killed Lieutenant Colonel Welch of 6th KSLI.

During the morning the Germans drove the French out of Mézières. At 3.15 p.m., 11th DLI was ordered to take part in the recapture of the village. Their ranks consisted of 10 officers and about 130 men. The 12th KRRC and 12th RB attacked the village from the south-west, while 11th DLI and 11th RB worked through the wood on the north-west, with a company from 2nd Scottish Rifles on their right. There was little in the way of artillery support. At 4 p.m., they launched their attack out of the wood that had been their overnight bivouac. Emerging from the trees, the Durhams faced a dash across open ground directly into trench mortar and machine-gun fire. Nevertheless, Captain Pemberton managed to reach the

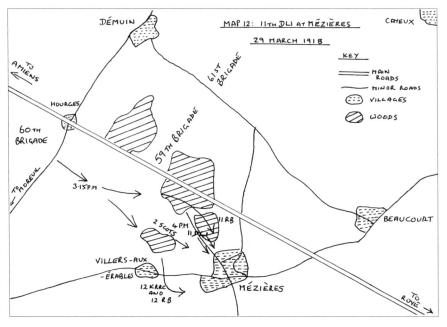

11th DLI at Mézières, 29 March 1918. (*Martin Bashforth, 2010*)

village with about twenty men, and remained there in an attempt to hold the village until only two men were left, before pulling back. Similarly, Second Lieutenant King reached the village with a Lewis gun, but by then all his men had been hit and they were forced to retire. Both officers were awarded the MC for their actions. A third group got into the village square and put three German trench mortars out of action. Despite the brave efforts by all the units involved, none were able to hold the village. Finding themselves trapped from behind by concealed parties of the enemy, they were forced to fight their way back to their original lines. The survivors were ordered back to take up a defensive line between Thennes and Hourges.

Inevitably the losses were heavy, in terms of those killed, wounded and captured. The battalion now consisted of a mere four officers and thirty-four men. Four of those killed are commemorated at Pozières: Second Lieutenant Frederick Arnott, and Privates Joseph Barnard, John O'Brien and Clifford Pollard. Sergeant J. M. Craggs is buried at Mézières. Private Victor Anderson died of wounds from a previous day and is buried at Namps-au-Val. Lieutenant Bushell, Second Lieutenant Ellwood and Second Lieutenant Applegarth were all taken prisoner. Applegarth had been shot in the chest and died from a tetanus infection on 8 April in a German Field Hospital near Beaufort-en-Santerre. His remains were exhumed after the war and buried at Caix, north-east of Moreuil, not far from where he fought his last battle.

On repatriation after the war, both Bushell and Ellwood were interviewed to provide accounts of their capture. Bushell (originally from B Company) had command of one officer and twenty-five men. They worked their way through a dense copse, but as they emerged came under such heavy fire that they had to lie down. The other officer was missing and several of the men were out of action. Bushell kept the others down in the hope of being able to make another advance when the enfilade fire died down. As they were only about fifty yards from the German machine-guns and in plain view, neither advance nor retreat were an option. When the firing did cease, it was because the Germans had worked their way round into the copse behind. Bushell had little option but to surrender.

Ellwood was in charge of what was referred to as D Company, consisting of himself, two officers and about thirty men, of whom some twenty-five were recently acquired reinforcements and new to action. His party worked their way through the wood into heavy machine-gun fire, coming from the houses directly opposite. He was hit and concussed. As with Bushell, he found himself surrounded by Germans who had worked their way round behind, and he and his two surviving men were forced to surrender. Lieutenant Colonel Hayes wrote later to reassure the family that there was hope that their missing son would be found:

> I am writing to you about your son, The only news that I can give you is not good. He fell badly hit and fell into German hands, consequently is reported wounded and missing. He was on my headquarter's staff as Lewis gun officer and was not only a fine subaltern, but a personal friend, and as a friend I refuse to believe the worst till I get proof of it.

He continued in much the same vein, praising Ellwood's coolness under fire and qualities as a friend and comrade: 'All we know is that he got up under terrific machine-gun fire and walked forward and said "Come on you fellows" and then he fell hit in the body.' Hayes was relying on second-hand testimony or imagination, as he had been away recovering from the effects of gas poisoning and did not arrive back to the battalion until the morning of 31 March.

30 March, Saturday

A further retirement was forced and the division established a new line on the Démuin–Moreuil road with 60th Brigade to the right, 59th in the centre and 61st to the left. After a quiet night, the Durhams were alerted that the Germans were in Moreuil Wood and shifted their formation to create a defensive line in that direction. The situation remained precarious, men being seen retiring to their left and the French pulling back on their right. Continuous attacks were held up throughout the day, but at 4 p.m. the thin defences of the 60th Brigade were penetrated. A cavalry attack with artillery support successfully recovered the position. Two DLI men were killed (Tom Evans, buried at Fouqeuscourt, and John Willingham, buried at Hangard), while Lance Sergeant W. Johnston died of wounds at a rear dressing station and is buried at Namps-au-Val.

31 March, Easter Sunday

Easter Day witnessed a similar pattern of events. The lines came under heavy artillery bombardment and, with both flanks being turned, fell back just south of the river Luce by late afternoon. Captain Pemberton organised 11th DLI on a hill south-east of Thennes. The Germans attacked almost immediately, but were repulsed. The remnants of 6th KSLI and 11th DLI joined cavalry in a counter-attack and by 8 p.m., aided by artillery fire from the divisional command post on higher ground at Domart, had secured the flanks. Captain Endean was wounded by a shell splinter in the upper thigh, inches from the spine. Sergeant Thomas Bonney was killed and is buried at Moreuil Communal Cemetery. Lance Corporal John Yates was also killed and is commemorated at Pozières.

Sergeant Thomas Bonney was killed on 31 March 1918. On his lapels are the crossed rifle and pick symbol of the Pioneers. (*Collection of David Kelly*)

Lieutenant Colonel Hayes arrived back during the morning to find what was left of his battalion. Unable to contact Pemberton, Hayes chose not to interfere with his command and instead took over a mixed party of men from other 20th Division units, remaining with them until they were relieved a couple of days later.

1 April, Monday

Further counter-attacks were mounted on 1 April, which managed to stabilise the front for a while, indicating that the German attacks were beginning to run out of steam. The remnants of 20th Division were at last withdrawn. The survivors of 11th DLI marched to the Amiens road and were taken by bus to Quevauvillers, twelve miles south-west of the city. By now the battalion of over 800 men had been reduced to 'the strength of a strong platoon'.[1] The divisional artillery remained in the field until 28 April as part of the continuing battles that finally stopped the German advance at Villers-Bretonneux.

Lieutenant Colonel Hayes tried to summarise the 11th DLI casualties, even listing the officers day by day. Taking a cautious view in line with the letter to the Ellwood family, he listed only one officer (Second Lieutenant Vincent Duckett) and sixteen other ranks as definitely killed. Officers listed as wounded were Second Lieutenants A. Naylor, E. W. English, N. F. Gibson, J. H. Dodds, A. E. Wilkinson, H. J. E. Whitfield, and Captains W. G. L. Sear and W. J. Endean. The missing officers were listed as Lieutenant Bushell and Second Lieutenants W. G. Craig, R. R. Galley, H. Rutherford, W. T. Alexander, W. Banks, F. Arnott, D. E. Ellwood, T. W. Applegarth and C. A. Morris, among whom three were reported to have been also wounded. Among the other ranks, 221 were reported wounded and 215 missing, with a further 3 having died of wounds. His mathematics suggested that on that basis he had lost 474 men leaving a nominal strength of 529 as of 31 March 1918. It was nothing like that in reality. As well as Duckett, both Galley and Arnott had been killed, while Banks and Applegarth were so badly wounded that they died a few days later. The Commonwealth War Graves Commission lists seventy-two men from 11th DLI as killed between 21 and 31 March 1918, while a further nine died of wounds in enemy hands before the end of April. Hayes' estimates were understandably optimistic, though the numbers would soon be made up with new recruits.

Awards, other than those already mentioned, went to Sergeant W. Bayfield of South Shields, who was wounded and received the DCM, and to Corporal B. Harrison, also awarded the DCM. These had been difficult times for the Pioneers, not intended for such intense fighting and following a complicated reorganisation. The experience had been difficult for the division of which they were part and the whole of the Fifth Army, which ceased to exist. However, there is no doubt that all involved had distinguished themselves. They fought the Germans to a standstill, conceding ground but extracting a heavy price as they did so. It probably did not feel like it at the time for the exhausted men, but it was a major turning point for the course of the war.

Lieutenant General Ivor Maxse, Commanding Officer XVIII Corps, to which the 20th Division and 11th DLI had been attached, was anxious to ensure that his appreciation of 20th Division was received right down to company commanders. An extensive two-page memorandum was sent out, dated 5 April 1918, setting out exactly what had been achieved in a detailed account. He was aware of what had happened to General Sir Hubert Gough and that gossip might reach the men under his command. He had no intention that survivors of the March Retreat should feel in any way diminished by a sense of defeat. He made sure that every brigade and unit received commendation, particularly singling out the initiative of the division in covering a widening gap between XVIII and XIX Corps at the most dangerous moment on 26 March. He concluded:

> I wish to thank all ranks of the 20th Division for their cheerful endurance under critical conditions of fighting, and for their gallant spirit whenever called upon to make a special effort. I would also remind them that still greater exertions will be required from them during the coming months and I am convinced they will respond to the call.[2]

Many families back in England experienced a wave of grief not surpassed since the Pals battalions had been decimated in a matter of a few days just two years before. Because of the confusion that accompanied the retreat, many families were left for weeks not knowing what had happened to their fathers, brothers and sons. During late April an official letter was delivered to 6 Bridge Terrace, Darlington. Florence Bashforth had last seen her husband only a few weeks before when he came home on leave to see his family and their new son. She was now a widow with three children and an uncertain future. She continued to be paid 30s 6d allotment of pay until 3 November, increased to a pension of 32s 6d. The grief for the wider family was further compounded, as shown in a memorial notice in the *Northern Echo* on Friday 3 May 1918.

> BASHFORTH – Sergeant T. Bashforth, better known as McGlasson, killed in action in France on Good Friday, March 29th, 1918, aged 29 years. Also his brother-in-law, G.R. Howe, who was killed in action on

March 27th, 1918. Deeply mourned by wives and children, mother, father, mother-in-law, sisters and brother, sisters-in-law and brothers-in-law. "They answered the call".

There was a mistake over the date, however, disguising from the family that the two brothers-in-law had in fact been killed on the same day, at opposite ends of the line of the German advance. George Robert Howe, 39621 Rifleman of C Company 2nd/7th Battalion, Prince of Wales Own West Yorkshire Regiment, and son of Thomas Howe of 22 Santon Street, Gosforth, was caught up in the launch of Operation Mars, the German offensive twinned with Operation Michael to the south. Killed near Arras, he is commemorated on the memorial there – he also has no known grave. George Howe was the husband of Thomas' half-sister, Margaret McGlasson. The husband of the oldest McGlasson daughter, Mrs Laura Flint, was badly wounded during the war and lost a leg. The publication of the memorial notice had one other strange twist. One day there was a knock on the door at Bridge Terrace. Matthew Kelly, now living in Middlesbrough, had come to offer help to the children of his illegitimate son, Thomas Bashforth. Florence turned him away, but the story continued to be told for generations to come.

For some families there was a much longer wait for news. Not untypical were the cases of Private Frank Crofts and Private Jonathan Bainbridge. They were finally struck off the battalion roll on 26 and 27 June respectively, there being no further news from those within the battalion, from the Red Cross or from the German authorities. The War Office was still writing to Private George Arthurs' family in Swansea as late as 5 November 1918 to see if they had heard any news. It was not until 17 July 1919 that he was finally presumed to have died.

The sheer volume of correspondence dealt with during this period added to the problems for the family of Private Arthur Bell from Horden Colliery. They were supposed to have been informed of his death on 27 April 1918 and, despite letters of enquiry from his father, who must have heard rumours from returning soldiers, it was not until 22 April 1919 that the clerical error was corrected. The difficulties for the family will have been further aggravated by difficulty in tracing the soldier's unit. Having only returned to France on 13 March after a long period of illness, he was shunted between battalions until he arrived with 11th DLI only two days before the German offensive.

An even stranger occurrence beset the widow of Private Mark Farn from No. 7 Platoon, B Company. She was properly informed at her home in Shotton Colliery of his presumed death as of 1 June 1918. Anne Farn had advised the authorities that she was expecting a baby since her husband's last leave and had to provide a birth certificate for the child to upgrade the pension allowance. Out of the blue, on 16 September 1922, she was sent her late husband's identity disc, which had turned up at Hamilton Infantry Records Office in an envelope from the General Hospital in Palestine and was assumed to belong to a member of the Highland Light Infantry. An investigation was launched to try to ascertain what had happened, but it petered out in mutual denials of responsibility.

It was no better for the families of officers. The confusion in the war diary regarding what happened to Second Lieutenant Ralph Rowland Galley of A Company on 22 March 1918, has already been noted. Was he killed or did he return with Captain Endean to fight another day? His identity disc turned up at the Central Office of Effects on 15 May 1918 with no details, forwarded by an Ambulance Corps. They had added a note to the effect that 'it is doubtful whether the owner is dead', but gave no reason for that assumption. It also took some distressing correspondence before it was established that Mrs Mary Rowlands Galley of Essex Lodge, Ravensbourne Park, Catford, was his mother and not his wife. As late as 12 July 1919 she wrote to the War Office:

> I could not accept his death after the message "doubtful whether the owner is dead" until I found out all I could. Whoever took the effects from his pockets could surely have sent a more definite message and I think it was up to the Authorities to make FULL enquiries and report the results to the next of kin, instead of leaving sorrowing mothers, wives &c to find out for themselves what had happened to their Dear ones.[3]

As late as 23 December 1919, the War Office was prepared to presume Galley's death, but not to issue a death certificate. Notwithstanding all the confusion, Galley's body was recovered and is buried in the northern part of Eppeville Old Churchyard, south-west of Ham. The location of the burial suggests he may have been carried to an Allied Field Ambulance unit, died and was buried before they pulled back from the area the following day.[4] However, nothing can explain all the other errors. There were fortunately no such errors in relation to Second Lieutenant Vincent George Duckett; the war diary records his small unit disappearing into the mist and never being seen again on 23 March 1918. Both Galley and Duckett had been clerks before the war and had made their way up through the ranks, receiving their commissions in December 1917, so any mistakes were unlikely to have been related to issues of class.

Two of the officers who died of wounds received during March 1918 were old boys of the Queen Elizabeth Grammar School, Darlington. Born in 1883 in West Hartlepool, Second Lieutenant William Banks had been a stores accountant before the war, married with a daughter born in 1916. He was transferred to 11th DLI when the 14th Battalion was broken up in February 1918. He was reported missing on 24 March 1918, but confused stories got back to the family. Both his widow, Lizzie Banks, and his sister Edith wrote letters asking for clarification, as they had received information from an unnamed officer of 11th DLI that Banks had been taken prisoner, had escaped and been killed in the British lines the following day. However, a letter from Private 71015 T. Brent, a stretcher-bearer with 11th DLI, gave a different and more detailed story. Writing from hospital in Boulogne on 3 June 1918, he explained that Banks had been hit in the stomach in a counter-attack near Ham on 23 March. Private Brent stayed with him and gave him water, until forced to retreat himself.

> I opened his tunic and found he had been shot on the right side of the abdomen. He was then alive. I remained with him about 1½ hours and gave him water. He was dead before I had to leave him. He said nothing except to ask who I was. The Germans later came over the ground where Lt Banks was lying.

The confusion is not helped by an official German report from Reserve Feld Lazarett at Ham, stating that he had died from a gunshot wound to the head, unless this had been a *coup-de-grace*. The widow was still trying to get the War Office to release his money, more than £80, sending black-edged cards as late as September and October of 1919.[5]

The background of Second Lieutenant Thomas William Applegarth, who was also taught at Darlington Grammar School, has been described. Having been commissioned after previous service as a private soldier, he was posted to 11th DLI in October 1917, joining A Company in time for the Battle of Cambrai. He was captured on Good Friday, 29 March 1918 at Mézières. He had been shot in the chest and the wound developed a tetanus infection, from which he died on 8 April. The family at the time would have still thought of him as missing, receiving a telegram to that effect on 10 April. With no further news arriving they turned to one of the local gentry for assistance. Mrs Ada McQueen of Cleatlam House, Winston, wrote on their behalf. Mrs Applegarth had been widowed at the same time and would have been distraught with grief when it was confirmed that her son's name was on a list of casualties received from the Germans. It would have been of some small comfort that his few effects were returned: a treasury note case, purse, comb, two regimental badges, letters, a whistle, handkerchief, some foreign currency and his identity discs. However, this was not quite the end of problems for Hannah Applegarth. She had to wait for her husband's will to be proven and send

Three embroidered postcards sent by Lt William Banks to his daughter Kathleen in Darlington. (*DLI Trust and Durham CRO, D/DLI 7/819/2*)

The entrance portico to the Pozières Memorial to the Missing of the Somme, 1918.
There are fifty-six men of 11th DLI commemorated here.
(*Martin Bashforth*)

The DLI section of the memorial at Pozières, showing the names of Lt Arnott, Lt Duckett, CSM Robson, Sgt Bashforth and Sgt Seggar of 11th DLI.
(*Martin Bashforth*)

a copy before the War Office would release the £47 6s 7d in her son's bank account. Finally a letter was sent on 12 October 1920 to notify that his remains had been exhumed from Beaufort German Cemetery and reburied at Caix New British Cemetery, north-east of Moreuil.[6]

NOTES TO CHAPTER ELEVEN

1   Miles, 1920, p. 271.
2   The National Archives, WO 95/2096, XVIII Corps Memorandum No.Ga.155/4, filed with 20th Division War Diary.
3   The National Archives, WO 339/111910, papers of Lt R. R. Galley.
4   However, the papers of Second Lieutenant William Banks indicate that the Germans had a Field Hospital in Ham as soon as a day later, so Galley may have died in German hands.
5   The National Archives, WO 339/112493, Papers relating to Second Lieutenant William Banks.
6   The National Archives, WO 339/81426, Correspondence and papers relating to Second Lieutenant T. W. Applegarth.

CHAPTER TWELVE

The Final Stages:
April 1918 to June 1919

The battalion of Pioneers that had marched up the hill from Le Havre in July 1915 was no more. Gone were the largely homogeneous companies of Durham men, mostly from mining communities. There were still some of these men alive, survivors among the handful who marched onto the Amiens Road on 1 April 1918 or men who had been on leave at the time of the German attack on 21 March. The battalion was now largely composed of new recruits, mostly conscripts and often very young, and also men brought in from other units that had now been disbanded, by no means all from other battalions of the DLI. This was probably true of all units in the British Army and it is they who would be the backbone of the final British advance alongside their allies from the Empire, America and France.

On 2 April, the remnants of 20th Division were billeted around Quevauvillers, ten miles south-west of Amiens, reorganising and taking in new drafts. The 11th DLI was heavily reinforced on 6 April, with 470 new men. Lieutenant Colonel Hayes and several other officers had rejoined the battalion, including Lieutenant A. Floyd and Lieutenant M. Cooper. The following day they set off marching from Quevauvillers to Lincheux. On 10 April, they continued to Huppy, where they were joined by another 108 recruits. The next day they carried on to Rieux, where they spent a week training everyone in the basics of musketry and Pioneer work. It was an opportunity to weed out those who were considered unsuitable and on 18 April no less than 191 men were despatched back to the Base Depot at Étaples. At the same time there was an influx of fourteen new subalterns.[1] Unfortunately, the commanding officer, Lieutenant Colonel Hayes, had not fully recovered from the effects of gas and reported sick. He was replaced by Lieutenant Colonel R. E. Boulton from 1st KOYLI, who was joined by Captain H. F. King from the 4th Suffolk Regiment as second-in-command.

Captain Pemberton, who had been covering this role, was transferred to the general staff of XVIII Corps as Education Officer.

Under their new leadership the battalion moved to Frévillers, where they settled in to more training, lectures and drill. The routine was as if the battalion had just arrived in France, which, for most of the men, was the case. Along with the rest of 20th Division, the Pioneers remained part of XVIII Corps, but were now attached to the First Army at Villers-Châtel, ten miles north-west of Arras. The battalion was almost up to full strength[2] and, from 1 to 3 May, the division relieved the 3rd Canadian Division in a sector of the front between Lens and Avion, defending the higher ground to the rear, and the approaches to Vimy Ridge. The 11th DLI marched to the Château de la Haie near Liévin and Carency, between which two villages the battalion was split. They were mainly involved in trench works, repairing, improving and building new ones.

A new departure for the Pioneers came on 23 May, when they were used to supply gas attacks. They would do this on several occasions, transporting the cylinders to and from the front line. On one particular day, virtually all the men were used to push seventy-five trucks, each containing twenty-one gas cylinders, along two tramways leading to the front line. Here the gas was discharged and the Pioneers then trundled the empties back again. Gas was used throughout the First World War by both sides and despite

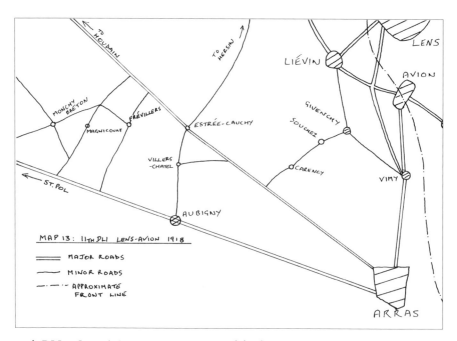

11th DLI at Lens-Avion, 1918. (*Martin Bashforth, 2010*)

some rather crude defensive equipment was equally as effective, whoever chose to use it. The Germans retaliated with mustard gas a few days later, over two successive days around Liévin. Among the officers from 11th DLI affected were Captains P. V. Kemp and A. Philip (both survivors of the March Retreat), along with several second lieutenants, including T. A. Atley, R. Conacher, G. F. Wood, E. R. Harbron, G. Cain, G. H. Ault and J. C. Ratcliffe, and 122 other ranks. Captain Kemp died a few days later, along with several of the men. During July, there was a further series of gas attacks, with the Germans initiating the exchange on 3 July and the pioneers retaliating ten days later.

Captain Percy Vickerman Kemp had been born in Sunderland, 16 July 1892, and was the son of the Revd James Vickerman Kemp, vicar of Witton Park, near Darlington. A pupil of St John's School, Leatherhead, and a graduate of St John's College, Cambridge, he had signed up in 1915 as a private in the Public Schools Battalion of the Royal Fusiliers; at the time he was a young schoolmaster. Following his commission on 4 August 1916, Kemp was assigned to 11th DLI, having expressed a wish to join a Durham unit. He proved a very capable officer and was mentioned in despatches for actions in the lead-up to Cambrai. He suffered early in the March Retreat and was pulled out of the line on 24 March 1918. The gas attack on 27 May caused severe complications and he died of pulmonary

Gas sentry from 20th Division making notes, near Liévin, 1918. (*Imperial War Museum*, Q 6699)

oedema on 31 May 1918 at hospital in Étaples. His father had been offered a travel warrant, but too late for him to visit his son. While Kemp had not been married, he wrote a codicil to his will on the day of his death, leaving all his investments (amounting to an estate worth more than £200) to a Mary Emmerson. Perhaps she was his fiancée? If so, it would have been some comfort to know that she was in his thoughts at the end.

The death of Private 91068 Henry Cunliffe on 5 June 1918 was a stark contrast, though it is not clear from the service papers whether his family ever knew the exact circumstances. A letter was immediately sent to his mother to say that he had been wounded and that they were doing everything they could, but he was dead before the letter arrived. Cunliffe was a conscript from Halifax and was one of a batch of 470 men who joined the battalion in early April. He was shot in his billet and died the following day. Lieutenant A. Floyd, one of the officers who had arrived with 11th DLI the same day as Cunliffe, took statements and made the report. Private 91036 C. Wilson had been stood next to Cunliffe, heard a shot and saw him fall. Across the hut one of the other men had his rifle pointing in their direction. Private 44899 J. Parkinson saw the latter man cleaning his rifle and heard the shot fired. Private 91083 S. Dodds gave his own account:

> On the morning of 5/6/18 before proceeding to forward area I loaded my rifle. On returning to camp about 8.30 a.m. I was very tired and forgot to unload the magazine. I slept till late in the day 12.30 p.m. About 8.15 I was cleaning my rifle, having removed bolt and magazine. I left it to go to the latrine and on return was ordered to fall in. I placed magazine in and then shot bolt home and pulled trigger forgetting it was loaded. Not having a cut-off on my rifle I loosed off a round which hit one of my comrades.

The bullet went through Cunliffe's hand into his abdomen.

Lieutenant Floyd's report accepted Dodds' account and Lieutenant Colonel Boulton passed the report forward to the divisional commander. He clearly placed the blame on Dodds, who was sent for trial by Field General Court Martial. The court found him guilty of neglect and he was awarded fifty-six days FP2. The punishment may seem small next to a death, but would have added to the young soldier's sense of shame. There would be little about the war that he would want to remember or that he would want people back home to know about. Cunliffe's few effects were returned to the family on 23 October 1918, including his identity disc, knife, diary, purse, five coins, two safety razor blades, stamp case and a letter. Henry Cunliffe had been the only child of George Henry and Jennie Lee Cunliffe.

Headstone of Henry Cunliffe at Aubigny Communal Cemetery Extension. Cunliffe was shot accidentally. The inscription reads 'Until the day breaks'.
(*Gaynor Greenwood*)

Outside of the mutual gas attacks, work mainly comprised monotonous trench improvement until August, mostly around Riaumont and in the reserve lines. The gas attacks, sniping and artillery bombardments resulted in further isolated casualties. Officers came and went, among them Second Lieutenant H. J. E. Whitfield to join the recently created Royal Air Force and Captain W. F. E. Badcock to take up a new post with 6th DLI. By way of entertainment, on 31 July 1918, the battalion held a Transport Horse Show.

Things began to change as the British launched a new and rapidly successful offensive, re-taking the Somme Salient in only five days, and making equally rapid progress in the Ypres Salient. On 14 August Lieutenant Colonel T. H. Carlisle, DSO, MC, arrived from the Royal Engineers to take command of 11th DLI. The battalion was moved further north with the rest of the division, to a line between Fresnoy and Avion. By now the more experienced men from 11th DLI were in demand for training new platoons and others were sent off to join 185th Tunnelling Company. The front line around Arras was being reinforced to act as a base for the new advance. The 20th Division began to contribute their own attacks, at first with little success against heavy resistance. For 11th DLI there continued the constant alternation between digging and gas, gas and digging. The Germans launched mustard gas attacks around Avion on 4 and 5 September.

The first significant breakthrough by 20th Division was made by 7th DCLI on 26 and 27 September, when they captured the enemy trenches south-west of Acheville. In the first week of October, the whole divisional front moved forward in a series of attacks involving all the infantry battalions, while the Germans began to withdraw. Captain Pemberton returned to 11th DLI with the rank of Major on 7 October. The following day the 20th Division was relieved by the 12th Division and moved to a training area around Monchy Breton. The 11th DLI were stationed at Estrée Cauchie where they continued their training of three platoons a day, including practice at attacking strongpoints.

On 30 October, the division was moved at short notice to join XVII Corps as part of General Byng's Third Army, with the DLI battalion arriving by train at Frémicourt and then on to Cambrai by bus. Here the 20th Division became part of the final advance. The artillery attached to the 19th Division played the major role which led the offensive. The infantry followed on 3 November and became involved in the care of civilian refugees streaming back from the east. The Pioneers followed the track of the advance through Rieux, Montrecourt, Sepméries, and Jenlain, arriving at St Waast-la-Vallée on 9 November.

On 10 November, the 20th Division advanced to hold the front line east of the Mons–Maubeuge road, replacing the 24th Division. The ceasefire at

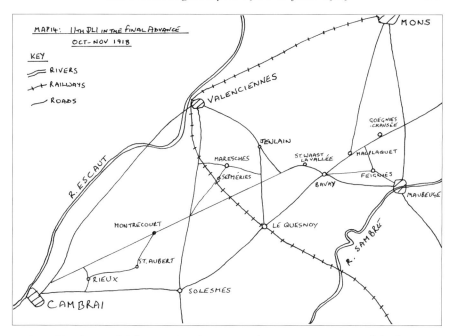

11th DLI in the Final Advance, October–November 1918. (*Martin Bashforth, 2010*)

11 a.m. the following morning found the division at a point some thirty-five miles east of Cambrai. The 11th DLI were on the march to Feignies when they were ordered to stand fast. It was a short rest as they were immediately set to work repairing the roads north of Maubeuge. They were constantly on the move thereafter, mainly employed in reclamation work, repairing roads and railways and filling craters. Travelling via Maresches and St-Aubert they reached Cambrai at the end of November. Orders were received to release 200 former miners, those who were deemed most fit to resume their old jobs. On 1 December the first 182 men left. On 2 December, the division was pulled out for a short rest at Marieux, a few miles south-west of Doullens. Those still serving with 11th DLI spent their remaining days in France based at Grenas, a small village adjacent to the Doullens–Arras road. Most of their time was spent improving billets, interspersed with bathing and drill, along with reclamation work in the local area. Most unusually, given the past four years' experience, bad weather over the Christmas period led to a suspension of work. By the end of December their numbers had reduced to thirty-four officers and 533 men.

During January 1919, the process of demobilisation gathered pace. By the end of the month there were only 25 officers and 294 men left in the battalion. The remnants were kept busy with farm work, clearing the rubbish of warfare, training and drill. There were classes in book-keeping, shorthand and medical lectures, as well as special training for ceremonial parades. The King's Colours were presented to the battalion by Major General Douglas Smith on 3 February 1919.

The battalion continued to be useful, restoring the infrastructure that had been destroyed during four-and-a-half years of wreckage and slaughter. They filled in trenches, cleared up disused camps, and salvaged light railway track and equipment. In February, several officers and 163 men transferred to 20th DLI, to serve in the Army of Occupation in Germany. In April, there were sports tournaments between the various battalions of the 20th Division, in which 11th DLI finally triumphed after successively defeating 11th KRRC and 6th KSLI in the preliminary rounds.

At the end of February, there were 8 officers and 127 men, falling to 7 officers and 84 men at the end of March, and 4 officers and 33 men at the end of April. In May, they carried out the final clear-up around Grenas before making their way to Pas-en-Artois, by which time they were down to a cadre of two officers and twenty men. Ten more men had gone by 16 June, when the remnant entrained for the final journey back to England. With them they managed ten general service wagons, seven limbers, three cookers, two water carts, one mess cart and one Maltese Cart (a two-wheeled cart used for carrying medical supplies). They unloaded all this at Le Havre on 19 June and four days later embarked for Southampton, where they handed over the battalion equipment to railway carriers. On this final act the battalion war diary closed.

They had returned the way the new battalion had come almost exactly four years before, but this was not the massed return of a conquering army. The final dozen men left hundreds behind in France and Belgium who would never return, some whose bodies would never be found or identified. Many more had been maimed in mind and body. Most of the survivors had now returned to civilian life, though perhaps not to what they had remembered. Many families were nursing a grievous loss, mostly within communities that shared their experience on an unprecedented scale. The war left its mark in many different ways, even for those involved with such an ordinary, unsung battalion as 11th DLI, and that experience has resonated through subsequent generations to an extent that may seem surprising. It is to this trail of remembrance and forgetting that the final chapters of the book will turn. Meanwhile, what can be said about the battalion from a military viewpoint?

One of the commonly used measures to assess a battalion's contribution is the list of honours received by the individuals who served with the unit. Pioneer battalions do not figure highly in this respect. The highest honour was the Victoria Cross and the battalion won none of these, though some

Portrait of Geoffrey Hayes, who rose from Adjutant to Lieutenant Colonel of 11th DLI and was awarded the DSO. (*DLI Trust and Durham CRO, D/DLI 7/309/4*)

were awarded to men in the infantry battalions of the 20th Light Division. In his discussion of awards made to Pioneer battalions, Mitchinson records only one Victoria Cross, awarded to Sergeant Carmichael of the 9th Battalion, North Staffordshire Regiment.[3]

The highest award for 11th DLI was the Distinguished Service Order won by Lieutenant Colonel Geoffrey Hayes for his actions during the German counter-attack at Cambrai. Captain W. G. L. Sear and Major R. L. S. Pemberton received the Military Cross and bar. The MC was also awarded to Major J. G. Taylor, Lieutenant D. C. Cooke, Lieutenant W. J. E. Endean and Second Lieutenant R. H. King. Hayes was twice mentioned in despatches, and eight officers were mentioned in despatches once. The awards were made principally regarding three sets of events: the capture of Guillemont and its aftermath in late 1916, the Battle of Cambrai in 1917 and the German Offensive of March 1918. The same pattern broadly applied to awards for other ranks. Sergeant J. Hook and Private F. Ingram were each awarded the Distinguished Conduct Medal following Cambrai. A further eight men received the Military Medal during 1918 and two received the Meritorious Service Medal. French awards were made to Privates R. Harsburgh and F. Irving (Croix de Guerre) and to Sergeant F. Williams (Médaille Militaire). Six men were mentioned in despatches.

These figures derive partly from papers filed with the battalion war diary that may not be complete. The number of men listed as mentioned in despatches for 1918 seems rather low considering the events of March. Awards could also come in other forms. Private 17447 Hugh Lavelle received a printed commendation from the divisional commander for his exemplary coolness and devotion to duty as a messenger for 11th DLI during the period from 22 March to 2 April 1918, as well as the Military Medal. The figures with the diary may represent someone's subsequent attempt to research the awards to the battalion rather than an official record. The *London Gazette* is not always clear as to the battalion with which men were serving, so a full list may never be known. The number and level of awards serves to underline the ordinariness of the battalion's contribution in terms of valorous actions.

A further way of comparing the contribution of battalions is the macabre totting up of fatalities and arranging these in league tables. Rarely involved in the first wave of infantry assaults, Pioneer battalions did not suffer the dramatic and concentrated losses of other infantry battalions. Only when Pioneers found themselves operating as conventional infantry did they suffer great losses. The majority of deaths among Pioneer units were received during the German offensives of 1918, their bodies never found and their names recorded on the memorials to the missing at Poziéres, Arras and Soissons. The list is headed by 22nd DLI, which had the misfortune to be caught twice in these rapidly moving advances, in

The citation for Hugh Lavelle's bravery during the March Retreat. He was awarded the Military Medal. (*Collection of Mike Lavelle*)

March 1918 and again in May. Accurate figures are anyhow difficult to ascertain. Mitchinson lists 293 fatalities for 11th DLI. The Commonwealth War Graves Commission provided a list to the author which contains 316 names. There are discrepancies between this list and that in *Soldiers Died in the Great War*, both containing errors. Comparing the two lists I have arrived at a maximum potential number of 325 men.[4] As individual service records have become accessible I have begun to discount several names, where men had transferred to other units at the time of their deaths. Equally, however, there will be cases where men attributed to other battalions had been transferred into 11th DLI and have been recorded against their previous unit, especially during the early part of 1918. Perhaps the balance lies around 310, plus or minus 5 per cent.

Whether one uses medals or deaths as a measure, neither serves to demonstrate the peculiar contribution of a Pioneer battalion. Firstly, their presence meant that every division had a complete and properly trained infantry reserve battalion at their disposal, instantly and without reference back to a higher authority. In the case of 11th DLI this proved its value in several contexts. In the late summer of 1916, after the taking of Guillemont, the 20th Division could call on the Pioneers to take over from exhausted infantry battalions and occupy the front line. In the period immediately after the capture of Langemarck they did this again and also reinforced the infantry assault brigades to complete their objectives when their numbers had become depleted. At Cambrai, 11th DLI were instantly able to drop their picks and shovels, pick up their rifles and form the backbone of the divisional line of defence, as a result of which the German counter-attack was prevented from causing a complete rout. During the events of March 1918 they worked virtually entirely as conventional infantry, but were also able to be called upon (as on 26 March) to take up picks and shovels again, dig a decent defensive line for other exhausted troops, before advancing and reverting once more to frontline infantry. Finally, with the division reduced to a pitiful remnant, they could add their little weight to an almost suicidal counter-attack at Mézières on Good Friday, 1918. These were no small achievements.

In addition, the amount of labour, both skilled and unskilled, to support an infantry division proved to be much more than originally estimated. Throughout the war the Army sought to supplement its labour force behind the lines. In the front line the Pioneer battalions were not the sole source of labour, since the conventional infantry frequently found themselves employed on work parties. Nevertheless, the Pioneers provided the fulcrum of labour planning in any action. At Guillemont, in 1916, 11th DLI followed instantly behind the first-line infantry assaults to facilitate holding operations, alongside field companies from the Royal Engineers.

Because they could provide their own cover and defence they contributed to the speed of the overall attack and its ultimate success, freeing the infantry to keep moving forward. At Langemarck the main problem was maintaining communications and supplies to frontline troops across the vast, boggy landscape. It was to that task the Pioneers could be devoted, though they later went on to be used as conventional infantry.

What distinguished the Pioneers from both conventional infantry and labour companies was this versatility. In terms of the work they were called upon to perform, the range was quite amazing. When 11th DLI first arrived in France they began with a form of basket-weaving, constructing hurdles out of willow to reinforce the sides of wet trenches. As time went on they learned new skills. The speed with which Durham men could dig new trenches was legendary, but this was not just a question of hard graft. Trench lines, dugouts, communications trenches, forward posts and so on demanded technical skills as well. The limited instructions to be found in the pre-war *Manual of Field Engineering* had been fine for conditions on the South African veldt, but had to be reinvented on the Western Front. The laying of wire, usually at night and under the close scrutiny of the opposing trenches, was a science in its own right. The amount of subterranean activity required had not been anticipated by an army trained in the concepts of open warfare and siege. The Durham miners were natural candidates for constructing dugouts for headquarters close to front lines and for tunnelling to lay mines under enemy lines, especially in the wet conditions of Ypres and Laventie. By the time the war ended, 11th DLI had built roads and bridges, dug cuttings and laid railways through them, hewed forests and cut trees to make props and duckboards, laid out models of a planned campaign for training purposes and then fought in the campaign itself. They had lifted and shifted, loaded and unloaded, transported and dumped every conceivable item of war materiel, which in tonnages is beyond measurement. There were rarely medals for this kind of work. Recognition came mainly in the form of occasional notes to their commanding officer from divisional HQ. But, as Mitchinson has pointed out, this has proved true for all the divisional support units: engineers, signals, medical, transport, even artillery.[5]

The merit of a battalion might be assessed in another way, by examining its record for behaviour. The registers of the Field General Courts Martial contain a summary of all reported trials of men on active service overseas. Between July 1915 and the end of December 1918, twenty-eight men from 11th DLI were arraigned before the FGCM, as listed in the registers. The worst offences were a few occasions where a private struck an officer, for which the sentence was imprisonment with hard labour, usually suspended. Three of those charged were found not guilty. Most offences were minor cases of absence, drunkenness or insubordination, resulting in periods of FP1 or FP2. The practice in 11th DLI seems to have been to carry out this punishment and it was only very rarely remitted. It was designed to be exemplary and to act as a deterrent to the individual concerned and to the rest of the unit. Fourteen men from 20th Division were sentenced to death, none from 11th DLI, and, in all cases but two the verdict was either suspended, or not confirmed, or commuted to penal servitude or imprisonment with hard labour. The record of misdemeanours for 11th DLI was as unspectacular as everything else about the battalion, even compared with the main infantry battalions, as the following comparison shows.

Table 3:
Reports of Field General Courts Martial[6]

20th Division Infantry Units

Battalion (listed by Brigade)	Number of offences
10th King's Royal Rifle Corps	32
11th King's Royal Rifle Corps	49
10th Rifle Brigade	21
11th Rifle Brigade	42
6th Ox and Bucks Light Infantry	16
6th King's Shropshire Light Infantry	11
12th King's Royal Rifle Corps	60
12th Rifle Brigade	34
12th King's Liverpool Regiment	28
7th Somerset Light Infantry	20
7th Duke of Cornwall's Light Infantry	45
7th King's Own Yorkshire Light Infantry	29
11th Durham Light Infantry (20th Divisional Pioneers)	28

Over the 416 recorded courts martial, the average for a battalion was thirty-two, which places the Pioneers slightly below average. The figures are not a foolproof measure. Apart from ensuring that one accurately picks up every occasion correctly when scanning through more than twenty large, handwritten volumes, looking for thirteen different units, not all instances found their way into the registers. In the confusion of war conditions, reports were mislaid, did not arrive or were not sent in the first place. More importantly, each battalion had its own culture regarding how it dealt with discipline, to a greater or lesser degree preferring to keep matters within the battalion, avoiding the potential for a court martial and perhaps drawing unwanted attention to the battalion's commanders.

If life in war had been unglamorous for the Pioneers, whether in terms of gallantry, casualties or military discipline, then it matched the life from which most of them had come and to which the survivors now returned, officers and men alike. The 11th DLI had experienced no great triumph, suffered no devastating defeat. Now the survivors had to cope with what they had witnessed and the mental and physical injuries they had sustained. Bereaved families and communities had to find a way of 'mercifully putting away what had been'.[7]

NOTES TO CHAPTER TWELVE

1   Second Lieutenants W. H. Charnley, M. M. Harrington, A. D. Hanfield, J. R. Kneale, R. E. C. Smith, W. Hunt, J. H. Taylor, T. T. Firth, A. H. Ainsworth, J. S. Dodson, G. Cain, G. F. Wood, G. H. Ault and J. C. Ratcliffe.

2   Throughout the middle of 1918 this amounted to an average of 35 officers and 850 men.

3   Mitchinson, 1997, p. 281.

4   See Appendix One: 11th DLI Roll of Honour

5   Mitchinson, 1997, p. 282.

6   The figures are derived from a survey of entries in the Registers of Field General Courts Martial, 1915–1918, at the National Archives, WO213/2–26

7   Words re-arranged from *Two Sonnets*, by Charles Hamilton Sorley, 12 June 1915.

CHAPTER THIRTEEN

Homecoming

Hugh Lavelle felt strange going home for the last time, wearing his Army greatcoat over ill-fitting civilian clothes. The uniform made him feel conspicuous in a way that he had not experienced before. His discomfort increased as the train pulled out of Stockton-on-Tees towards Stillington on the last leg of his journey. It was almost as unsettling as it had been when he first set off to join his Army unit. Then it had been an adventure – now it was something very different. Was there such a thing as the reverse of an adventure? Soldiering was over for Hugh Lavelle.

The guard checked his ticket and asked: 'Are you Hugh Lavelle? You look a bit different from when I last saw you, lad.' Hugh nodded, a little puzzled, as he didn't recognise the man. 'There'll be loads of folk at the station waiting for you, I bet. You'll get a real hero's welcome, and well done says I.' Not at all what Hugh wanted to hear, he didn't like a lot of fuss, and the last thing he felt just then was any kind of hero, despite his Military Medal. There was a small station halt before the village, for the local steelworks. He got off there and cut along a back lane to the village, keeping well away from the station. There were kids in the alley behind the row of terraces, but they were too young to know who he was and carried on with their little games. Hugh sneaked in through the back gate, dodging the washing and into the back kitchen. No hero's welcome for him – not if he could help it.

For every man who came home there was a story. Every story was different, except in one respect. For the most part they are now forgotten, unrecorded. We have no idea what they felt like, what they experienced, the thoughts that went through their heads. We don't know whether they were happy, nervous, excited, relieved or what they expected. We can only imagine. Hugh Lavelle did come home to Stillington, he did get off the train

Hugh Lavelle at the time of his recruitment and training, 1914–1915. (*Collection of Mike Lavelle*)

to avoid a reception committee and he did walk home along the back lane. The rest of the above is imagination, with help from contemporary railway timetables. The basic story is remembered by subsequent generations of Lavelles. Such stories are subject to a process of editing and elaboration as memories fade, people struggle to recall details, and as the story passes by word of mouth down the generations. Hard facts about the homecomings for the men of 11th DLI, as for all the other returning millions the world over, are hard to come by.

We know a little about some survivors. There are a few records of those who claimed pensions for their war service. There are family stories, though mostly these are about those who died, who seem somehow more memorable for that – perhaps because we are officially encouraged to remember them. There are other records of a darker nature: newspaper reports of incidents of violence and disturbance by returned soldiers who found it hard to readjust; registers and reports in old asylum records when minds had given up the struggle to make sense of the world; indications in employment registers that returning men could not settle back into their old jobs, some deciding to stay in the Army to manage the occupation of the Rhineland. What follows is an attempt to use such sources where they exist for 11th DLI men, to paint a picture of how it was for the former Pioneers.

An average pattern of experience for the former recruits would be useful. A register from Shildon Wagon Works lists all the employees who left to join the armed forces, giving information about their trades, their age, their family connections, their original regiment and what happened to them.[1] Shildon lies in south-west Durham. The wagon works employed a mixture of skilled and unskilled men roughly comparable to the pattern in the mines from which the bulk of 11th DLI was recruited. While only a few men from Shildon can be directly linked to 11th DLI, many others joined the 17th Northumberland Fusiliers. The 17th NF (Pioneers) was recruited by the North Eastern Railway Company from its own employees and had similar experiences to 11th DLI. Just as there was work in the mines, steelworks and foundries for the majority of employees to return to, so was it the case for the Shildon Works men. The NER encouraged a strong sense of community. The Shildon employees can be used, with caution, to establish an average pattern of experience.

Out of the 751 men who enlisted from Shildon Works across the course of the war, only 47 chose not to resume work there, representing only 6.3 per cent. The great majority resumed work, 77 of these (10.3 per cent) during the course of the war as a result of wounds, or becoming too old or unfit to serve. At the end of the war, 527 (70 per cent) returned to the works as part of the normal process of demobilisation. Roughly four out of five returned to their former employment. With caution, we can assume a similar proportion for the men of 11th DLI, though we need to acknowledge that, by 1918, the battalion was no longer drawn from the original, relatively homogeneous source in the Durham coalfields. There were men from a much wider variety of trades, a much broader geographical range and a significant number had been transferred into 11th DLI because they were deemed unfit for other types of service.

Out of the 751 men from the Shildon Works, 100 were killed in action, died of their wounds or returned in such poor health that they died shortly afterwards and were classed as war casualties. This proportion of 13.3 per cent is broadly comparable with the national average. Ten men were listed as having suffered from gas inhalation but returned to work, while eleven spent time as prisoners of war, of whom one died in Germany. Eight-seven men were recorded as having been wounded but later resumed work at Shildon, though it is not recorded as to whether they were able to continue working for long or suffered continuing ill health.

It was against this general background that men went through the process of demobilisation. As 11th DLI was disbanded, not every man could go home at once – there was work still to be done in France and Flanders, and the logistics of such an operation would have been overwhelming. As a soldier was being discharged he was given a medical and handed Army Form Z22, on which he could claim for any disability resulting from military service. Some made speculative claims using these forms. A certificate was issued, recording the condition of any equipment remaining in the soldier's possession, so that he could be held responsible for any further loss or damage before it was finally handed over. The soldier was transported to one of the coastal Infantry Base Depots such as those at Étaples and Boulogne, to await a ferry. Once in England, he was directed to a dispersal centre, often in the region from which he originated. Many north-eastern men were discharged through the camp at Ripon. The dispersal centres, with their tents and huts, would have been eerily familiar to those who had signed on in 1914, looking much like the camps that had been hastily erected in the Home Counties for training the Kitchener battalions.

At the dispersal centre there were more forms, chief among them form Z11. This acted as identification, entitling the bearer to draw his final pay at a post office, to apply for unemployment benefit if required and to show his status as a demobilised soldier. It also served as a rail warrant for his home town, but indicated that he was part of the Army Reserve and could be recalled to service until such time as he was finally discharged.[2] Hugh Lavelle, for example, would also have been issued with a form to hand in at a railway station along with his Army greatcoat, in exchange for £1.

For most former soldiers of 11th DLI, this was their experience. It remains unrecorded, unreported and unremarkable except for the men themselves and their families, localities and workplaces. The majority returned to a private existence from which, if they came to the notice of official record creators at all, it was not as men specifically from 11th DLI.

It might have been expected that former prisoners of war would have been released more quickly, but this varied. Most of the camps were in Germany, which was not immediately occupied. It was some time after the Armistice before arrangements were in place. The basic principles of repatriation were similar to demobilisation. Many of the prisoners were in poor medical condition and needed treatment to get them fit to travel. Former prisoners were interviewed about the circumstances of their capture and their subsequent treatment by the Germans. Among the interview records at the National Archives there is only one mention of a surviving 11th DLI ranking soldier, Private Thomas Oates, but no details are given.[3] In the case of other ranks, the questions tended to be about conditions and treatment, especially as most of them had been worked hard, fed poorly and treated roughly. Those who had suffered badly found themselves hospitalised and some died before arriving home.[4]

Transcripts of some interviews of officers survive among their service papers at the National Archives. The two examples for officers of 11th DLI indicate a subtext of defensiveness. Whether this was the manner of the interviewing officer or discomfort on the part of the interviewee, it is difficult to know, though we can compare responses as both related to the same incident.

Lieutenant Raymond Bushell was captured at Mézières during the courageous action on 29 March 1918. The report of his interview is entitled 'Statement regarding circumstances which led to capture.' Although Bushell was in command of his section, he uses the passive tense when describing what happened. The men 'came under withering fire' from machine-guns and trench mortars, and, 'the men were ordered to lie down'. It is an odd turn of phrase for the man giving the orders. The rest of the report maintains this sense of being helpless to communicate or retire, until forced to surrender.[5]

Lieutenant Dan Ellwood was in charge of D Company and was captured in the same way. He was concussed and, with two remaining out of his group of twenty-five, was taken prisoner. Ellwood was at pains to explain that they had been 'without the aid of artillery or machine-guns of any description' and he enclosed a copy of a letter sent to his family by Lieutenant Colonel Hayes outlining Ellwood's brave conduct.[6] It would seem that for both officers, one unhurt and the other only slightly injured, there was some sense of shame attached to their hapless fate.

Ellwood remained in the Army briefly following the war, serving at the DLI depot. Unfortunately, he contracted syphilis and continued to suffer physically from the after-effects. He left service on 1 November 1919 and the following April relinquished his commission, while retaining his rank. He retained affection for the Army, applying to join the Officers' Legion in 1927.

For all those waiting to go home, a serious problem in the winter of 1918/19 was the influenza epidemic. The disease ravaged dispersal centres, depots, hospitals and camps. Immune systems and resistance to disease were low, especially where lung conditions were involved. Soldiers may have survived the war, or survived the prison camps, only to succumb to influenza before they got home. There is little evidence of this happening to men of 11th DLI while still in service. A possible exception might be Private 24121 Frank Blakeway, who died in hospital on 23 February 1919 at Pont-Rémy near Abbeville. One officer succumbed while serving with the Army of Occupation, and there may have been other men, formerly from 11th DLI but attached to 20th or 56th Battalions.

A very small number of Army Pension papers have survived.[7] Although the five relating to men from 11th DLI cannot be taken as representative, there is sufficient variety to illustrate the range of experience of those who suffered ill-health as a result of war service. Private 13392 Joseph Batty was a former miner from East Stanley who served with 11th DLI from 3 August 1915 until he was taken prisoner on 21 March 1918. On 8 December 1918, he was repatriated to the DLI Depot. He used form Z22 to make a claim for rheumatism, but an examination detected none and he was recorded as 'nil disability'. It was likely that Batty was suffering ill effects in some way, both during service with 11th DLI and as a prisoner, but it seems he was one of those who took the opportunity of the form to make a speculative claim in the hope of recompense for what he had suffered.

Sergeant 11639 William Dowding was also a miner, from Chopwell in County Durham, though he had been born in Stafford. He served with 11th DLI for the duration of the war until discharged to DLI Depot in April 1918, having been awarded the Military Medal in June 1916. He was wounded during the German offensive and had his left foot amputated. Although the details of any pension award are not recorded in his papers, his previous twelve years of service as a regular soldier was taken into account. At the age of forty-two, with a wife and several young children, he might have been reasonably recompensed according to the standards of the time. Some assessment will have been made of his level of disability, according to a scale of percentages. It is known, for example, that men went back to work with quite severe physical problems. John William

Tombling, a steel worker from the Hartlepools, was badly injured by a flamethrower and left in cold conditions overnight in No Man's Land. He lost all his toes due to frostbite, but returned to work after the war, packing the front of his steel-capped boots with newspapers and rags.[8] No evidence of a disability award survives. Private 13524 Wilfred Fortune from Croxdale provides an idea of the value of disability awards. He was wounded in the left knee on 26 March 1918. He claimed a pension because of soreness and swelling to his knee after walking about a mile. The case was judged to be less than 20 per cent disability and he was awarded only a temporary pension of 5s 6d, for fifty-two weeks from 9 January 1919. As he was a miner by trade, this seems a rather minimal recompense. It must have affected his ability to work underground.

Another former regular soldier like Dowding was 11914 John Thomas Ellison, who was discharged from 11th DLI to Class Z reserve on 16 July 1919, at the rank of Acting Quartermaster-Sergeant. Before the war he had been a postman, after previously serving eighteen and a half years with 4th DLI, and he served most of the war with 10th DLI as Colour Sergeant.[9] Like Dowding he had married late in life, returning home from the war to his wife Agnes and their son John Thomas, born 1915, and to his job in the post office at Gateshead. The pension he received was not for disability and was not awarded until 1 October 1944 when he was seventy years of age. It was the equivalent of a retirement pension, set initially at £74 3s 9d. He died on 7 October 1950 of a cerebral haemorrhage caused by hypertension.

The saddest case relates to Private 12412 Israel Walton, although his actual connection with 11th DLI was short-lived. Walton was a miner from Dunston and joined 3rd DLI on 17 August 1915, but disappeared shortly afterwards. He was reported absent without leave and struck off the battalion strength on 3 October 1915. He remained at large until 21 July 1917 when he was caught by the civil authorities. He was convicted for desertion and losing his equipment on 30 August 1917, and was sentenced to three years' detention. The sentence was remitted on 19 September, providing he returned to the ranks, and he was sent to join 11th DLI. On 25 September, he was transferred to 12th DLI in Italy. He went absent without leave on 10 December, gave himself up a week later and was sentenced to ninety days' FP1. He went absent again on 15 March 1918 and received six months' hard labour, commuted to another ninety-day bout of FP1, during which he 'offered violence' to a superior officer and was sentenced to two years' hard labour. The sentence was quashed, as Walton was declared insane. He was posted back to England for home service at the Depot, from which he was finally discharged on 11 March 1919, declared no longer fit for war service. The surviving papers do not spell out whether he was awarded a pension or whether the many problems with discipline will have disqualified him. It was normal practice to discount any periods of absence from pension awards and Walton was absent from his unit more than he was present.

Other men with black marks in their service records found it hard to resume steady employment after the war. J. W. Pickard was a smith's labourer at Shildon Works before the war and was also in the Territorial Army, 5th DLI. He progressed through the ranks and by 1916 was a Sergeant in 11th DLI. On 12 August 1916, at a Field General Court Martial 'held in the field' he was sentenced to six months' hard labour for absence and reduced to the ranks.[10] He remained with 11th DLI and was wounded, being discharged on 18 July 1917 as unfit for military service. No pension claim has survived. After his discharge he returned to work at Shildon, but left the North Eastern Railway Company service on 19 September 1918, no reason being stated in the records.

The number of men with jobs and homes to return to, who chose to remain in the forces and serve with the Army of Occupation was relatively small. The 11th DLI battalion war diary on 27 February 1919 recorded that 'several officers and 163 other ranks' transferred to 20th DLI to serve with the Army of Occupation. Apart from this reference there is nothing to tell us about the ordinary soldiers, who they were, why they chose this option and what happened to them. Among officer's records, there is some information about those remaining in service and the kind of work that they did, whether in Germany or back in the DLI Depot in England.

Lieutenant George Stanley Dennis was one of two officers who transferred to the Army of Occupation about whom there are surviving records. He joined the Army at the age of thirty-four in 1914, originally with 19th Royal Fusiliers as a private. He took a commission in 1916 and arrived with 11th DLI on 5 October of that year. He was fortunate to avoid the March Retreat in 1918, having been seconded for home service for six months. He returned to 11th DLI on 14 November 1918 and took charge of B Company as Acting Captain. Dennis had served an apprenticeship in mechanical engineering before the war, working at Farbe Lehrmeyer & Co. in Aachen, Germany. His familiarity with the country and the language was an advantage when he volunteered to serve with 2nd Intelligence Corps Company in Cologne, while nominally attached to 20th DLI for record purposes. He arrived in March 1919, but became a victim of influenza within a very short time. His widowed mother was telegraphed on 30 June to say that he was dangerously ill, but by the next day he was dead. Fortunately, he left an estate of several hundred pounds and she would have been entitled to ask for a pension as sole dependent.[11]

Lieutenant Endean had a similarly short service with the Army of Occupation. He joined 11th DLI from 14th DLI in February 1918 and distinguished himself during the March Retreat, being wounded in the action at Mézieres. He was hit 'by a piece of shell which entered the right buttock and passed through emerging near the tip of the coccyx'; once recovered he went to serve with 52nd DLI in Germany until 13 July 1919, when he was repatriated overseas as a result of the recurrence of problems with his old wound. Although Cornish by birth, the son of a retired mine manager, Endean had been in South Africa in 1914. He returned there to work for Rand Mines Ltd, Johannesburg.[12]

Captain Walter Sear was another officer to return to the colonies after the war. Already the recipient of the Military Cross for action at Ypres in 1917, he was wounded at Mézières. He was shot through the left shoulder and lung by a machine-gun bullet and was coughing up blood for six hours afterwards. He was treated at No. 5 Southern General Hospital, Portsmouth before going on to the Prince of Wales Hospital for Officers at Marylebone to recuperate. There was no chance of him going back into service after such a wound and he was demobilised on 2 May 1919, retaining his rank and being transferred to the Reserve until 21 October 1920. Before the war he had been Superintendent at the Colonial Sugar Refining Company in Sydney, went back there after the war and was last recorded in his service papers living in Melbourne in 1934.[13]

Another returning to normal civilian life was Lieutenant George Hugh Tollit. He had been born in 1872 and had served with the regular Army in India before volunteering in 1914 at the age of forty-two. His military background made him a candidate for battalion administration and he began service as Honorary Lieutenant and Quartermaster. In October 1917, he was promoted to Captain and became Adjutant, in which capacity he distinguished himself at Cambrai. This was despite recurrent bouts of rheumatism that had occasioned periods of sick leave. He remained in service until 13 November 1919, some months after the battalion had returned to England and been disbanded. He returned to civilian life at the age of forty-eight.[14]

Tollit had replaced Captain Arthur Dawson as Adjutant, a man of similar age. Dawson had been born in 1873 and was a schoolmaster from Jarrow. He did not enjoy good health at any point during his service. He was diagnosed with 'trench fever' in 1916. He was sent home on sick leave on 21 August 1917, suffering from a general nervous breakdown. He did not recover sufficiently until May 1918, a factor which probably saved his life, given the experiences of the battalion during his absence. He does not appear to have returned overseas, but achieved the rank of Acting Major. He was demobilised at Ripon on 20 January 1919, and on 21 December 1921 given the entitlement to the rank of Major. The records do not state, but it can be presumed that he returned to his career as a schoolmaster.[15]

Richard Laurence Stapylton Pemberton represents a sharp contrast to Tollit and Dawson. He was born 10 April 1891 into a county family in Durham, with a long tradition of landownership, coal owning and distinguished public service. Educated at Eton and Oxford, Pemberton applied for a commission from the start and went overseas with 11th DLI on 20 July 1915. He quickly rose to command a company, winning the MC at Cambrai and a bar to the MC for his conspicuous gallantry at Mézières when in temporary command of 11th DLI. In December 1918, he briefly officially commanded the battalion. Before returning to England on 20 January 1919, he took a few days leave in Pau, and was demobilised at Ripon on 24 January. He returned to civilian life as a landowner and company director, but kept up his association with military affairs, assisting the Ministry of Labour at Newcastle with the Disabled Officers and Soldiers Committee until 1922. Commuting between his estate near Sunderland and his offices at St James', London, he continued to be a public figure as a Justice of the Peace. On 4 May 1938, Pemberton put his name forward for a scheme to enrol former officers. He was accepted onto the Officers Emergency Reserve with an end date of April 1946, when he would have been fifty-five. When war broke out he was given the temporary rank of second lieutenant and served with Light Anti-Aircraft Batteries. However, as soon as sufficient younger men became available, he was requested to stand down, with effect from 15 November 1941, although he did not actually leave the reserve until well after time expiry on 1 September 1948. He would have cut an imposing figure, standing 5 feet 11 inches tall, weighing 196 pounds, with a chest expanding to 42 inches.[16]

His former CO, Geoffrey Hayes, was a regular officer in 1914, serving with the DLI in India, but home on leave at the outbreak of the war. Beginning as Adjutant at Temporary Captain, he had a succession of temporary appointments up to the rank of Lieutenant Colonel in charge of 11th DLI from 13 December 1916. His service with the battalion was distinguished; he was twice mentioned in despatches and was awarded the Distinguished Service Order for his leadership of the battalion at Cambrai. He was forced to relinquish command of 11th DLI during the March Retreat after being gassed and, although he returned to the unit briefly in April 1918, his health was too poor and he returned to England for hospital treatment and sick leave. Once recovered he took command of 2nd/5th Norfolk Regiment in the UK until 10 November 1919, after which he reverted to his substantive rank of Captain for unspecified military duties as part of the winding down of the armed forces. From May 1926 to August 1928 he was posted to the West African Regiment, was promoted to Major and then returned to the full establishment in India. Although it had proved a long and probably frustrating struggle to re-establish himself, by the late 1920s, Hayes was well respected and reports on him by senior officers were complimentary as to his leadership and military skills, though all noted a certain tactlessness. This was to prove his undoing when he returned to 2nd DLI in India in 1930, where he found himself in a clash of personalities with Lieutenant Colonel Turner.

Hayes' surviving papers largely deal with this exchange of views.[17] There are some interesting facets to Turner's comments, not least that, in contrast to previous reports from other commanders, he regarded Hayes as little more than average in terms of his physical and intellectual qualifications, no more than satisfactory at his duties and 'well up to the average in military ability: but below average in some requirements of his rank'. Others had described him as of good judgement, sound initiative, quick decision, a good trainer, keen on his men and his profession, against which qualities his tactlessness and occasional irascibility were seen as minor complaints. For Turner this was a complete reverse – Hayes' manners overshadowing and cancelling out any other qualities, though he admitted in 1930 that 'I have not previously informed this officer of his deficiencies'.

Hayes was clearly hurt by the criticisms, accused Turner of having 'disliked me for over 20 years' and demanding, not unreasonably, specific evidence of the complaints against him, especially when these were repeated in 1932 and a request made that he be transferred to the Judge Advocate General's Department. The reasons become clearer in Turner's final comments, which amount to a condemnation that he did not fit in to the Officer's Mess. He was disliked by subordinate officers. In this Turner was backed by General Shea, Commander-in-Chief, Eastern Command, India: 'I have every confidence in the reporting officers: and consequently agree with them. I cannot report from personal knowledge as I have seen little of Major Hayes.'

Hayes returned on sick leave to England in April 1933 while a board discussed what to do with him and concluded that he be asked to retire. He was placed on half pay from 6 December 1933, and retired at the rank of Lieutenant Colonel on 9 June 1934. The final assessment by the board went back over all his reports since 1910 and picked out his lack of tact and failure to address it satisfactorily. Against that his service in the Great War counted for nothing, other than giving him the right to a rank he had never substantively acquired. That Turner had not even had the decency to speak to him directly about his failings and to provide more specific evidence of them stands more as a condemnation of Turner than it does of Hayes. It certainly does not measure up to modern standards of personnel management, even if it reflects the culture of the Army at the time. It is sad that such a courageous and diligent officer as Hayes had to suffer such treatment from an army that had reverted to its pre-war type. If the 'land fit for heroes' did not exist in the UK for former civilians, it was equally true in the regular armed forces. Geoffrey Hayes died in Aberdovey on 3 July 1976, by which time his grandson was also a serving officer in the Light Infantry.

The only documentary references we have of the life of 11th DLI soldiers after the war are the details of those who returned home and died as a consequence of their war service. Death certificates provide scant detail, but the following four cases will give an indication of life for those returning in poor health.

Private 22525 Thomas Edward Dawson made it home very quickly after the Armistice. Prior to the war he had been a putter, working at Boldon Colliery. He was married and aged twenty-eight. He returned to the north-east of England just as it was being swept by the outbreak of Spanish influenza. He died from the effects of influenza and pneumonia on 30 November 1918 at Sunderland War Hospital. Some from Dawson's family were with him as his mother-in-law, Mrs M. Robinson, registered his death and that she had been present.

Private 31767 George Henry Elsy, a cart-man, aged thirty-eight, died of the same causes on 14 March 1919 at his home, 36 Edith Street, South Shields. His sister from North Shields was present and registered his death. It is disturbing to know that two others with precisely the same surname and forenames died in South Shields within weeks of each other, one an infant and one an old man, almost certainly close relatives.

On 3 July 1919, former Lance Corporal 53298 George Highslip Woods Gedney died, aged twenty-three, at the Tuberculosis Hospital, Cottingham, near Hull. He had been admitted there from the Grove Military Hospital in Tooting, London. The death certificate indicates that he had been suffering from tuberculosis of the lungs and peritoneum for as long as two years. The death was registered by his sister Mrs V. M. Hoe and he was buried at Hull Western Cemetery.

Private 18854 Francis Reay Bates was demobilised at Notley on 23 January 1919. He had enlisted at Birtley on 11 September 1914 and went out to France with 11th DLI in July 1915. However, he was admitted to 1st Australian General Hospital Rouen in 1916, suffering from contusion to the back and shell shock. Following recovery, he was attached to 86th Prince of Wales Company, Labour Corps with a new number: 566355. On his final discharge he was adjudged to be 40 per cent disabled due to his war service and was awarded a pension of 11s a week rising to 16s from 2 September 1919. He returned home to Birtley, living at 248 South Street, Ouston, but was unable to resume work underground. He was re-employed at the pit as a timekeeper. His ill health continued and he died 23 April 1920 at the Royal Victoria Infirmary, Newcastle-upon-Tyne, of ulcerative endocarditis and cardiac failure. The disease causes bacterial infection to circulate through the bloodstream and must have been in some way related to his earlier injury, as he was classed as a war casualty and his grave at Pelton Cemetery is maintained by the Commonwealth War Graves Commission.

The present popularity of family history may help to recover the untold stories of survivors from the war who did not come to the attention of the official record keepers. By this we know a little about Sergeant 16996 John Doyle. Born in Darlington in 1888, he married Mary Ellen Kane in 1907 at St Augustine's Roman Catholic Church, and in due course they had four children. He was previously a labourer at a local railway engineering works. There are no service records, but, as he was not awarded the 1914–15 Star, we can deduce that he was called up during 1916. By 1918, he had risen to the rank of Sergeant. He was captured in the March Retreat, illustrated by a note in the 1918 Absent Voter's Register recording him as a prisoner of war. According to family stories, he and several comrades escaped through a tunnel and made it into the American lines. After repatriation he was in poor health, suffering from nephritis, and was bedridden for several months. When he had recovered sufficiently, he obtained work as a caretaker at a local school. He died 8 June 1922 of heart disease at the age of only thirty-four. Though his war experiences clearly contributed to his death, he is not officially classed as a war casualty.[18]

At the commencement of this chapter, I described the homecoming of Hugh Lavelle, the only example known to me of a former 11th DLI ranking soldier returning to a normal existence, uncomplicated by disease, injury or other impairment. He married a local girl, Norah Stevenson, and became a labourer at the local ironworks, until it failed during the Depression. He got a job with the London & North Eastern Railway, retiring in 1957. He served in the Home Guard during the Second World War and took part in the capture of the crew of a German bomber shot down at the nearby village of Great Stainton in 1943. He died in 1966 and was buried in an unmarked grave in the local churchyard. Branches of the family still live in the area.[19] Unusually, he gets a mention on the local war memorial, though not by name, as it notes the 113 men who returned as well as the names of those who died. Even the road alongside which the rather pretty memorial park is situated conveys the memory of the war, being called Messines Lane. It is to the issue of memory and remembrance that I turn to in the final chapter.

Hugh Lavelle and Norah Stevenson at the time of their marriage in 1922. (*Collection of Mike Lavelle*)

Hugh Lavelle in old age, in the 1960s. (*Collection of Mike Lavelle*)

NOTES TO CHAPTER THIRTEEN

1 Copy from Locomotion: The National Railway Museum at Shildon.
2 A number of reservists from Shildon Works were called up during a national strike in 1921.
3 National Archives, WO 161/100/427, p. 3168.
4 Van Emden, 2000.
5 National Archives, WO 339/60723, papers relating to Lieutenant R. Bushell.
6 National Archives, WO 339/69379, papers relating to Lieutenant D. Ellwood.
7 National Archives, WO 364, from which the examples quoted have been taken.
8 Personal information from his great grandson, Ed Matthews.
9 He therefore possibly figures in the early photograph of 10th and 11th DLI sergeants in 1914.
10 National Archives, WO/213/10, Register of Field General Courts Martial.
11 National Archives, WO 339/60079, papers relating to Lieutenant G. S. Dennis.
12 National Archives, WO 339/69860, papers relating to Lieutenant W. J. Endean.
13 National Archives, WO 339/50265, papers relating to Captain W. G. L. Sear.
14 National Archives, WO 339/16636, papers relating to Captain G. H. Tollit.
15 National Archives, WO 339/20827, papers relating to Captain A. Dawson.
16 Army Historical Records, papers relating to R. L. S. Pemberton.
17 Army Historical Records, papers relating to G. G. Hayes.
18 Information about John Doyle from his great granddaughter, Emma Laycock. An attestation form from the International Committee of the Red Cross shows that Sergeant Doyle of B Company, 11th DLI, was captured on 23 march 1918 at Aubigny. He was imprisoned at Giessen, Meschede, Stargard and Altdamm successively. The last two camps were near Sceczin (Stettin) in modern-day Poland and were particularly unpleasant. He was repatriated via Leith on the SS *Lacour*, shortly after the Armistice on 23 November 1918. He may have escaped at some point, but this suggests that he was recaptured and moved east.
19 Information about Hugh Lavelle from his grandson, Mike Lavelle.

CHAPTER FOURTEEN

Death Divides but Memory Clings

The way in which we remember those who fell during the First World War has changed dramatically in recent years. The war has been rediscovered by a new generation. Conventional forms of commemoration continue, but a more personal style of remembrance has emerged, accompanied by the growth of family history and the emergence of public records of individuals into the popular domain.

On Remembrance Sunday, 9 November 2008, three old men in wheelchairs took centre stage at the Cenotaph in London. Uncannily, these last surviving UK veterans of the First World War each represented a different branch of the armed forces. William Stone, the youngest at 108, had barely finished his basic training in the Royal Navy when the Armistice was signed. Henry Allingham, the oldest, had served in the Royal Naval Air Service and the Royal Air Force, at the Battle of Jutland and on the Somme. Harry Patch was the sole, wounded survivor of a team of Lewis gunners from 7th DCLI, victims of shelling at Pilckem Ridge in 1917. As 7th DCLI was a unit in the 20th Light Division, he also represented a connection to 11th DLI. War remains a contemporary experience, and each of the veterans was accompanied by a member of the equivalent branch of the armed forces, recently serving with distinction in Iraq and Afghanistan. Although their wheelchairs were lined up together in front of the Cenotaph, Henry, Harry and William were kept at a distance from each other – close enough to form a group, but too far apart for any informal fraternisation. This was an act of public theatre, whatever their private thoughts.

Despite the official choreography of 9 November 2008, the emotional impact of their flesh and blood presence provided a human link for the many observers who remembered men and women, missed and missing,

Headstone of Stephen
Ferry at Ferme-Olivier
Cemetery, Elverdinghe.
The inscription reads
'Death divides, but
memory clings'.
(*Jon Miller*)

from almost a century of warfare. Henry Allingham's brave attempt to
stand and lay his own wreath was, testament to his humanity, courageous
but fragile. They were living representations, remembered for this one final
instant. It is an event that can never be repeated. These were remarkably
old men. It was their last time together and the last time any of them
would attend such a ceremony. In the following months each of them died
– William, Henry and finally Harry.

Whatever had been the official intent behind the theatrical appearance
of these three actors, there will have been a multitude of meanings placed
upon it, by those attending in whatever capacity, by the television audience,
and by those attending similar ceremonies elsewhere in villages, towns and
on battlefields across the world. Not least, at this precise moment, will
have been the private thoughts of the three men themselves. We cannot
exactly know what was in their minds at 11 a.m., as the traditional two-
minute silence enveloped the assembly. Henry Allingham took every
public opportunity to make his point about the futility and waste of war.
Harry Patch mostly remembered his comrades from the Lewis gun team
on the anniversary of the date they were killed by shellfire, rather than on

Remembrance Sunday or Armistice Day. William Stone, who dismissed any idea that he had been a hero, was nonetheless a conventionally patriotic man who was proud to have 'done his bit' in a later war and took a childlike thrill from having helped to drive trains during the General Strike in 1926.

The event on 9 November 2008 was unique in its focus on recognisable and named individuals who were not famous generals or admirals or national war leaders. It provided a glimpse beyond the dominant official discourse concerning remembrance, to a more human form of witness, usually subterranean and, to a degree, subversive of the conventional paradigm. The contest between the personal and the official vision of how to commemorate those who survived and those who died in the First World War began during the war itself. This tension continues today, both in relation to past wars and to those serving in present wars.[1] If anything, it may be argued, the dominant official vision is somewhat in retreat. One of the principal reasons has been the phenomenal growth in family history as a means by which the individual can engage with the past in a highly personalised way, free from the constraints of official discourse, though not necessarily from its influence. Another reason has been the visibility of ordinary soldiers and their families in media coverage of current wars, the pilgrimages to Wooton Bassett on the return of the fallen from Iraq and Afghanistan, the popularity of the campaign 'Help for Heroes', and, even, public sympathy for Lance Corporal Joe Glenton, during his court-martial in 2010. Remembrance may sometimes continue to use the old language, but has been democratised.

Almost as soon as men enlisted in 1914, and within a short period of the first casualties, families and communities in the United Kingdom, as well as the men on the battlefields, began to discuss how best to deal with the absence and loss engendered by war. They acted among and for themselves, with their relatives, loved ones, friends, workmates and comrades uppermost in their intentions. In localities as far apart as Hackney and Hull, local people set up shrines, often rather rough and ready, made from what was to hand. Many parish churches made lists inside the church enumerating the men of the parish who had signed up for service overseas. Very few of these forms of commemoration survive today. Most of the street shrines fell into disrepair, were bombed during the Second World War or fell victim to housing development. Some fell into disuse following the dreadful losses on the Somme in 1916, when the numbers to record became too harrowing to commemorate. Five street shrines still exist in Hull and one has recently been restored at Stoneham in Hampshire.[2] What both street shrines and parish notices held in common was the lack of any physical representation of the soldier other than names. These recorded real individuals, not archetypes, not icons.

Workplaces were often even quicker than the general public to organise forms of remembering. They could hardly fail to notice the sudden loss of members of staff enlisting. They had structures through which to organise a response. The North Eastern Railway Company had long produced a monthly staff magazine. The issues in the last quarter of 1914 established a pattern that was emulated by other railway companies, notably the Great Eastern Railway and the Great Western Railway. Early articles in the North Eastern Railway magazine were rather general, such as noting that by September 1914 almost 5,000 men had joined the Colours and that a call for volunteers to form a battalion of North Eastern Railway men had been oversubscribed by a factor of three in a matter of a few days.[3] The following month witnessed a shift towards the reporting of individual cases. There was a list in double columns and over several pages of all those who had already enlisted (pages 265–271). The first 'Roll of Honour' listed six casualties, each with a photograph and a short pen portrait. By December, a format was established under regular headings: 'From the Front' (news and reports including letters), 'Railway Work of the Army' (covering civilian workers alongside the armed forces), 'NER Commissioned Officers' listing those who had taken commissions, 'NER Men with the Colours' listing those in other ranks, and four more names, photographs and pen portraits in the 'Roll of Honour'. The articles provide a remarkable array of names, images and personal details of value to the present-day family historian. Among the men remembered in this way were several who served in 11th DLI.

The records of individual departments and workplaces, like the street shrines, were at first ephemeral, replaced after the war with more permanent memorials. Notices and plaques were affixed to walls in workplaces, always commemorating those who had died, but often listing all those who were serving. A rather battered example is in the collection at the National Railway Museum. The Sheet Department of the Great Western Railway based at Worcester created a colourful illuminated roll of honour, listing all those who served and carrying photographs of the six men who had lost their lives.[4]

Families treasured and displayed the postcard-sized photographs that many recruits obtained shortly after enlistment or after receiving their first full uniform. Some reservist soldiers wore full dress uniform, but the most common image is that of the Kitchener volunteer in his ill-fitting khaki uniform, often looking rather ill at ease. Where photographs taken later in the war have survived (such as the family portrait of Thomas Bashforth in chapter 4), it is often noticeable how much the individual had changed from being a civilian, uncomfortable in his military disguise, to a more self-assured man, conscious of his status in uniform. Such men had, through their training and their new form of dress, crossed a line from being a private individual to being a public figure. These photographs remain powerful symbols for remembrance, even to descendants who never knew the men portrayed.

By comparison, the photographs of soldiers in newspapers, war magazines and film newsreels tended to be of men in groups, rather than of individuals – men marching, doing physical exercise, practising drill or posed on the battlefield. They are anonymous and, while they may be more martial in tone and content, they are a long way from the graphic line drawings that provided artistic impressions of battlefield heroism common in magazines such as *War Illustrated*. Nevertheless, even these images are part of the cultural background from which we draw our sense of what it was to be a Great War soldier, mediated through frequent exposure to particular iconic images – men falling on the wire as they go over the top, the shocked man shouldering his wounded comrade along a trench and officers standing in the featureless landscape around Ypres. Nevertheless, the most common, archetypal and powerful image for the family is the postcard of a missing grandfather, uncle or cousin. This is the image that haunts the family historian and sends them into the archives to find out more.

The archives themselves are a form of remembrance. The online records of the Commonwealth War Graves Commission, recording the name and personal details of each Commonwealth soldier, sailor or airman who lost their life during the two world wars of the twentieth century, have this explicit purpose. The records originated as a means of maintaining data on all the cemeteries looked after by the Commonwealth War Graves Commission. This organisation was the brainchild of Sir Fabian Ware, who began his work while serving with the Red Cross in 1914–1915. In 1917, the work was formally instituted as the Imperial War Graves Commission. Over 31,000 graves had been registered by October 1915. The sheer weight of bureaucracy involved, married to the basic principles on which the organisation was set up (especially the idea of uniformity of representation and equality of treatment), ensure that what is presented carries with it little ideological baggage. The major exception to that is the modern name given to the online database: 'The Debt of Honour'. This phrase immediately takes what was in essence simply a bureaucratic record and provides an added ethical significance as part of the dominant paradigm of 'Remembrance'. The growth of family history has caused many more archives to be placed online, including medal index cards, pension records and service records.

At a local level are the various memorials and rolls of honour. These include village monuments, plaques in churches, workplaces and clubs, or larger books of remembrance in cathedrals, museums and town halls. The Book of Remembrance in Durham Cathedral lists all the men of the Durham Light Infantry by calendar day. Thus on the 27 March page you will find the DLI men who died in 1915–1919 in year order. The North Eastern Railway Book of Remembrance lists men alphabetically by surname with initials, and, where known, the department and location from which they originated. In instances like these, the amount of surrounding context is as varied as the numbers and locations in which they are found. The DLI Book of Remembrance is in a chapel dedicated to the regiment and is surrounded by religious and military iconography. The NER book occupies a quiet corner of the National Railway Museum. Typically, local memorials bear words about glory, sacrifice, and honour, and are a focus of annual ceremonies.

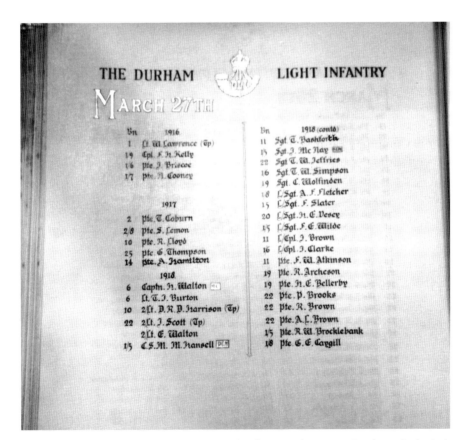

The first page in the First World War Book of Remembrance at Durham Cathedral, showing the names of those who died on 27 March, each year of the war. Eight names from 11th DLI are recorded in 1918. (*Martin Bashforth, courtesy of the Dean and Chapter, Durham Cathedral*)

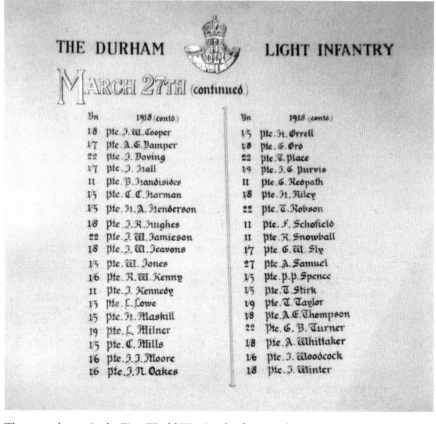

THE DURHAM — LIGHT INFANTRY

MARCH 27TH (continued)

Bn	1918 (contd.)	Bn	1918 (contd.)
18	Pte. J. W. Cooper	1/5	Pte. H. Orrell
1/7	Pte. A. G. Damper	1/8	Pte. G. Oro
22	Pte. J. Doving	22	Pte. T. Place
1/7	Pte. J. Hall	19	Pte. J. G. Purvis
11	Pte. B. Handisides	11	Pte. G. Redpath
1/5	Pte. C. C. Harman	18	Pte. H. Riley
1/5	Pte. H. A. Henderson	22	Pte. T. Robson
18	Pte. J. R. Hughes	11	Pte. F. Schofield
22	Pte. J. W. Jamieson	11	Pte. R. Snowball
18	Pte. J. W. Jeavons	1/7	Pte. G. W. Sly
1/5	Pte. W. Jones	27	Pte. A. Samuel
1/6	Pte. R. W. Kenny	1/5	Pte. P. P. Spence
11	Pte. J. Kennedy	1/5	Pte. T. Stirk
1/5	Pte. F. Lowe	1/9	Pte. T. Taylor
15	Pte. H. Maskill	18	Pte. A. E. Thompson
19	Pte. F. Milner	22	Pte. G. B. Turner
1/5	Pte. C. Mills	18	Pte. A. Whittaker
16	Pte. J. J. Moore	1/6	Pte. J. Woodcock
16	Pte. J. N. Oakes	18	Pte. J. Winter

The second page in the First World War Book of Remembrance at Durham Cathedral, showing the names of those who died on 27 March, each year of the war. Eight names from 11th DLI are recorded in 1918. (*Martin Bashforth, courtesy of the Dean and Chapter, Durham Cathedral*)

Several regimental museums have websites and displays that acknowledge the individual soldier. The Durham Light Infantry Museum has a substantial collection of medals and associated material relating to individual former soldiers of the DLI, some of which is now accessible online. The form of presentation is an example of how institutions continue with the prevailing paradigm in relation to remembrance. Follow the links on the website to the 'Medal Room' and there is an opportunity to search for names of what are referred to as 'Local Heroes'.[5] There are several sets of medals from 11th DLI men, including Geoffrey Hayes, and each entry provides a pen portrait and photograph of the recipient.

There are major sets of material held at the Imperial War Museum, the National Archives and available from the Historical Disclosures section of Army Records. Each of these archive sources has its own individual characteristics. They can be combined imaginatively to look at particular groups of men. They might be from the same town or locality; they might also be connected to one particular unit. In composite, they provide a totally different image of the soldier from the conventional paradigm, because they allow one to rediscover the man, in himself and in his group. They sometimes provide a link to those people, around the time that the war ended, who were forced to retreat into silence in the face of the centralised and bureaucratic way in which the state and local grandees sanctioned a form of remembrance that was imposed on the majority of families. Such detailed research can reaffirm the essential humanity of the individual soldier against the conventional image portrayed in state functions, official ceremonies, news bulletins, recruitment advertising and populist journalism. It may be too strong to say that this offers a way to comprehensively subvert the conventional paradigm, but it certainly offers an evidence-based contrast.

The personal perspective actually has its roots during and immediately after the First World War. The surviving service papers reveal the enormous impact on bereaved families, which was not assuaged by bureaucratic attempts to compensate. When the personal pain felt by widows and bereaved parents is visible in these papers, there is sufficient indication, coupled with the memories handed down through families, to suggest that we need to penetrate the fog of official remembrance to fully understand the profound personal and social pain caused by the first major industrialised war. It is no longer sufficient to simply rewrite the campaigns and battles, and to explain and justify the generals.

I can now only surmise what my grandmother experienced, piecing it together from tiny snippets of information. I had no opportunity to talk to her about the subject, while loyalty to a subsequent husband might well have prevented her from saying very much. Hers was a grief buried, with no known grave and no grave marker, just like the body of her former husband. The reality of her loss has been passed down the generations through family myths and this is probably true of many families so affected. The most poignant is a rather garbled story relating to when my father was called up for war service in 1939. He was a soldier in the Territorial Army, away at annual camp near Scarborough. My gran is supposed to have commented that this was just like his father at the outbreak of his war. However, my grandfather was never in the Territorials. He would, however, have been in training camp in the first week of September 1914, as a Kitchener volunteer. The grain of truth was amplified by my gran's fear for her son, that history might be repeated for him like his father before. The story that Thomas Bashforth contemplated desertion in January 1918 was similarly embroidered in the light of what subsequently happened.

It was one of those 'what if' tales beloved of family myth and redolent of how we construct our personal culture of remembrance.

Although as a child I knew about my grandfather's death in the Great War, the matter was never discussed. My grandfather was never denied, but any emotional issues were well buried, only to emerge at times of anxiety. It was a pattern repeated by my parents who never discussed my mother's first husband, who had been killed in the first week of September 1939 in a freak accident. They spoke disparagingly of the annual Remembrance Day parades and never wore poppies. They regarded the parades as nothing to do with ordinary people and as being tainted by the hypocrisy of a class who continued to send young men to their deaths. The battle between personal grief and remembrance on the one hand, and the official clichés on the other, began before Armistice Day was first celebrated. It is in family life and family memories that we find a more authentic remembrance, the implications of which have often been experienced in tensions and dysfunction in relationships.[6]

Robert Bennett's letters, quoted so extensively in this book, initially survived because his mother kept them under the kitchen sink, in her private domain. When she died around 1930, the letters were taken and hidden again by Robert's sister, Catherine. She had been thirteen when Robert died and was profoundly affected by the death of her beloved older brother. As was commonly the case with mothers, sisters and wives impacted by grief, she kept the letters to herself.

Elizabeth (Lizzie) Bonney (née Greener) similarly kept all the letters from her husband, Sergeant Thomas Bonney. These, along with medals and commemorative plaque, were kept faithfully even after she emigrated to Canada and was married to Charles Curry, who appears to have always acknowledged that Tommy had been the first love. Sadly the letters were lost in the course of a house burglary and have not been recovered, but the memory of Thomas Bonney has been passed down, even among the Curry descendants.[7]

It was not always the case that family harmony followed loss; anger and jealousy can break out in the aftermath of grief. Cases of dispute occasionally emerge in the service papers. Most of the undamaged papers relating to Private 16228 Charles Hargreaves relate to a family dispute over the medals. At the time of Hargreaves' death in October 1916, his older brother and elderly father lived with his sister Margaret Ann Corbett. Hargreaves' medals were originally sent to the father. However, one of the younger sons, Robert Hargreaves, appears to have persuaded his father to move from Durham to live with him in Darlington. Robert wrote to the Army to recover the medals from Durham as his letters there were allegedly being ignored. The eldest son, John Hargreaves, returned the medals to the War Office on 5 January 1922, with a covering letter commenting:

> I am forwarding only to you the Medals required on behalf of my Sister Mrs Corbett. My Father has always stayed with her since my Mother died owing to his old age but since my Brother came home he never rested till he got my father from her and that is how the medals went to her. My Father told her she could keep them but my Brother says not and this is the result.[8]

The Army could only act according to any surviving wills or information as to next of kin. Such was also the case in relation to the effects of Private 16237 Robert Snowball from Felling. He died in a German field hospital on 27 March 1918 and the Germans returned his disc and effects. Everything went to his widow, Mrs Jane Snowball, though his mother wrote from Gateshead claiming to be the beneficiary of his will. The War Office acted according to a later will in his pay book.

It is difficult to know whether the constant contact with bereaved families by the War Office was a blessing or a curse. There were battles over pension entitlements for the widow of J. A. Bowlt in 1915 that took until the summer of 1916 to resolve after the intervention of the Hartlepool branch of the Soldiers and Sailors Families Association, because of the accidental nature of Bowlt's death.

The widow of Sergeant 25774 James O'Neill from Birtley suffered terrible anxiety while a decision was made about her entitlement to a pension. Her husband had returned home in December 1916 to serve with 276th Training Reserve Infantry Battalion after service overseas with 11th DLI. On 21 October 1917, he was run down by a motor bus, suffering severe injuries to skull, spine, pelvic girdle and femur. He died of the injuries but because his death was not 'in the performance of military duty' his widow was not entitled to the usual pension. She was awarded 15s a week for herself and three children as a temporary measure, from 29 April 1918. It is not recorded just how temporary this award was or whether she was later awarded an amount more fitting to her needs.

Kate Farrell, the articulate and assertive mother of John Farrell, who had served under the name of Brady, fought until 1920 to have his medals and grave notice re-inscribed. The events are emphatically marked in stone as a personal inscription on Farrell's gravestone: 'Son of Mrs Farrell and the late James Farrell, Broxburn Scotland, R.I.P.' Although Thomasina Brydon, the widow of Private 13952 Ernest Brydon from Annfield Plain, was not denied a pension for her husband, missing since 26 March 1918, it was not until the second anniversary of his presumed death that she finally got a letter from the War Office 'that it must now be definitely accepted that the soldier was killed in action or died of wounds on or since 26.3.1918'.

There were constant reminders for up to five years. Private 15002 Mark Farn from Shotton Colliery was reported missing with effect from 23 March 1918. The bizarre return of his identity disc in September 1922, having become mixed up with papers relating to a Highland Light Infantry man in Palestine who died in 1919, not only caused an internal enquiry at the War Office but further emotional distress for the widow.

The return of personal effects was of emotional importance to many families, these being the last connection to their loved one. The service records often include references to the return of personal items and, in a proportion of cases, list them. These lists, which relatives were asked to sign and return as a form of receipt, would make an interesting study in themselves but even a cursory sketch reveals some interesting features. The mention of any valuables is exceedingly rare and that is as true of officers as of other ranks. While there was the occasional bag of small coins and wallets, the only specific reference I have found was to a nine-carat gold ring belonging to Private 22063 Austin Barraclough. Most commonly the effects comprised letters, postcards, discs, photos and combs. Smoking materials such as pipes, cigarette cases and tobacco tins were frequently listed, as were personal care items such as combs and nail clippers. Occasionally watches and knives were returned and a variety of religious items such as chains, books and rosaries. For many families there was only an identity disc returned from German authorities, at worst nothing, despite requests such as that by Mrs Jane McLean in relation to her son, Thomas. This was especially true following major actions, virtually without exception during the retreats at Cambrai and St Quentin.

Perhaps the least welcome reminders, though necessary and proper from the authorities of the War Graves Commission, were the notifications of exhumation and reburial caused by the concentration of the thousands of smaller cemeteries. These letters would be sent out mostly during 1920 and principally affected those buried in cemeteries attached to casualty clearing centres at various places in the Somme battlefield area, including Guillemont, near Cambrai and in the area raced over during the March 1918 retreat. The letters from Infantry Records were sensitively worded. A typical example is that for Private 12531 Robert Cain to his widow at Monkwearmouth, dated 24 October 1919:

> I beg to inform you that it has been necessary to exhume the remains of the late No 12531 Private R Cain, 11th Battalion Durham Light Infantry, for proper burial at Gouzeaucourt New British Cemetery, 11 miles North East of Peronne.

The new grave has been duly marked with a Cross bearing all the soldier's particulars.

The removal was undertaken with every measure of care and reverence, and the reinterment conducted by an Army Chaplain.[9]

These reminders, along with the issue of medals, commemorative plaques and memorial scrolls continued alongside the emergence of official ceremonials and memorials created locally and nationally. The history of these phenomena has been covered by other writers and it would be inappropriate to cover the matter in a book dedicated to a single battalion. Of more relevance is the continued significance of these memorials to descendants today. The centenary of the First World War will commence in 2014 and, soon after, the centenary of many of the war memorials.

The families were allowed to add their own personal inscriptions to the official grave markers overseas and these are usually carved close to the base. Among those inscriptions found on graves of 11th DLI men, one of the most common is the phrase 'Peace Perfect Peace', as is the case with John Acomb, Joseph Logan and John George Cummins. Such inscriptions included simple expressions like 'Ever remembered by his loving wife and children' for Matthew Craggs and 'In Loving Memory, Sadly missed by his

Postcard photograph of Pelton Fell War Memorial, 1922, in cenotaph style. Thomas Bonney is commemorated here. (*Collection of David Kelly*)

loving brothers and sisters' for Private C. Hildreth. Austin Barraclough is remembered with a short four-line poem, 'Keep on dear son / Take your rest / We miss you most / Who loved you best', while Robert Barron is commemorated with the traditional religious phrase 'In the midst of life we are in death'. A few are conventionally heroic, like 'Steadfast in life, Valiant in death', which appears on William Bonney's grave. The confines of space tend to produce some of the most simple and thereby emotive phrases: 'Until the day breaks' for Harry Cunliffe; 'Far to sight, near to heart' for Charles Hargreaves; and the one that heads this chapter, 'Death divides but memory clings' for Stephen Oliver Ferry. They contrast quite markedly with the more official phrases found on local memorials such as 'Make them to be numbered with Thy Saints in Glory everlasting', found on Stillington War Memorial, and 'When you go home, tell them of US and say – for your tomorrows, WE GAVE OUR TODAY' on the renovated memorial at Wheatley Hill.

Example of personal inscriptions on CWGC headstones: Joseph Logan, 'Peace Perfect Peace'. (*Gaynor Greenwood*)

Example of personal inscriptions on CWGC headstones: Matthew Craggs, 'Ever remembered by his loving wife and children'. (*Gaynor Greenwood*)

Example of personal inscriptions on CWGC headstones: William Bonney, 'Steadfast in life, valiant in death'. (*Gaynor Greenwood*)

Example of personal inscriptions on CWGC headstones: Charles Hargreaves, 'Far to sight, near to heart'. (*Jon Miller*)

Men from 11th DLI are not recorded anywhere on a single memorial to the battalion. There are two memorials to the 20th Light Division, one at Langemarck and one at Guillemont, but these have little personal significance. Apart from those who have a grave-marker in Europe or in their home towns when they died in the UK, most share a memorial. Many are listed in France and Flanders on various memorials to the missing from significant battles and campaigns. Most are represented on memorials constructed locally.

My own grandfather's name can be found recorded on the walls of a chapel of remembrance at the Memorial Hospital in Darlington. In a town noted for its Quaker heritage, it is no surprise that the local powers settled on the construction of a hospital as the most suitable memorial, rather than some grandiose monument. Thomas Bashforth shares the memorial with several other 11th DLI men from Darlington, among them Lieutenant Banks. Bashforth's name also appears in his parish church (St John's at Bank Top), and Banks can be found recorded on wooden panels in the main assembly hall of the Queen Elizabeth Sixth Form College, formerly the Grammar School. His name is among all those from the school who served, and close by that of his officer colleague, Second Lieutenant

The interior of the hall at Darlington Memorial Hospital showing the wall plaques commemorating the names of the town's fallen. (*Martin Bashforth, courtesy of the hospital management*)

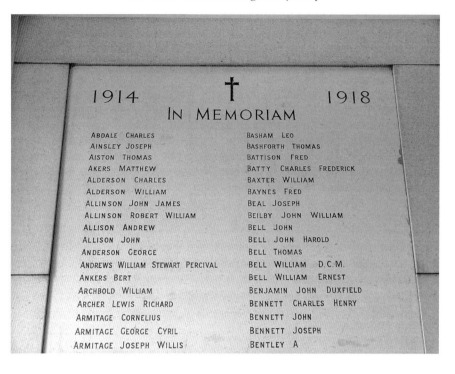

† 1914 IN MEMORIAM 1918

ABDALE CHARLES	BASHAM LEO
AINSLEY JOSEPH	BASHFORTH THOMAS
AISTON THOMAS	BATTISON FRED
AKERS MATTHEW	BATTY CHARLES FREDERICK
ALDERSON CHARLES	BAXTER WILLIAM
ALDERSON WILLIAM	BAYNES FRED
ALLINSON JOHN JAMES	BEAL JOSEPH
ALLINSON ROBERT WILLIAM	BEILBY JOHN WILLIAM
ALLISON ANDREW	BELL JOHN
ALLISON JOHN	BELL JOHN HAROLD
ANDERSON GEORGE	BELL THOMAS
ANDREWS WILLIAM STEWART PERCIVAL	BELL WILLIAM D.C.M.
ANKERS BERT	BELL WILLIAM ERNEST
ARCHBOLD WILLIAM	BENJAMIN JOHN DUXFIELD
ARCHER LEWIS RICHARD	BENNETT CHARLES HENRY
ARMITAGE CORNELIUS	BENNETT JOHN
ARMITAGE GEORGE CYRIL	BENNETT JOSEPH
ARMITAGE JOSEPH WILLIS	BENTLEY A

Above: A section of one of the plaques at Darlington Memorial Hospital showing the name of Thomas Bashforth. (*Martin Bashforth, courtesy of the hospital management*)

Left: Part of the left-hand panel of the Great War Roll of Honour for the pupils of Darlington Queen Elizabeth Grammar School, showing the names of former pupils Thomas Applegarth and William Banks of 11th DLI. (*Martin Bashforth, courtesy of the management of Queen Elizabeth Sixth Form College*)

Applegarth. As a pupil of the school in the early 1960s, I had no idea that I would one day find myself researching and writing about names on that memorial. As somewhat irreverent teenagers we would persuade the headmaster, Dr Hare, when he covered a teacher's absence, to explain the use of a periscope in the trenches, as he had served in the Great War himself and happily repeated this story as physics in action. As a rebellious sixth-former, I would wear a CND badge in the middle of the obligatory poppy for Armistice Day assembly. I have since found a better way to dissociate myself from what I regard as militaristic officialdom and now pay a more personal and heartfelt respect to my forebears.

Some individuals are to be found recorded but some are listed on small plaques inside the churches of tiny villages, such as that at High Coniscliffe where Private 32827 William Longstaff is listed. Others can be found on multiple official memorials in the same town, as in Barnard Castle, where church and chapel had their own memorials and the town had another more elaborate one in the grounds of what is now the Bowes Museum. Lance Corporal 17728 John William Hunt is recorded in the parish church as well as on the town memorial.

Memorials have sometimes had to be moved or renovated as a result of danger or neglect. At Wheatley Hill, a former pit village near Durham, the original memorial has been rescued and stands adjacent to the village hall in the town cemetery. The names, among them several from 11th DLI, have been re-inscribed on granite slabs next to the original memorial cross, along with names from the Second World War and the Korean War. The village hall itself has become the heritage centre for the locality and provides the focus for community remembrance. Local volunteers have published a book containing memories of the men from the area who served in the First World War, including several from 11th DLI.

The practice of remembrance has developed in recent years into an all-year-round pursuit, taken up by groups and individuals from all walks of life, many joined together by the common link of First World War ancestry – sometimes a survivor, more often one of those who lost his life. This book began when, in my fifties, my father suddenly presented me with a photograph of my grandfather, which I had never before seen, gruffly commenting that 'he was not my real father'. I was lucky enough to obtain copies of my grandfather's service papers. It was then a short step to finding out about the unit with which he served, drilling down from Gough's story of the Fifth Army, through a second-hand copy of the divisional history and a book on the DLI battalions, until I had some idea of where and when he had served. With an extract from the battalion war diary I could pinpoint where he died. One September afternoon, a year later, I stood at the side of a road near the village of Arvillers, looking

The renovated war memorial at Wheatley Hill, County Durham, includes several names from 11th DLI. (*Patricia Bashforth*)

out across the field where he had been killed. This book, composed many years later, forms my tribute of remembrance. In the process came a personal transformation, developed through a sense of loss and grief for the grandfather I never knew – my real grandfather. The antipathetic teenage schoolboy now knows much more about two of the names on the school war memorial and can better appreciate the personal consequences that lie behind them. While not altering my opinions of the state's role in both war and remembrance, I cannot watch the coffins returning from Iraq and Afghanistan through the village of Wooton Bassett without sharing feelings with the bereaved families involved. My family and I have borne the effects of the loss of my grandfather in many subtle ways over three generations and more. Yet I can keep my feelings for the soldiers and their families entirely separate from my opinions as to the politics of the wars in which they suffer. It is not the same for everyone, for grief touches us in many contradictory ways. In my case I had to confront my own sense

A group of four graves at Bouchoir British Cemetery, with John Kennedy of 11th DLI on the right. The author adopted the left-hand grave for an unidentified DLI soldier to represent his missing grandfather, Thomas Bashforth, killed nearby. (*Martin Bashforth*)

of loss for a grandfather I never knew, while exposing the loss felt by my father for the father he never knew. The research was therapy for both of us. The pain began to be put to rest when I adopted the grave of an unknown DLI soldier at Bouchoir Cemetery, 2 kilometres from Arvillers, leaving a bouquet of poppies and a message in the visitor's book. But even recalling that event causes the grief to surface again.

The great, great nephew of John Cummins similarly began his interest as a result of discussing a photograph with his grandfather. In 1993, he visited the battlefields out of general interest. Two years later the interest had become more focused and he visited Cummins' grave at Grove Town Cemetery. Now Sean Gregory is active in the Western Front Association as a speaker and organiser, and he continues his researches and makes sure that the fruits are made available to local libraries. He regularly goes to France and visits both Cummins' grave and that of Ivison, a comrade who died in the same incident. He explores the places with which his great, great uncle was associated. John George Cummins is never far from Sean's mind, as Thomas Bashforth remains in mine.

Sean's study of the war leads him to conclude that it was not a waste of young men's lives and that they did not die in vain. Despite the horrors, despite the mistakes, the war had to be fought to avoid the domination of Europe by German militarism. Sean has occasion to spend time with the families of soldiers serving in the Middle East, knows their suffering first hand and recognises the deep similarity that there is between families now and families in the Great War. Talking of these families, he says: 'I feel as proud of this community as I feel about the Great War community. Even though over ninety years separate them there is a bond.'[10]

Mike Lavelle, grandson of Hugh Lavelle, remains proud of his ancestor's acknowledged bravery, as well as the unassuming ordinariness of his subsequent life. Mike has travelled extensively around the Western Front, seeking out places associated with 11th DLI, and noting the gravestones and memorials bearing the names of its members. He hopes to keep alive these memories for subsequent Lavelle generations, so that the ordinary men are not forgotten.[11]

Gaynor Greenwood is related to Robert Bennett, whose letters form such a large part of the first half of this book. She is the granddaughter of Robert's younger brother David, often mentioned in the letters. She developed her interest in the Great War from talking to her maternal grandfather, a survivor from 18th DLI. She visited France in 1980 and traced Robert's name on the Thiepval Memorial. The idea that his grave had never been recovered after the war was deeply upsetting to David, who had imagined things differently. This sense of loss for the 'missing' still remains painful to families many decades on. Gaynor's access to the letters has occasioned a special connection to the human emotions arising from the war, encouraging her to travel widely across the Western Front (and in southern England) in search of the places from which they were written. Combining the letters with a sense of place has helped her develop an enormous empathy with her great-uncle. Her father went on to serve in the RAF in the Second World War, and survived. With two successive generations plunged into global warfare and the seemingly endless sequence of smaller wars since, she feels 'that there is something in human nature which is naturally territorial and also in some for a desire for power'.

What is true for all who take an interest in the First World War, and for whom this interest has a personal and family connection, is that we feel obliged to ask questions. Was the war justified? How has it affected our families? How has it affected other families? How should we remember both the war and those involved? How does it make us feel about wars today and in general? People were not of one mind in this regard in 1914, nor again in 1919, 1939, 1945, and not now. We are numerous individuals who have each found a personal way through conflicting ideas and emotions and may continue to change the way we think and feel. There is no 'one size fits all' pattern that can be crammed into some officially designated formula of remembrance and this was equally true in 1919. As 'descendants' of the First World War, we are now closer to the families of

Stillington War Memorial, 2009. (*Patricia Bashforth*)

A section of names on
Stillington War Memorial
includes John Cummins, 11th
DLI. (*Martin Bashforth*)

The reverse of the Stillington
War Memorial also
commemorates the survivors,
including Hugh Lavelle.
(*Martin Bashforth*)

G v R 1

HE whom this scroll commemorates was numbered among those who, at the call of King and Country, left all that was dear to them, endured hardness, faced danger, and finally passed out of the sight of men by the path of duty and self-sacrifice, giving up their own lives that others might live in freedom.
Let those who come after see to it that his name be not forgotten.

Serjt. Thomas Bashforth
Durham. L. I.

Memorial scrolls, like this one for Thomas Bashforth, were sent to bereaved families. (*Collection of David Bashforth*) that time than one would ever have thought possible. As Gaynor wrote: 'I just wish my Great-Grandmother (Robert's mother) knew that her son would be remembered by his descendants. And what would Robert have thought of his letters being of such great interest all these years later?'[12]

NOTES TO CHAPTER FOURTEEN

1 On 6 November 2010, six former soldiers wrote to the *Guardian* asserting that 'The Poppy Appeal is once again subverting Armistice Day'. They accused the annual launch of 'glitz' and specifically attacked the abuse of the word 'hero', stating: 'there is nothing heroic about fighting in an unnecessary conflict'.

2 Information from: http://www.bbc.co.uk/humber/content/articles/2007/11/09/street_shrine_feature.shtml, accessed 20 January 2009 and from: http://www.northstoneham.org.uk/warshrine/history/movement.html, accessed 20 January 2009.

3 *North Eastern Railway Magazine*, October 1914, p. 237.

4 National Railway Museum, poster collection, inventory number 2005-7681.

5 Website: http://county.durham.gov.uk/sites/dli/Pages/WelcomePage.aspx, accessed 9 June 2010.

6 I have explored the personal aspects of this in 'Absent Fathers, Present Histories', chapter 10 of *People and their Pasts*, ed. Hilda Kean and Paul Ashton (Palgrave, London, 2009).

7 Information from David Kelly, a descendant.

8 The National Archives, WO 363, papers of Charles Hargreaves.

9 The National Archives, WO 363, papers of Pte Robert Cain.

10 Email to the author, June 2010, with permission.

11 Email to the author, June 2010, with permission.

12 Email to the author, June 2010, with permission.

Bibliography

1. Original Documents from Private Sources

Appleby, Arthur: information supplied by William Appleby, Great War Forum.

Bashforth, Thomas: papers and photographs jointly supplied by the author and David Bashforth; oral memories from the late Thomas Bashforth and the late John Raymond Bashforth; family history research by the late Thomas Sidney Bashforth and by David Bashforth and the author.

Bennett, Robert David: Letters to his family 1914–16, by permission of Mr Kenneth Banks; transcripts and family history information from Gaynor Greenwood.

Bonney, Thomas: information, papers and photographs supplied by David Kelly.

Cummins, John: information, papers and photographs supplied by Sean Gregory.

Doyle, John: information regarding life and family history from Emma Laycock.

Fletcher, Noel William Scott: information about school background from Kate Wills, Great War Forum.

Lavelle, Hugh: information, papers and photographs supplied by Michael Lavelle.

Thew, Thomas: family information supplied by Moss Hardy.

Tombling, John William: information from Ed Matthews, Great War Forum.

2. Original Documents from
Durham County Records Office:

Banks, William: D/DLI/7/819/1–4; Field Message Book with notes from cadet training and embroidered postcards addressed to his daughter, Kathleen Banks.

Dunn, Thomas Henry: D/DLI/781/1; Letter to Family 4 November (no year).

Freeman, William Winters: D/DLI/7/231/1; In Memoriam – Order of Service, 23 December 1917, St Alban's church, Windy Nook.

Garrity, Peter: D/DLI/7/245/1 The Small Book of Peter Garrity; D/DLI/7/245/2 decorative discharge scroll.

Hayes, Geoffrey G.: D/DLI/7/309/1–4; papers and photograph relating to his war service.

McEvoy, Patrick: D/DLI/7/434/1–2; correspondence from War Office to Mrs E. M. McEvoy, 1919–22.

Rogers, William: D/DLI/950/1; Service Book.

Seymour, James: D/DLI/7/623/1; Field Service Postcard to Miss F. Seymour.

Stafford, George Brabazon: D/DLI/7/662/2; album of material relating to his war service, including periods at Penkridge Bank Camp, Rugeley, with 16th DLI.

Turner, Alfred: D/DLI/7/719/1–6; D/DLI/7/981/1–2; Correspondence and records relating to the war service of Alfred Turner.

Various School Log Books 1900–19 as referenced in the text.

3. Original Documents from
the Liddle Collection, University of Leeds

GS 0358: Papers of John Copeland (diary and transcript of tape recordings).

GS 1036: Papers of G. D. J. McMurtrie, 7th Somerset Light Infantry (typescript).

GS 1788: Papers of Ralph Worfolk.

4. Original Documents from
The National Archives

WO 95/415, Records of 34 Casualty Clearing Station (Third Army), Nov. 1915 – Jun. 1919.

WO 95/2094-2097, 20th Division, Headquarters and Services: General Staff, Jul. 1915 – Jan. 1919.

WO 95/ 2108, War Diaries: 11th Battalion Durham Light Infantry, Jul. 1915 – Jun. 1919, Divisional Signal Company, Jul. 1915 – Apr. 1919.

WO 95/2109, War Diaries, 60th, 61st and 62nd Field Ambulance Units, Jul. 1915 – Apr. 1919.

WO 95/ 2111–2127, War Diaries, 59th, 60th and 61st Brigade HQ and constituent infantry battalions, 1915–19.

WO 97/3364, Royal Hospital Chelsea, Soldiers Service Documents 1883–1900.

WO 161/100/427, Committee on the Treatment of British Prisoners of War, Interviews and Reports, Other Ranks.

WO 213/4–26, Registers of Field General Courts Martial, May 1915 – Jan. 1919.

WO 329/1601–1631, Service Medals and Award Rolls, First World War, British War Medal and Victory Medal, Durham Light Infantry.

WO 329/2769–2792, Service Medals and Award Rolls, First World War, 1914–15 Star, Durham Light Infantry.

WO 339, Officers War Service Records (individual references as quoted).

WO 363, Army Service Records (individual references as quoted).

WO 364, Army Pension Records (individual references as quoted).

WO 372/3 Service Medal and Award Rolls Index, First World War.

5. Original Documents from The Imperial War Museum

11994 PP/MCR/69: Private Papers of I. V. B. Melhuish, 7th Somerset Light Infantry.

6. Contemporary Published Sources and Memoirs

Cox & Co. Ltd, *List of British Officers Taken Prisoner in the Various Theatres of War between August 1914 and November 1918* (London 1919, reprinted 1988).

Gough, General Sir Hubert, *The March Retreat* (Cassell & Co. Ltd., London, 1934).

Inglefield, Captain V. E., *The History of the Twentieth (Light) Division,* (Nisbet & Co. Ltd., London, 1921).

Miles, Captain Wilfred, *The Durham Forces in the Field 1914-1918 (Vol II The Service Battalions of the Durham Light Infantry)* (Cassell & Co. Ltd, London, 1920).

North Eastern Railway Magazine 1914–19 (copies at National Railway Museum).

Northern Echo, 1914–19 (microfilm copies at Darlington Local Studies Library).

7. Modern Publications: Books

Ashplant, T. G., Dawson, G. and Roper, M. (editors): *The Politics of War Memory and Commemoration* (Routledge, London and New York, 2000).

Audion-Rouzeau, S. and Becker, A., *1914–1918: Understanding the Great War* (Profile Books, London, 2002).

August, A., *The British Working Class 1832–1940* (Pearson Longman, Harlow, 2007).

Austin, J. and Ford, M., *Steel Town: Dronfield and Wilson Cammell 1873–1883* (Private, Sheffield 1983).

Barton, P., Doyle, P. and Vandewalle, J., *Beneath Flanders Fields: The Tunnellers' War 1914–1918* (Spellmount, Staplehurst, 2004).

Beckett, I. F. W., *Home Front 1914–1918: How Britain Survived the Great War* (The National Archives, Richmond, 2006).

Berg, A., *War Memorials from Antiquity to the Present* (Leo Cooper, London, 1991).

Bet-El, I. R., *Conscripts: Forgotten Men of the Great War* (Sutton Publishing, Stroud, 2003).

Beynon, H. and Austin, T., *Masters and Servants: Class and Patronage in the Making of Labour Organizations* (Rivers Oram Press, London, 1994).

Bilton, D., *The Home Front in the Great War: Aspects of the Conflict 1914–1918* (Leo Cooper, Barnsley, 2003).

Blacker, C. P. (ed. Blacker, J.), *Have You Forgotten Yet? The First World War memoirs of C. P. Blacker, MC, GM* (Leo Cooper, Barnsley, 2000).

Bourke, J., *Dismembering the Male: Men's Bodies, Britain and the Great War* (Reaktion Books Ltd, London, 1999).

Brown, M., *The Imperial War Museum Book of the Somme* (Pan Books, London, in association with the Imperial War Museum, 2002).

Brown, M., *Tommy Goes to War* (Tempus Publishing Ltd, Stroud, 1999.)

Cecil, H. and Liddle, P. (eds), *Facing Armageddon: The First World War Experience* (Leo Cooper, Barnsley, 2003).

Chaplin, S., *Durham Mining Villages* (Working Papers in Sociology No. 3, University of Durham, 1971).

Cooper, B., *The Ironclads of Cambrai: The First Great Tank Battle* (Cassell, London, 1967).

Corns, C. and Hughes-Wilson, J., *Blindfold and Alone: British Military Executions in the Great War* (Cassell, London, 2002).

Fussell, P., *The Great War and Modern Memory* (Oxford University Press, Oxford and New York, 1975).

Gliddon, G., *Somme 1916: A Battlefield Companion* (Sutton Publishing Ltd, Stroud, 2006).

Gregory, A., *The Silence of Memory: Armistice Day 1919–1946* (Berg, Oxford, 1994).

Gregory, A., *The Last Great War: British Society and the First World War* (Cambridge University Press, Cambridge, 2008).

Grodnitzky, B., *The Great Mining Family on the March: An Analytical Study of the Durham Miner's Gala* (University of York, 2005, unpublished thesis).

Hall, A. D., *A Pilgrimage of British Farming 1910–1912* (John Murray, London, 1913).

Harris, J., *Private Lives, Public Spirit: Britain 1870–1914* (Penguin Books, Harmondsworth, 1993).

Heathorn, S., *For Home, Country, and Race: Constructing Gender, Class and Englishness in the Elementary School 1880–1914* (University of Toronto Press, Toronto, Buffalo and London, 2000).

Hodgkins, K. and Radstone, S. (eds), *Contested Pasts: The Politics of Memory*, (Routledge, London and New York, 2003), chapter 3, Carr, G., 'War, History and the Education of Canadian Memory'.

Holmes, R., *Tommy: the British Soldier on the Western Front 1914–1918* (HarperCollins, London, 2004).

Horsfall, J. and Cave, N., *Battleground Europe: Cambrai: The Right Hook* (Leo Cooper, Barnsley, 1999).

King, A., *Memorials of the Great War in Britain: The Symbolism and Politics of Remembrance* (Berg, Oxford and New York, 1998).

Kuhn, A. and McAllister, K. E. (eds): *Locating Memory: Photographic Acts* (Berghahn Books, New York and Oxford, 2006): Briggs, M. A., chapter 5: 'The Return of the Aura: Contemporary Writers Look Back at the First World War Photograph'.

Lloyd, D., *Battlefield Tourism: Pilgrimage and the Commemoration of the Great War in Britain, Australia and Canada 1919–1939* (Berg, Oxford and New York, 1998).

MacDonald, L., *1914: The Days of Hope* (Penguin, London, 1989).

MacDonald, L., *1915: The Death of Innocence* (Penguin Books, London, 1997).

MacDonald, L., *Somme* (Michael Joseph, London, 1983).

MacDonald, L., *They Called It Passchendaele* (Michael Joseph, London, 1978).

MacDonald, L., *To the Last Man: Spring 1918* (Viking, London, 1998).

McPhail, H. and Guest, P., *Battleground Europe: St Quentin 1914–1918* (Leo Cooper, Barnsley, 2000).

Messenger, C., *Call to Arms: The British Army 1914–18* (Weidenfeld and Nicholson, London, 2005).

Middlebrook, M., *The Kaiser's Battle: 21 March 1918 – The First Day of the German Spring Offensive* (Penguin, London, 1983).

Middlebrook, M., *Your Country Needs You: From Six to Sixty-Five Divisions* (Leo Cooper, Barnsley 2000).

Mitchinson, K., *The Pioneer Battalions: Organized and Intelligent Labour* (Leo Cooper, London, 1997).

Moorhouse, B., *Forged by Fire: The Battle Tactics and Soldiers of a World War One Battalion, The 7th Somerset Light Infantry* (Spellmount, Staplehurst, 2003).

Patch, H. and Van Emden, R., *The Last Fighting Tommy: The Life of Harry Patch,* the only surviving veteran of the trenches (Bloomsbury, London, 2007).

Prior, R. and Wilson, T., *Passchendaele: The Untold Story* (Yale Nota Bene, New Haven and London, 2002).

Putkowski, J. and Sykes, J., *Shot at Dawn* (Leo Cooper, London, 1989).

Roper, M., *The Secret Battle: Emotional Survival in the Great War* (Manchester University Press, Manchester and New York, 2009).

Samuel, R., *Theatres of Memory Volume 1: Past and Present in Contemporary Culture* (Verso, London and New York, 1994).

Samuel, R., *Theatres of Memory Volume 2: Island Stories: Unravelling Britain* (Verso, London, 1998).

Stedman, M., *Battleground Europe: Guillemont* (Leo Cooper, Barnsley, 1998).

Steel, N. and Hart P., *Passchendaele: The Sacrificial Ground* (Cassell & Co., London, 2000).

Thompson, P., *The Edwardians: The Remaking of British Society* (Routledge, London and New York, 1992, 2nd edition).

Todman, D., *The Great War: Myth and Memory* (Hambledon and London, London and New York, 2005).

Van Emden, R., *Prisoners of the Kaiser: The Last PoWs of the Great War* (Leo Cooper, Barnsley, 2000).

Ward, S. G. P., *Faithful: the History of the Durham Light Infantry* (Nelson & Sons Ltd., London, 1962).

Westlake, R., *Kitchener's Army* (Spellmount, Staplehurst, 2003).

Winter, D., *Death's Men: Soldiers of the Great War* (Penguin, London, 1979).

Winter, J., *Sites of Memory, Sites of Mourning: The Great War in European Cultural History* (Cambridge University Press, Cambridge, 1998, Canto edition).

8. Modern Publications:
Journal Articles

The Ephemerist, Journal of the Ephemera Society, No. 129, Summer, 2005: Batten, S., 'World war headstone ephemera'.

Journal of British Studies: April 2005; 44, 2: Roper, M. 'Between Manliness and Masculinity: The "War Generation" and the Psychology of Fear in Britain, 1914–1950.'

Midland History, Vol. 24 (Birmingham 1999): John Hartigan, 'Volunteering in the First World War: the Birmingham Experience, August 1914 – May 1915'.

9. Websites
and Online Sources

Ancestry, http://www.ancestry.co.uk, accessed frequently for British Army World War One Medal Rolls; British Army World War One Pension Records 1914–20; British Army World War One Service Records, 1914–20; U. K. Soldiers Died in the Great War, 1914–19.

Commonwealth War Graves Commission: Debt of Honour Register, http://www.cwgc.org/debt_of_honour accessed frequently for reference, and a printed abstract of 11th Durham Light Infantry casualties.

Commonwealth War Graves Commission: *A History of the Commonwealth War Graves Commission* (London, undated).

Journal of the Centre for First World War Studies: Batten, S., 'Forgetting the First World War' (Birmingham, undated).

The Long, Long Trail: http://www.1914-1918.net/, accessed periodically for background information. Also through the same site, The Great War Forum, to contact other researchers.

The North East War Memorials Project: http://www.newmp.org.uk/ for information on local war memorials.

Public History Review No. 15 (Sydney, 2008): 47–59, Scates, B., 'Memorialising Gallipoli: Manufacturing Memory at Anzac.'

Public History Review No. 15 (Sydney, 2008): 135–52, Murray, L., 'Comparing Criteria: Assessing the Significance of Memorials.'

The Restoration of Stoneham War Shrine, http://www.northstoneham.org.uk/warshrine/history/movement.html, accessed 20 January 2009.

Roll of Honour, 11th DLI

The following names, listed in alphabetical order regardless of rank, represent those who served in the battalion for whom information has been found. The majority lost their lives, but the list also includes several survivors and a few names of those, attributed to 11th DLI by the Commonwealth War Graves Commission, but who served with other units when they died. Page references are in brackets.

Acomb, John. Private 21491, killed in action, aged 23, 10 November 1915. (78, 79, 84 n10, 229)

Adams, Second Lieutenant, transferred to RFC. (124)

Ainley, Allen. Private 81885, killed in action, 18 August 1918, aged 19.

Ainsworth, Second Lieutenant, joined 18 April 1918. (202 n1)

Alexander, W. T. Second Lieutenant A Company, captured. (160, 162, 181)

Allan, Paul. Private 26404, killed in action, 26 October 1916.

Amour, William. Private 17554, died of wounds, 28 March 1918. (177)

Anderson, Victor. Private 43746, died of wounds, 29 March 1918, aged 20. (178)

Angel, John William. Private 14945, missing in action, 24 March 1918. (167)

Appleby, Arthur. Sergeant 17176, a regular soldier attached to 11th DLI in 1914, was later wounded and, after treatment and recovery, transferred to the Royal Engineers, 252528. He served as a lieutenant in the Home Guard in Darlington in the Second World War. (243)

Applegarth, Thomas William. Second Lieutenant, died of wounds, 8 April 1918, aged 24.

Arkless, Peter. Private 16249, survived the war. On 31 March 1917 he was driving a lorry that overturned at Le Transloy. Arkless was judged to be blameless, but the injury may have resulted in him being returned to England. (see index)

Armstrong, Thomas. Corporal 24139, gave evidence in the Arkless enquiry 1917.

Arnott, Frederick. Second Lieutenant, missing in action, 29 March 1918, aged 22. (171 n7, 178, 181, 188)

Arthurs, George Frederick. Private 74990, mason's labourer from Swansea, missing in action, 23 March 1918. (164, 183)

Atkinson, Frederick William. Private 376385, from Leeds, missing in action, 27 March 1918. (176)

Atkinson, John. Private 12204, railwayman from South Shields, killed in action, 2 August 1916. (108)

Atley, F., Lieutenant, at Langemarck and Cambrai. (140, 143)

Atley, T. A., Second Lieutenant, gassed. (191)

Austin, Ernest. Private 74971, foreman maltster from Taunton, died of wounds as a prisoner of war, Langensalza, 8 May 1918.

Bailey, James. Private 16616, labourer from Gateshead, died of wounds, 13 January 1917.

Bainbridge, Harold. Private 22659, farm labourer from Hornby, Great Smeaton, missing in action, 30 November 1917.

Bainbridge, Jonathan. Private 15348, miner aged 24, from Bishop Auckland, missing in action, 23 March 1918. (164, 183)

Baker, John Thomas. Corporal 25771, from Felling, killed in action, 23 February 1916.

Banks, William. Second Lieutenant, died of wounds while a prisoner of war, 6 April 1918. (see index)

Barker, Bertie. Private 16622, platelayer aged 25, from Chester-le-Street, died of wounds, 24 December 1916.

Barker, Harry. Private 23295, miner aged 30, from Bill Quay, killed in action, 5 October 1916.

Barker, William. Private 33026, quarryman from Tow Law, killed in action, 5 October 1916. (126)

Barnard, Joseph. Private 78790, missing in action, 29 March 1918. (178)

Barraclough, Austin. Private 22063, springsmith's striker aged 20, from Kimberworth, died of wounds, 15 September 1917. (228, 230)

Barrasford, Robert. Private 18/443, miner from Durham, originally with 18th DLI in Egypt, killed in action, 30 November 1917. (151–2)

Barron, Robert Wharton. Private 16224, miner aged 28, from Durham, died of wounds, 11 April 1916. (230)

Barrow, Rowland Charles. Private 53552, born Wolverhampton, works manager, enlisted Barnet, aged 42, missing in action, 30 November 1917. (152–3)

Headstone of Austin Barraclough at Dozinghem Military Cemetery.
(*Gaynor Greenwood*)

Headstone of Robert Barron at Gouzeaucourt New British Cemetery.
(*Gaynor Greenwood*)

Bashforth, Thomas. Sergeant 14956, aged 29, plasterer from Darlington, missing in action, 27 March 1918. (see index)

Bates, Francis Reay. Private 18854, miner aged 26, from Pelton, died of cardiac failure, 23 April 1920, buried Pelton Cemetery. (214)

Batty, Joseph. Private 13392, miner from East Stanley, enlisted 27 August 1914, with 16th DLI, to 11th DLI 3 August 1915, taken prisoner 21 March 1918, repatriated December 1918, demobilised 6 April 1919. Survived the war.

Beever, George Harold. Private 90934, aged 19, drill grinder from Grenoside, Sheffield, died from pleurisy aggravated by TB, 22 June 1918.

Beilby (Beilry), George Sidney. Private 375150, aged 35, from Hull, killed in action, 22 March 1918. (162)

Bell, Arthur Wesley. Private 9911, miner from Horden Colliery, missing in action, 23 March 1918. (164, 183)

Bennett, Robert David. Private 17203, miner aged 22, from Shotton Colliery, killed in action, 20 September 1916. (see index)

Berry, George. Private 25252, from Stanley, missing in action, 21 March 1918. (160)

Biglin, Joseph Edward. Private 85086, railway clerk from Hull, conscripted 1917, joined 11th DLI April 1918 until end of war and transferred to 20th DLI in Germany until 1919. (IWM, Oral History 11342)

Blackburn, George. Private 25721, aged 26, from Newcastle-upon-Tyne, killed in action, 5 September 1916.

Blakeway, Frank. Private 24121, from Manchester, died, 23 February 1919. One of several brothers who died in war service. (208)

Bond, Richard Nicholson. Private 32862, aged 27, fish curer from South Shields, died of wounds, 5 October 1916. (126–7)

Bonner, Edward. Private 18093, from Dunston, killed in action, 23 October 1915.

Bonney, Thomas. Sergeant 18688, miner aged 22, from Ouston, near Birtley, killed in action 31 March 1918. (see index)

Bonney, William. Lance Corporal 24145, aged 25, from Birtley, killed in action 20 September 1917. Brother of Thomas Bonney. (230–1)

Boulton, R. M., Lt-Col., CO 11th DLI 17 April 1918 – 13 August 1918. (189, 192)

Bousfield, William. Company Sergeant Major 25203, court-martialled 1915 for being drunk on duty, stripped of rank but later served with the Labour Corps. Survived the war. (78)

Bowlt, James Alexander. Private 17199, aged 33, dock labourer from West Hartlepool, died after sleep-walking out of an upstairs window, 4 August 1915. (65, 67, 84 n4, 227)

Bowlt, Thomas Short. Private 14970, died on 1 May 1918 while prisoner of war. Although originally assigned to 11th DLI, he transferred to 14th DLI on 31 December 1917 and then 22nd DLI.

Boyne, James A. Corporal 21508, mentioned in despatches LG on 25 May 1917. (125)

Boynton, Francis Robert. Private 231358, cowman from Murton, North Yorkshire, missing in action, 25 March 1918. (169)

Bradley, Frederick Charles. Private 76898, bricklayer aged 32, from Lyminge, Kent, died of wounds, 30 November 1917. (153)

Brady, John (alias – see Farrell).

Brent, T. Private 71015, stretcher bearer, witness to death of Lt Banks. (185)

Briddick, James. Private 2526, attributed incorrectly to 11th DLI by CWGC. Died 26 April 1915 with 5th DLI at Ypres. (61, n115)

Briscoe, James Henry. Acting Lance Corporal 25209, aged 32, from West Hartlepool, died of wounds, 6 November 1915.

Broughton, James. Private 12199, bricklayer's labourer from Middlesbrough, killed in action, 7 October 1916.

Browes, Horace. Private 25254, aged 23, from Meersbrook, died of wounds, 4 December 1917.

Brown, Francis. Private 14966, boiler fireman aged 23, from Darlington, died of wounds, 4 September 1916. (108)

Brown, George. Private 14964, miner aged 24, from Castle Eden Colliery, died of wounds, 25 March 1918. (123–4, 130 n9, 169)

Brown, George. Sergeant 3/11449, miner and former soldier from Birtley, aged 41, joined 11 September 1914 and served as sergeant bugler until 18 October 1915, suffering from shell shock. Served with 16th DLI in UK until discharged 12 May 1916, due to his condition.

Brown, James. Lance Corporal 15313, miner aged 26, from Brandon Colliery, missing in action, 27 March 1918. (37, 176)

Brown, Joseph. Private 17222, enlisted West Hartlepool 30 August 1914, married to Mary Edith (née Smith) of Durham. Joined Battalion on 25 August 1915. Survived the war. (111)

Brown, Joseph. Private 18420, miner aged 24, from Houghton-le-Spring, killed in action, 18 September 1916. (110)

Brydon, Ernest. Private 13952, miner from Stanley, missing in action, 26 March 1918. (171, 227)

Buckle, Charles. Private 25775, from Consett, killed in action, 16 August 1917. (139)

Busby, Arthur. Private 17492, miner from South Moor, Stanley, missing in action, 28 March 1918. (177)

Bushell, Raymond. Lieutenant, served as private soldier with 21st Royal Fusiliers, commissioned 11th DLI on 19 September 1916, B Company.

Wounded and captured at Mézières, 29 March 1918, repatriated 19 December 1918, demobilised 12 February 1919. An engineer, he took over his father's agricultural machinery firm in York. (see index)

Cain, George. Second Lieutenant, joined 18 April 1918, gassed. (191, 202, n1)

Cain, Robert. Private 12531, labourer from Monkwearmouth, killed in action, 30 November 1917. Witness at the Bowlt Enquiry 4 August 1915. (151–2, 228)

Cameron, Alexander. Private 31157, aged 35, originally from Appleton Wiske, but enlisted Stanley. Reported missing 21 March 1918, taken prisoner and died 9 December 1918 at Toul.

Carlisle, T. H. Lt-Col., DSO, MC, CO 11th DLI from 14 August 1918 until demobilisation 1919. (194)

Carr, John. Private 24736, from Houghton-le-Spring, killed in action, 10 March 1917. (122)

Carthy, James (alias see Connfey).

Chadwick, Arthur Dyson. Private 36533, aged 33, from Rochdale, died of wounds 21 February 1918. Originally 11th DLI, died serving with 18th DLI.

Chapman, William Robert, Second Lieutenant. Methodist theology student from Easington. Served with RAMC until commissioned with 11th DLI in 1917. Wounded at Ypres. Later served with 15th DLI and wounded again in 1918.

Charnley, W. H., Second Lieutenant, joined 18 April 1918. (202 n1)

Chipchase, Christopher John. Private 20/411, architect and surveyor aged 19 from Darlington, killed in action, 21 December 1916.

Clark, Robert William. Private 85115, crane driver with North Eastern Railway Company, aged 19, from Hull, died at Netley Hospital from gas shell burns, 14 July 1918.

Clasper, Henry Andrew. Sergeant 11498, fireman aged 30, from Gateshead, died of wounds 27 August 1916. (98)

R. W. Clark,
Hull Docks.

Portrait of Robert Clark from the *North Eastern Railway* Magazine, 1918. (*Courtesy of British Rail Board* (*Residuary*) *Ltd*)

Clough, Ernest Rowan Butler. Second Lieutenant, aged 22, from Bristol, died of wounds 27 June 1916. (21, 90–1)

Clover, Ernest. Private 375902, from Sheffield, missing in action, 22 March 1918. (162)

Coates, Alexander. Private 21944, miner from Crook, died of wounds, 10 November 1915. (78, 82, 84 n10)

Cole, James Sidney. Private 76788, plumber from Gateshead, died of wounds, 1 December 1917. (153)

Collingwood, Alfred William. Private 376457, aged 22, from Darlington, missing in action 24 March 1918. (167)

Collingwood, Harold Edwin. Private 85108, aged 19, from the Cycle Shop, Nafferton, died at Ripon from bronchial pneumonia aggravated by gas, 19 October 1918, buried Nafferton All Saints New Churchyard.

Collins, A. E. Major, later Lt-Col., CO 11th DLI 16 October 1915 – 15 December 1916. (57, 76, 116)

Collins, Edward. Private 12934, miner and former soldier aged 46, born Barnsley, from Newcastle-upon-Tyne, died of wounds, 5 April 1918. (30 n8)

Conacher, R. Second Lieutenant, gassed. (191)

Connelly, George Arnold. Private 53556, labourer aged 31, from Leyton, killed in action, 25 May 1917.

Connfey, James (served as James Carthy). Private 25211, aged 38, from Sunderland, died of wounds, 13 February 1917. (122, 129 n8)

Connolly, Patrick. Private 16202, labourer, born Kilkenny, from Newcastle-upon-Tyne, died of wounds, 5 September 1916. (56, 109, 110, 112)

Cook, George Nesbit. Private 11904, from Newcastle-upon-Tyne, killed in action, 23 March 1918. (165)

Cook, J. T. Lance Corporal 23506, aged 25, from South Shields, died at home post-war, 6 January 1919, buried Harton Cemetery, South Shields.

Cook, William. Private 24787, from Willington, died of wounds, 25 July 1918.

Cooke, Douglas Edgar. Lieutenant, Adjutant, March 1918, awarded MC. (160, 166–7, 197)

Cooper, Myles. Second Lieutenant, born 28 February 1895, son of Canon Cooper of Durham, former pupil of Durham School. Discharged 19 February 1919. (160–1, 163-5, 167–8, 171, 189)

Copeland, John. Private 20849, timber merchant from Seaham, served with 20th DLI in France and Italy, later with 14th DLI before joining 11th DLI 4 February 1918 until discharge.

Cornish, John James. Private 16233, miner aged 32, from Brandon Colliery, died of wounds, 11 September 1916. (38 n18)

Coulter, James. Private 25820, from Wingate, killed in action, 18 September 1916.

Cowell, Gawin. Lance Corporal 18830, miner from Birtley, killed in action, 13 October 1915.

Cox, Regimental Sergeant Major, to England, February 1917. (122)

Coxon, Matthew. Private 34999, farm labourer from Tyne Dock, died at home, 19 August 1916, buried Harton Cemetery, South Shields. Although listed by the Commonwealth War Graves Commission as 11th DLI, he served in 25th (Works) Battalion DLI and then the Army Service Corps. He was killed in an accident at Brigg in Lincolnshire.

Craggs, Jonas May. Sergeant 25905, from Escomb near Bishop Auckland, killed in action, 29 March 1918. Brother of Thomas Johnson Craggs. (178)

Craggs, Matthew. Private 21340, aged 31, from Wheatley Hill, died of wounds, 30 October 1917.

Craggs, Thomas Johnson. Sergeant Major 3/10383, from Bishop Auckland, awarded Médaille d'Honneur, London Gazette 14 July 1919 and DCM. Survived the war and died 1941. Brother of Jonas May Craggs. (162, 183)

Craig, Walter George. Second Lieutenant, aged 27, from Gateshead, died of influenza at Grandenz PoW Camp, 5 November 1918. (160, 162, 171 n8, 181)

Crofts, Frank. Private 71051, labourer aged 20, from Holmesfield, near Chesterfield, missing in action, 23 March 1918. (164, 183)

Cummings, James. Private 25716, aged 27, born Sheffield, from Durham, died of wounds, 20 February 1916.

Cummins, John George. Private 16984, coke worker aged 27, from Stillington, died of wounds, 21 September 1916. (see index)

Cunliffe, Henry. Private 91068, aged 19, joiner from Otley, accidentally shot, died of wounds, 6 June 1918. (192–3, 230)

Cunningham, W. F. Lieutenant, assisted in the Bowlt Enquiry, 4 August 1915. Survived the war. (58, 65, 97)

Curd, Henry Arthur. Private 24123, from Notting Hill, London, missing in action, 23 March 1918. (164)

Davies, Stephen. Private 20879, rolling mills labourer, born Bilston, from Stockton-on-Tees, killed in action, 4 September 1916. (109–10)

Davison, David. Sergeant 21999, miner from Wardley Colliery, killed in action, 13 December 1916.

Davison, G. M., Brevet-Colonel, CO 11th DLI, August 1914 – 15 October 1915. (40, 57)

Davison, Joseph William. Private 16046, miner from Willington, killed in action, 5 October 1916. (127)

Dawson, Arthur William. Captain, schoolteacher from Jarrow, born 1873. Served as Adjutant. Demobilised 20 January 1919 with the rank of Major.

Dawson, John, Sergeant 13308, mentioned in despatches LG 25 May 1917, later Second Lieutenant with 9th DLI, dies 22 July 1918 age 25. From Washington, Co. Durham. Buried Sezanne Communal Cemetery. (124, 125)

Dawson, Thomas Edward. Private 22525, miner aged 28, from Boldon Colliery, died of infleunza, Sunderland War Hospital, 20 November 1918. (214)

Dennis, George Stanley. Lieutenant, died of influenza, 1 July 1919, serving with Intelligence Corps in Army of Occupation. (120–1, 210)

Devey, John Henry Charles. Second Lieutenant, leave 1917. (121)

Dobson, John George. Lance Corporal 16268, miner from South Moor, Stanley, died of wounds, 23 March 1916. (37)

Dobson, Tom. Private 18/1518, aged 27, from Sunderland, missing in action, 23 March 1918. (164)

Dodd(s), Samuel. Private 91083, accidentally shot Henry Cunliffe, 6 June 1918. Survived the war, transferring to 52nd Battalion as 66809. (192)

Dodds, J. H., Second Lieutenant, wounded March 1918. (166, 171 n7, 181)

Dodson, J. S., Second Lieutenant, joined 18 April 1918 (202 n1)

Donkin, Nathan. Private 20757, labourer and former soldier from Sunderland, killed in action, 16 August 1917. (136–9)

Donoghue, Frank. Private 39099, from Southwick, missing in action, 22 March 1918. (162)

Douglas, Second Lieutenant, officer at embarkation 1915. (58, 71)

Douglass, William. Private 15536, from Southwick, missing in action, 24 March 1918. (167)

Dowding, William. Sergeant 11659, miner from Chopwell, former regular, enlisted 7 September 1914, to 11th DLI, Military Medal 1916, wounded March 1918. Survived the war, discharged 1920 and applied for pension. (208–9)

Doyle, John. Sergeant 16996, former railway works labourer, taken prisoner 23 March 1918. Died in 1922 of illness aggravated by the effects of the war. (9, 215, 217 n18)

Duckett, Vincent George. Second Lieutenant, aged 22, bank clerk from Preston, missing in action, 23 March 1918. (156, 163, 165, 181, 184, 188)

Duffy, William. Private 25232, from Heworth, killed in action, 10 November 1915. (78–9, 84 n10)

Dunn, Thomas Henry. Private 36618, miner aged 24, from Evenwood, died of wounds to thigh, 26 December 1916. (117, 119, 129)

Headstone of John George Dobson at Lijssenthoek Military Cemetery.
(*Gaynor Greenwood*)

Ellis, James Henry. Private 45832, signal fitter from Bardney, Lincolnshire, died of wounds, 7 October 1916. Originally served with York and Lancaster Regiment. (127)

Ellison, John Thomas. CSM 11914, postman from Hetton-le-Hole, former regular, enlisted 11 August 1914, served with 10th DLI until transferred to 11th DLI 6 April 1918. Became Acting Quartermaster-Sergeant. Demobilised 16 July 1919. (209)

Ellwood, Dan Edmunson. Lieutenant, timber agent from Hartlepool, enlisted 18th DLI 5 October 1914, sent for commission 22 December 1916. Commissioned 7 February 1917, joined 11th DLI 9 September 1917. Wounded and taken prisoner at Mézières 29 March 1918, repatriated 18 December 1918. Remained in service until 1 November 1919. Survived the war. (144, 160, 166, 178–9, 181, 207–8)

Elsy, George Henry. Private 31767, coachman aged 39, from South Shields, died at home of influenza, 14 March 1919. (214)

Endean, William John. Born St Austell, Cornwall, 1888; worked as an accountant in mining in South Africa; enlisted there 1915. Commissioned Cambridge 21 March 1917 and sent to 14th DLI. Transferred to 11th DLI February 1918. Wounded 31 March 1918, but recovered and served with 52nd DLI in the Army of Occupation until 13 July 1919. Awarded the Military Cross. (see index)

English, E. W. Second Lieutenant, wounded March 1918. (160–1, 164, 181)

Evans, Thomas Guy. Private 77640, aged 19, shoe maker from Leicester, died of wounds in German hospital at Beaufort, 30 March 1918. (180)

Fallas, John Geoffrey. Private 81923, aged 19, grocer's assistant from Barnsley, died of wounds, 19 September 1918.

Farn, Mark. Private 15002, miner aged 28, from Shotton Colliery, missing in action, 23 March 1918. (165, 183, 228)

Farrell, John (served as John Brady). Private 21547, aged 22, from Broxburn, Renfrew, died of wounds, 13 March 1916. (56, 93–4, 227)

Fenton, Thomas. Private 17000, miner aged 41, from Fencehouses, missing in action, 24 March 1918. (167)

Ferguson, John. Private 81764, aged 18, from Backworth, Northumberland, died of wounds, 9 July 1918.

Ferry, Stephen Oliver. Private 22591, aged 32, from Sunderland, killed in action, 16 March 1916. (94, 219, 230)

Fieldhouse, John William. Private 75623, aged 19, from Bradford, missing in action, 24 March 1918. (167)

Fillingham, J., Second Lieutenant, later Captain and transferred out of 11th DLI. (82, 103, 120)

Findlater, Arthur Ernest. Private 81045, aged 19, carpenter's apprentice from Walsall, died from gas, 21 July 1918.

Firth, T. T., Second Lieutenant, joined 18 April 1918. (202 n1)

Fleming, Second Lieutenant, wounded. (140)

Fletcher, Noel William Scott. Second Lieutenant, aged 19, from Ipswich, died of wounds, 7 March 1917. (122, 126, 1280

Floyd, A., Lieutenant, took statements from witnesses for the Cunliffe Enquiry, 6 June 1918. Survived the war. (58, 71, 97, 189, 192)

Fortune, Wilfred. Private 13524, from Croxdale, enlisted 11 September 1914, to France 11 September 1915, wounded in left knee, 26 March 1918. Demobilised 8 January 1919. (209)

Fox, Henry George. Private 18/1739, aged 20, from Sherburn Hill, missing in action, 26 March 1918. (171)

Fox, Jim. Private, conscripted 1917, joined 11th DLI April 1918 and served intermittently with C Company. (IWM Oral History 9546)

Freeman, William Winters. Second Lieutenant, aged 27, from Gateshead, killed in action, 30 November 1917. (148–50)

Gaine, Lieutenant, officer at embarkation 1915. (58, 71)

Galley, Ralph Rowlands. Second Lieutenant, aged 27, from Monkwearmouth, killed in action, 22 March 1918. (160, 162, 165, 171 n8, 181, 184)

Garrity, Peter. Private 14931, from County Mayo, platelayer's labourer in Jarrow, enlisted 12 August 1914. Wounded and disabled, discharged 29 June 1918.

Gedney, George Highslip. Lance Corporal 53298, aged 24, from Hull, died at Cottingham Hospital of TB, 3 July 1919, buried Hull Western Cemetery. (214)

Gibson, Alfred. Private 17503, from South Moor, Stanley, died 16 April 1918. (93)

Gibson, N. F. Second Lieutenant, wounded March 1918. (163, 181)

Given, J., Private, wounded, 12 September 1915. (73)

Gowans, George Alexander. Private 16257, aged 28, from Gateshead and Paisley, killed in action, 12 November 1915.

Graham, John. Private 14851, aged 23, from Dunnington, killed in action, 15 April 1917.

Grant, Cameron. Private 53226, aged 41 from Liverpool and Leeds, died of wounds, 24 September 1917.

Gray, Ralph. Private 20993, miner aged 22, from Burnopfield, killed in action, 5 September 1916. (110)

Griffin, John. Sergeant 25199, aged 31, from South Bank, Middlesbrough, killed in action, 5 October 1916.

Grimshaw, Frederick. Private 18686, miner aged 28, from Birtley, killed in action, 13 December 1916.

Hall, Thomas. Private 14899, from Choppington, Northumberland, missing in action, 28 March 1918. (177)

Headstone of Cameron Grant at Dozinghem Military Cemetery.
(*Gaynor Greenwood*)

Hamilton, Lance Corporal, witness to death of Pte William Barker. (126)

Hamilton, William, Private 12762, court martial, awarded MSM. (78, Appendix 2)

Hammill, W., Sergeant V/346242, died at home 23 November 1918, buried Bishopwearmouth Cemetery, Sunderland.

Handisides, Bertie. Private 15027, brewer's labourer aged 29, from Stranton, West Hartlepool, killed in action, 27 March 1918. (176)

Hanfield, A. D. Second Lieutenant, joined 18 April 1918. (202 n1)

Hannah, Thomas. Private 17493, aged 39, from Carlisle, missing in action, 30 November 1917.

Harbron, E. R. Second Lieutenant, gassed. (191)

Hargreaves, Charles. Private 16228, labourer aged 32, from Durham, killed in action, 5 October 1916. (226, 230, 232)

Harker, Thomas. Private 12384, from Loftus, died of wounds, 16 January 1918.

Harkness, William Norman. Private 85167, aged 19, apprentice bricklayer from Blackhill, Consett, died of gas poisoning 1 June 1918.

Harland, Reuben. Private 18859, aged 24, labourer from Birtley, missing in action, 28 March 1918. (177)

Harrington, M. M. Second Lieutenant, joined 18 April 1918. (202 n1)

Harris, George W., Private (Corporal) 25648, from Castleford, killed in action, 31 August 1918.

Harrison, Bert. Corporal 53700, MSM 1918, DCM 1919. (181)

Harsburgh (Horsburgh), Robert. Private 15045, Croix de Guerre. (197)

Hatton, Alfred. Private 13486, from Gateshead, embarked 20 July 1915, killed in action, 15 September 1917.

Hayes, Geoffrey G. Regular officer with DLI in India. Captain and Adjutant 11th DLI from 18 September 1914, rose to Lieutenant-Colonel until sick leave April 1918. Mentioned in despatches twice and awarded Distinguished Service Order. Remained in service following the war until retirement 9 June 1934. Died from heart disease, Tywyn Nursing Home, 4 July 1976. (see index)

Henderson, John. Lance Corporal, miner and former soldier, from Gateshead and Dudley (Northumberland), died of wounds, 19 December 1915. (82–3)

Hennessey, Michael. Private 11591, D Company, witness at the Brown Enquiry, 4 April 1917. Survived the war. (123)

Heslop, George Christopher. Temporary Captain, awarded Military Cross 'for consolidation work under machine gun and artillery fire at the Somme, September 3rd and October 7th 1916'. Survived the war.

Hewitt, James. Private 16000, miner from Willington, died of wounds, 21 March 1916. (94)

Headstone of Alfred Hatton at Bard Cottage Cemetery, Boesinghe.
(*Gaynor Greenwood*)

Hewitt, John Cousin. Private 13306, labourer aged 26, from Blaydon, killed in action, 11 February 1916. (93–4)

Higgins, R. F., Captain, left behind sick 20 July 1915. (62)

Hildreth, Charles. Private 45678, miner aged 20, from Tow Law, killed in action, 16 August 1917. (136, 139, 230)

Hill, Allan. Private 75610, from Stillington, missing in action, 28 March 1918. (177)

Hill, Tabez. Private 376565, aged 40, from Leicester, died 8 April 1918.

Hill, William Henry. Private 11843, from Hexham, died of wounds, 16 November 1915.

Hindle, William. Private 36163, slater and tiler aged 37, from Darlington, died from mustard gas poisoning in hospital in Colchester, 29 September 1918, buried Darlington West Cemetery.

Hinksman, James. Private 18276, aged 27, from Felling, died of wounds, 5 October 1916.

Hodges, Albert E., Sergeant 18823, promoted to WO Class II. (114)

Hodgson, Henry. Private 21/24, aged 32, from Barnard Castle, died of wounds, 16 August 1917. (137)

Holt, Redfern. Private 76882, from Mirfield, missing in action, 30 November 1917.

Hope, Ernest. Private 75586, aged 19, from Wakefield, missing in action, 26 March 1918. (171)

Hopkinson, John. Sergeant 13451, aged 23, from Gateshead, died of wounds, 25 March 1918. (169)

Hook, John. Private 18754, promoted Colour Sergeant, awarded DCM after Cambrai. (197)

Hopkins, Second Lieutenant, sickness. (116)

Horner, Walter. Private 21665. Transferred in from 14th DLI, captured 24 March 1918, held as PoW in Germany and repatriated 28 December 1918. From York. (courtesy Steve Mattock)

Howells, David J., Private 17019, aged 21, from West Hartlepool, killed in action, 2 August 1916.

Huddart, Joseph Ethelbert. Private 32882, aged 31, from Hebburn, Jarrow, died of wounds, 18 April 1918.

Hughes, Thomas. Private 25043, from Dipton, died of wounds, 31 May 1918.

Hughes, William. Private 12716, from Belfast, enlisted Darlington, missing in action, 22 March 1918. (162)

Hume, W., Private 12209, probably B Company, gave evidence to the Arkless Enquiry, 31 March 1917. Survived the war.

Hunt, Arthur William. Private 15047, miner's labourer aged 23, from Hendon, Sunderland, killed in action, 16 August 1917. (138–9)

Headstone of William Hindle, Darlington West Cemetery, County Durham. (*Martin Bashforth*)

Headstone of Arthur Hunt at Bard Cottage Cemetery, Boesinghe. (*Jon Miller*)

Hunt, John William. Lance Corporal 17728, aged 23, from Middleton-in-Teesdale, died at home 11 January 1916, buried St Mary's churchyard, Barnard Castle. (235)

Hunt, W. Second Lieutenant, joined 18 April 1918. (202 n1)

Hurst, William. Private 13786, from Gateshead, killed in action, 22 March 1918. (162)

Inglis, William Wiley. Lieutenant, aged 26, from Stockton-on-Tees, killed in action, 20 November 1917. (103, 149)

Ingram, F., Private 15055, awarded Distinguished Conduct Medal, *London Gazette*, 25 November 1917. Survived the war. (197)

Irving, Frederick. Private 17970, Croix de Guerre. (197)

Isaac, Thomas Alfred. Private 24129, from Gloucestershire, killed in action, 10 November 1915. (78–9, 84 n10)

Iveson, John. Private 20731, miner aged 26, from Birtley, died of wounds, 21 September 1916. (56, 105)

Jackson, Sidney Bill. Private 302822, from Biggleswade and Doncaster, killed in action, 22 September 1917.

Jardine, William S. Private 20997, wounded at Laventie, later served with Royal Defence Corps and West Yorkshire Regiment. (76)

Jee, Ralph. Second Lieutenant, awarded the Military Cross for actions at Cambrai. Prominent during the March Retreat. (87, 146–7, 160–70)

Jerrison, William. Private 14075, aged 29, from Shotley Bridge, killed in action, 2 October 1915.

Jobes, Herbert Edward. Private 30839, barman aged 28, from Annfield Plain, died of fractured skull, 6 October 1916.

Johnson, Frederick Lilly. Lance Corporal 45846, originally from Connington, platelayer with Great Central Railway, enlisted Barnsley, died as prisoner of war in hospital at Giessen, 11 July 1918.

Johnston, William. Lance Sergeant 16009, from Stanley, died of wounds, 30 March 1918. (125, 180)

Jones, Simon. Private 76865, stonemason from Portmadoc, died of pneumonia as prisoner of war, 23 July 1918.

Jones, T., Private 18008, from Newcastle-upon-Tyne, died at home 8 July 1918, buried St John's, Westgate, Newcastle.

Kane, Thomas. Private 16024, aged 30, from Heworth, Felling, died at home, 31 January 1915, buried St Mary's churchyard, Heworth. (48)

Kear, Thomas Enoch. Private 79362, miner from Castleford, died of wounds in German Hospital at Flavy-le-Martel, 25 March 1918. (169)

Keegan, Francis. Private 25272, from West Stanley, died of wounds, 1 September 1916.

Kemp, Percy Vickerman. Captain, aged 25, from Darlington, died from gas, 31 May 1918. (103, 121, 160, 191–2)

Kennedy, John. Private 4/9342, miner from South Shields, killed in action, 22 March 1918. (162, 237)

King, H. F., Captain, joined as second in command from 4th Suffolk Regiment, 17 April 1918 - 8 November 1918. (189)

King, Robert Henry. Second Lieutenant, awarded Military Cross for actions at Mézières, 29 March 1918. (164, 168, 171 n7, 178, 197)

Kipling, William Alfred. Private 22193, from Snape, near Bedale, killed in action, 30 November 1917. (151–2)

Kitchen, Henry. Private 75557, farm labourer from Swinehead, Lincolnshire, killed in action, 23 March 1918. (165)

Kneale, J. R. Second Lieutenant, joined 18 April 1918. (202 n1)

Knighton, Edgar. Private 76704, painter from Wellingborough, missing in action, 30 November 1917.

Lambert, Edward James. Corporal 13086, later Sergeant then CSM, wrote to Bennett family. (106–7, 166)

Lascelles, A. M., Second Lieutenant, assisted at the Brown Enquiry, 4 April 1917. This may be Arthur Moore Lascelles, on detachment from 14th DLI, who later won the MC and VC before being killed 7 November 1918. (123)

Lavelle, Hugh. Private 17449, enlisted September 1914, was mentioned in despatches and awarded the Military Medal in 1918. Survived the war and died in 1966. (see index)

Laws, Thomas. Private 21754, miner from Chester-le-Street, killed in action, 20 September 1917.

Laws, William. Private 18920, miner aged 30, from Felling, killed in action, 30 September 1916. (110)

Leadley, William. Private 21455, from Scarborough and West Hartlepool, missing in action, 22 March 1918. (162)

Ledger, George William. Private 18685, miner aged 30, from Birtley, killed in action, 13 October 1915.

Leonard, Henry. Private 12870, railway platelayer aged 22, from West Hartlepool, died of wounds, 27 June 1916. (91–2)

Liddell, J. Second Lieutenant, joined 20 September 1916. (103, 120)

Liddle, John. Lance Corporal 16026, aged 31, from Felling, died of wounds, 19 September 1916. (103)

Lincoln, John. Private 78777, aged 24, from East Molesey, missing in action, 24 March 1918. (167)

Lindsay, Joseph. Private 15895, miner from South Shields, killed in action, 15 April 1917.

Lister, Daniel. Private 17430, miner aged 29, from Wingate, killed in action, 16 September 1915. (73–4)

Lister, John. Private 25745, aged 34, from South Moor, Stanley, killed in action, 5 October 1916.

Lloyd, Henry Percy. Major, from Bishop Auckland, Territorial in 7th DLI before the war, initially served as Captain with 11th DLI, C Company. Presided at the Bowlt Enquiry 4 August 1915. Wounded October 1915. Mentioned in despatches for courage at Cambrai in December 1917. (58, 65, 100, 148)

Lloyd, James. Lance Corporal 17957, aged 25, from Stanley, missing in action, 30 November 1917.

Logan, James. Private 18677, miner from Ouston, near Birtley, missing in action, 24 March 1918. (167)

Logan, Joseph. Private 30817, grocer aged 30, from Tantobie, killed in action, 5 October 1916. (229–30)

Lomas, Robert. Private 376247, aged 41, from Richmond, Surrey, missing in action, 26 March 1918. (171)

Long, John Salkeld. Private 16241, aged 27, from Gateshead, killed in action, 14 February 1917. (122)

Longstaff, George. Private 25661, aged 38, from Wingate, missing in action, 23 March 1918. (165)

Longstaff, William. Private 32827, aged 33, head horseman from High Coniscliffe, near Darlington, died of wounds to the back, 9 December 1917. (235)

Lowerson, John Thomas. Private 21779, miner aged 34, from Lumley Colliery, missing in action, 28 March 1918. (177)

Luke, William. Private 21752, miner aged 32, from Murton Colliery, killed in action, 20 September 1917.

MacLaren, Second Lieutenant, officer at embarkation 1915. (58, 71)

Marples, Lieutenant, suffers from measles. (89)

Martin, Second Lieutenant, in March Retreat 1918. (160, 164)

Martland, Arthur William. Private 76675, from Birkenhead and Egremont, died of wounds, 3 April 1918.

McAllister, James. Private 32883, clothing assistant aged 28, from Jarrow, died of wounds to the head, 20 December 1916.

McAllister, James Edward. Private 17958, aged 23, from Stanley, died of wounds, 12 October 1916.

McCarthy, James. Private 25276, from West Hartlepool, killed in action, 13 October 1916.

McCaughey, John William. Private 14820, labourer aged 27, from Consett, died of wounds, 14 December 1916.

McCormack, M. Private, court martial. (78, Appendix 2)

McDonald, Hugh. Private 17478, miner from Stanley, killed in action, 28 September 1915. (76, 79, 84 n10)

McEvoy, Patrick. Regimental Sergeant Major 15084, labourer aged 28, from Sunderland, died of wounds, 20 April 1918. (122, 129 n7, 147)

McFarlane, Anthony. Private 16467, pipe maker's labourer aged 37, from Blaydon, killed in action, 30 November 1917. (151–2)

McGill, Joseph. Private 3/11659, aged 46, from Monkwearmouth, killed in action, 25 March 1918. (169)

McGreehin, F. G. Second Lieutenant, in March Retreat 1918. (171 n7)

McGregor, William. Private 3/10374, from Pity Me, Durham, killed in action, 13 October 1915.

McKay, John Davison. Private 18867, labourer aged 22, from Birtley, died of wounds, 17 December 1916.

McKenzie, Roderick. Private 15082, witness at the Bowlt Enquiry, 4 August 1915. Survived the war. (65)

McKie, Thomas. Private 16721, iron worker from Consett, killed in action, 23 August 1916.

McLean, Albert. Private 15081, metal labourer from Witton Park, killed in action, 2 August 1916.

McLean, Thomas. Private 16721, ship plater's helper from Whitby and West Hartlepool, aged 27, killed in action, 5 October 1916. (73, 228)

McLean, William G., Corporal 18569, brother of Thomas McLean. Survived the war. (73)

McMahon, Francis. Private 16277, aged 23, from Felling, died at home 31 October 1915, buried St Mary's churchyard, Heworth.

McSoley, James. Private 20257, aged 36, from Bishop Auckland and Otley, died of wounds, 30 September 1915. (76)

Meek, Norman. Private 70906, labourer aged 21, from Seaham, killed in action, 24 March 1918. (167)

Mesham, Thomas. Private 16579, miner aged 29, from Wingate, died of wounds, 29 August 1916.

Miller, William Henry. Private 14880, miner aged 24, from Elswick, died of wounds, 24 October 1915.

Milligan, John. Private 25277, from Gateshead, killed in action, 5 September 1916.

Mohun, Robert. Private 15220, from Cramlington, Northumberland, killed in action, 4 September 1916.

Monger, Llewellyn William. Sergeant 8884, aged 27, from Bradford-on-Avon, missing in action, 23 March 1918. (165)

Morrill, Robert. Private 39917, aged 21 from West Hartlepool, rivet heater at Gray's Shipyard, missing in action, 23 March 1918. (165)

Morris, C. A. Second Lieutenant, taken prisoner March 1918. (160, 162, 181)

Mudd, Charles Henry. Private 30335, aged 21, from Staindrop, died of wounds, 1 September 1916.

Munro, Walter. Private 16027, aged 25, from Gateshead, killed in action, 11 November 1917.

Murphy, John. Private 53589, aged 47, from Haggerstone, London, died of wounds, 28 May 1917. (126)

Murray, Thomas. Private 25228, from West Cornforth, died of wounds, 10 November 1915. (78, 84 n10)

Myers, John Henry. Private 22316, labourer aged 22, from Durham, killed in action, 19 December 1916.

Myers, John James. Second Lieutenant, killed in action , 22 October 1917. Served originally with 11th DLI, but was serving with 15th DLI when he was killed.

Naylor, A. Second Lieutenant, wounded March 1918. (160, 164–5, 181)

Neale, James. Private 25673, aged 43, from Teddington, killed in action, 30 November 1917. (151)

Newman, Frederick. Private 18866, metal cleaner from Birtley, died in England during training, 6 December 1914, buried Brookwood Cemetery, Surrey. (48)

Noble, John. Private 13761, painter from Penrith and West Stanley, died of wounds, 4 September 1916.

Oakley, James. Private 23136, from Middlesbrough, missing presumed killed in action, 21 March 1918. (160)

Oates, Thomas. Private 19499, enlisted 2 March 1915, served with 19th DLI and then 11th DLI, when taken prisoner in 1918. Discharged, 13 January 1919. (207)

O'Brien, John. Private 43201, from Grimsby, died of wounds, 29 March 1918. (178)

Oddy, Charles. Private 43200, aged 33 from Leeds, killed in action, 21 April 1917.

O'Neil, William James. Private 16243, aged 25, from Gateshead, died at home, 7 January 1920, buried Gateshead East Cemetery.

O'Neill, James. Sergeant 25774, from Killenny and Birtley, died in England, 21 October 1917, when attached to 276th Infantry Training Battalion, buried St Joseph RC church, Birtley. (93, 227)

O'Neill, Patrick. Private 25752, from Birtley, killed in action, 5 January 1916. (93)

Ord, Matthew. Lance Corporal 25768, age 28, from Blyth, died of wounds, 11 December 1916.

Ormston, John. Sergeant 14065, from Blaydon, died of wounds, 5 December 1917.

Packard, Thomas Henry. Sergeant 53713, scythe grinder from Heeley, Sheffield. Taken prisoner 23 March 1918, died of wounds in a German Field Hospital at Flavy-le-Martel, 25 March 1918. (169)

Page, William. Private 18883, metal cleaner from Birtley, died of wounds, 21 September 1917. (274)

Palmer, C. Captain, D Company, presided at the Brown Enquiry 4 April 1917. Mentioned in despatches, *London Gazette*, 25 May 1917, p. 5163. (58, 122–3, 125, 144)

Palmer, John Henry. Private 376697, postal worker from Durham, served with Gloucestershire Regiment, Ox and Bucks Light Infantry and 27th and 6th DLI before allocated to 11th DLI, 25 December 1917. Discharged on 3 March 1919.

Parfitt, James Robert Stanley. Private 376261, from Clapham, London, missing presumed killed in action, 27 May 1918, while then serving with 22nd DLI.

Parker, Robert Benjamin. Private 23525, packer from Hackney, killed in action, 10 August 1916. Although still formally attached to 11th DLI, he died while serving with 9th Northumberland Fusiliers.

Parker, William Ewart. Private 44066, clerk aged 19, from Blyth, died of wounds to head, chest and hand, 22 September 1917.

Parkin, H. S. Lieutenant, at Cambrai. (148)

Parkinson, James. Private 44899, witness at the Cunliffe Enquiry, 6 June 1918. Had previously served with the Cheshire Regiment, Labour Corps and Middlesex Regiment. Survived the war. (192)

Parry, Robert Thomas. Private 17544, from Wrexham and Birtley, died of wounds, 12 April 1918.

Pattison, James Thirlaway. Private 21415, aged 24, from Tanfield, died of wounds, 24 May 1917.

Pattullo, George Simpson. Corporal 19293, clerk, enlisted Newcastle 1914, promoted Sergeant, commissioned 1916 and served as an officer with 21st and 23rd Northumberland Fusiliers. Originally from Scotland of Spanish descent, previously played football for Barcelona FC. Retired to Spain after the war until 1939. Died London 5 September 1953.

Paynter, Reginald P., Sergeant 15825, later QMS, commissioned Second Lieutenant. (58)

Pearson, George. Lance Corporal 13002, aged 23, from Carlisle and Bensham, died of wounds, 14 October 1915.

Pemberton, Richard Laurence Stapylton. Commissioned 14 August 1914, with 11th DLI on embarkation 20 July 1915. Rose to rank of Major. Awarded the Military Cross and bar for actions at Cambrai 1917 and Mézières 1918. Second in command 9 November 1918 until demobilised 20 January 1919. (see index)

Philip, A. Second Lieutenant, gassed 1918. (121, 125, 191)

Pickard, John W. Sergeant 24547, smith's labourer at Shildon Works, joined 11th DLI 2 September 1915, court-martialled 12 August 1916 for absence and reduced to the ranks with six months' hard labour. Later wounded and returned home, serving briefly with the Training Reserve, before being discharged as medically unfit, 18 July 1917. (210, 283)

Pickering, Harry. Private 53726, glass-maker aged 31, from Barnsley, captured 23 March 1918, died 28 June 1918, at Stendhal.

Pickering, James Harold. Sergeant 18836, signalman aged 27, from Selby and Birtley, missing in action 25 March 1918. (169)

Plaice, Herbert. Private 25279, from West Hartlepool, died of wounds, 31 August 1916.

Pollard, Clifford. Private 53250, hairdresser from Leeds, missing in action, 29 March 1918. (178)

Potter, Charles Robert. Lance Corporal 22506, aged 29, from Gateshead, died of wounds, 6 September 1916. (101–2)

Pounder, Thomas. Private 32765, colliery labourer aged 28, from Shildon, died of wounds, 6 October 1916.

Prickett, Richard. Private 45840, plasterer from Accrington and Wakefield, died of wounds, 3 September 1917, while serving with P. B. Labour Company at Dunkirk.

Raffle, Robert. Corporal 16324, from South Shields, embarked 11 September 1915, died of wounds, 3 July 1918.

Ramsey, Charles Albert. Private 21837, miner aged 21, from Fenham, Newcastle-upon-Tyne, died of wounds, 8 October 1916.

Ramshaw, John. Private 13421, C Company, witness at the Bowlt Enquiry 4 August 1915. Survived the war. (65)

Ratcliffe, J. C. Second Lieutenant, joined 18 April 1918, gassed. (191, 202 n1)

Redpath, George. Private 32718, colliery weighman aged 41, from Fencehouses, died of wounds, 27 March 1918. (176)

Rees, D. J. Lieutenant, aged 37, barrister from Swansea and Shrewsbury, died in England, 7 July 1919, buried Putney Vale Cemetery, Wandsworth. D Company, assisted at the Brown Enquiry 4 April 1917 as Second Lieutenant. (119, 123, 130 n9)

Reidy, Fred. Private 23538, labourer from Gateshead, died of wounds, 11 October 1915.

Renhard, John. Private 79728, from Wakefield, killed in action, 24 October 1918.

Richardson, George. Private 17936, aged 45, from Edmondsley, died of wounds, 12 August 1918. Killed in an air raid at No. 6 Rest Camp, Calais, while convalescing.

Richardson, Robert. Private 15209, from Broom Park, killed in action, 11 April 1916.

Rigby, R. S., Lieutenant, at Laventie. (71)

Robson, David Sinclair. Company Sergeant Major 9647, regular soldier aged 34, from Wark near Hexham, missing in action, 23 March 1918. (163, 165, 188)

Rogers, William. Company Sergeant Major 12621, foreman miner, enlisted 12 August 1914, served with B Company. Service book at Durham County Records Office indicates he was paid until 19 June 1918 and may have been invalided out. Some notes in the book suggest he may have run some sort of football pools syndicate. (244)

Rolfe, John George. Private 18952, miner aged 26, from Leadgate, died of wounds, 12 September 1916.

Roper, Thomas Frederick. Private 9992, miner aged 24, from Spennymoor, died of wounds, 22 June 1917.

Rundle, John William. Private 17552, from Pelton Fell, missing in action, 24 March 1918. (167)

Rust, Richard. Private 73167, from Tantobie, platelayer with North Eastern Railway Company, killed in action, 24 March 1918.

Rutherford, H. Second Lieutenant, taken prisoner March 1918. (160, 162, 181)

Sadler, Joseph Charles. Private 76806, motor-coach body-maker aged 23, from Coventry, missing in action, 22 March 1918. (162)

Schofield, Fred. Private 79143, aged 19, cloth-finisher from Huddersfield, missing in action, 27 March 1918. (176)

Scott, George. Private 16257, aged 28 from Gateshead and Paisley, killed in action, 12 November 1915.

Scott, George. Private 23513, miner from Gateshead, killed in action, 12 November 1915.

Scott, Joseph Norman. Lance Corporal 21437, aged 20, from Lanchester, died of wounds, 5 September 1916.

Sear, Walter George Lane. Australian by birth, commissioned Second Lieutenant from 17 November 1915, attached 21st DLI. Transferred to 11th DLI rising to Captain. Wounded 29 March 1918, shot through the chest. Demobilised 2 May 1919, he returned to Australia. Awarded the Military Cross in 1917. (see index)

R. Rust,
East Tanfield.

Portrait of Richard Rust from the *North Eastern Railway* Magazine. (*Courtesy of British Rail Board (Residuary) Ltd*)

Seggar, Harry. Sergeant 16814, grocer aged 28 from Croft Spa near Darlington, missing in action, 28 March 1918. (125, 188)

Seymour, James. Private 25600, aged 23, from Newcastle-upon-Tyne, killed in action, 20 November 1917. (244)

Shafto, Thomas Edward. Private 13997, aged 25, labourer from New Shildon, died, probably as a prisoner of war, 25 April 1918.

Shanley, Francis. Private 14810, aged 27, from Newcastle-upon-Tyne, killed in action, 7 October 1916.

Sheehan, William. Private 16818, ironworks labourer from Stockton-on-Tees and West Hartlepool, killed in action, 7 October 1916. (65, 84 n4, 112)

Shephard, George William. Private 49616, farmer's horseman, from Boston and Grantham, missing in action, 22 March 1918. (162)

Shield, John. Lance Corporal 16106, miner aged 32, from South Moor, Stanley, died of wounds, 17 September 1916. (278)

Short, William Harold. Private 25762, fireman from Consett and Devon, killed in action, 15 April 1917. (84 n10)

Shuttleworth, Private. Witness to death of Pte William Barker. (126)

Siddle, William Clennell. Sergeant 18955, from Consett, killed in action, 10 November 1915. (84 n10)

Simpson, Edward. Lance Corporal 25761, aged 35, from Stanley, died of wounds, 12 December 1917.

Sinclair, William Henry. Private 46369, aged 32, from Sunderland, died of wounds, 25 October 1918.

Skillcorn, John. Lance Corporal 12949, miner aged 22, from Pelton, died of wounds, 10 March 1917.

Smart, Walter. Private 55591, from Anstey, Leicester, died of acute nephritis at Lincoln General Hospital, 16 January 1917, buried Anstey Cemetery. Actually served in England with the 11th Infantry Works Company, DLI. (122)

Smith, Alexander. Private 17553, miner from Pelton, born Fifeshire, aged 30, killed in action, 5 September 1916.

Smith, James (alias see Steel)

Smith, R. E. C. Second Lieutenant, joined 18 April 1918. (202 n1)

Smith, Thomas. Private 53427, from Canterbury, missing in action, 22 March 1918. (162)

Snowball, Robert. Private 16237, miner from Felling, court martial, died of wounds, 27 March 1918. (176, 227, Appendix 2)

Spooner, Thomas. Sergeant 14018, labourer Shildon Railway Works, enlisted 31 August 1914, promoted Sergeant 17 March 1916. Wounded 29 June 1916, but recovered and later served with the Army of Occupation.

Headstone of John Shield at Bard Cottage Cemetery, Boesinghe.
(*Gaynor Greenwood*)

Steel, S., Private 13441, from Airdrie and Gateshead, died of wounds, 6 March 1916. Served as James Smith. (278)

Stephenson, James. Private 25763, aged 20, from Newcastle-upon-Tyne, died of wounds, 24 October 1915.

Stobbart, Thomas. Private 16006, accidentally shot at Laventie, survived the war. (73)

Stones, Willie. Private 53238, textile worker aged 24 from Leeds, died in England, 27 October 1918 from multiple wounds, buried Beeston Cemetery, Leeds.

Stonestreet, Reginald. Private 76916, carpenter from Robertsbridge, taken prisoner, 24 March 1918, and died from lung disease in a German hospital, 3 July 1918.

Stott, Richard. Private 15144, miner from Wingate, killed in action, 15 April 1917.

Sturman, Sydney E. Private 25237, from Kirton-in-Lindsey and Stanley, died 28 February 1917.

Sturt, C. G. Second Lieutenant, assisted at the Bowlt Enquiry, 4 August 1915. (58, 65)

Suddick, Robert. Private 17561, miner from Birtley, died of wounds, 10 October 1916.

Surrey, John J. Private 12115, labourer aged 24, from Blaydon, killed in action, 30 December 1915.

Tait, Second Lieutenant, officer at embarkation. (58, 71)

Tansey, Joseph Alfred. Private 16073, aged 34, from Hinckley, Leicestershire, killed in action, 16 August 1917. (137)

Taylor, J. G. Second Lieutenant, later Major, awarded MC. (87, 197)

Taylor, J. H. Second Lieutenant, joined 18 April 1918. (202 n1)

Taylor, Robert. Private 15151, miner aged 32, from Haswell, Co. Durham, killed in action, 16 August 1917. (137)

Taylor, William. Private 18820, miner from Portobello, Birtley, killed in action, 30 November 1915.

Taylor, William Henry. Private 46378, aged 26, from Liverpool and Bradford, died 19 November 1917.

Thew, Thomas. Private 3/10394, railway platform porter aged 30, from Warkworth, captured, 24 March 1918, died at Stendhal, 12 June 1918.

Thompson, Austin Sampson ('Sam'). Private 16472, aged 32, from Gateshead, missing in action, 22 March 1918. (162)

Thompson, James. Private 22751, glass-maker from Gateshead, died in Germany as prisoner of war awaiting repatriation, 13 November 1918.

Thompson, James Martin. Private 12291, from Chester-le-Street, killed in action, 20 September 1916. (106)

Thompson, William. Private 12802, from Seaham, died of wounds, 14 July 1918.

View of Lijssenthoek Military Cemetery with the headstone of Private S. Steel (alias James Smith) at the front centre. Several other 20th Division men are buried close by and in the further ranks. (*Gaynor Greenwood*)

T. Thew,
Warkworth.

Portrait of Thomas Thew from the *North Eastern Railway* Magazine. (*Courtesy of British Rail Board (Residuary) Ltd*)

Thrower, John. Private 16685, miner from Byker, Newcastle-upon-Tyne, killed in action, 3 September 1916.

Toll, Frederick Samuel. Private 376883, aged 26, from Handsworth, Birmingham, missing in action, 23 March 1918. (165)

Tollit, George Hugh. Former regular soldier, enlisted Walthamstow and appointed Honorary Lieutenant and Quartermaster, 11th DLI. Adjutant and Captain from 15 September 1917. Demobilised 13 November 1919 and lived in Essex. (148, 211–2)

Tombling, John William. Private, accidental burning February 1917, story of flamethrower incident. (122, 209)

Towers, Private. Tried to rescue Sgt Thomas Bashforth 1918. (176)

Traynor, James. Private 17471, miner aged 29, from Beamish, killed in action, 25 August 1916.

Turner, Alfred. Private 22536, labourer aged 20, from Low Fell, died of wounds, 2 October 1915. (76–7, 244)

Unsworth, James Cuthbert. Lance Corporal 21022, coal heaver aged 28, from London and Dunston, died of wounds, 5 October 1916.

Urwin, Fergus William. Private 17968, miner aged 22, from Burnhope, died of wounds, 6 October 1916.

Uttley, Lawrence. Corporal 53710, Turkish Bath attendant aged 24, from Ecclesall, Sheffield, missing in action, 23 March 1918. (165)

Vaccare, Domnick. Private 52623, docks labourer from Hull, wounded 22 September 1917, died 2 October 1917.

Vans, Robert. Private 14759, from South Shields, killed in action, 12 October 1916.

Wade, William Thomas. Private 81645, from Leicester, missing in action, 29 May 1918.

Walton, H. P., Reverend. Joined as chaplain November 1916, at Cambrai 1917. (117, 148)

Walton, Isaac. Private 21346, from Wheatley Hill, died of wounds, 27 August 1916.

Walton, Israel. Private 12412, deserter, found to be insane. (209–10)

Warnock, Joseph. Private 21545, labourer from Glasgow and Sheffield, missing in action, 30 November 1917.

Watson, George Edwin. Private 376028, aged 22, from Nottingham, missing in action, 23 March 1918. (165)

Webb, Harry James. Lance Corporal 21524, blacksmith aged 25, from Oxford, died of wounds, 4 November 1915.

Welch, Thomas. Private 16653, miner aged 44, from West Stanley, died of wounds, 9 September 1916.

Whatling, Lee Samson. Private 76814, aged 27, laundry worker from East Bergholt, wounded (face, arm and left thigh) 22 December 1917, died next day.

Whitfield, H. J. E. Second Lieutenant, wounded on March 1918, later transferred to RFC. (171, 181, 194)

Wilkes, George Edward. Private 81873, aged 18, fitter's assistant from Bilston, Wolverhampton, died of wounds, 5 May 1918.

Wilkinson, A. E. Second Lieutenant, wounded March 1918. (181)

Wilkinson, Harry. Temporary Quartermaster and Lieutenant, awarded Military Cross (*London Gazette*, 3 June 1919).

Wilkinson, Herbert. Private 18584, docks labourer from Stranton, West Hartlepool, died of wounds, 13 November 1917.

Williams, Frederick. Sergeant, later CSM, awarded Médaille Militaire, commissioned April 1917. (78, 124, 197)

Willingham, John Turner. Private 52624, aged 38, glazier from Hull, reported missing 29 March 1918, died of wounds as prisoner, 30 March 1918. (180)

Wilson, Albert. Private 17467, miner aged 36 from South Moor, Stanley, killed in action, 3 September 1916.

Wilson, Charles. Private 18091, injured 1915. (75)

Wilson, Ernest. Private 91036, witness at the Cunliffe Enquiry 6 June 1918 (incorrectly listed as C. Wilson). Later transferred to 52nd Battalion, as 66963. (192)

Wilson, John. Private 3/10828, hawker from Fencehouses, killed in action, 2 September 1916.

Wilson, John William. Private 15343, from Brandon Colliery, killed in action, 7 October 1916.

Wilson, Thomas. Lance Corporal 17974, miner from Consett, killed in action, 13 December 1916.

Wilson, Thomas. Private 33236, labourer aged 35 from Throckley, Northumberland, missing in action, 1 December 1917.

Wilson, William Peart. Corporal 53550, grocer aged 20 from New Shildon, died of wounds, 23 September 1917.

Wood, Second Lieutenant, officer at embarkation. (58)

Wood, G. F. Second Lieutenant, gassed. (191)

Woodcock, William. Private 53706, miner aged 35, from Barnsley, wounded 1 April 1918, died two days later.

Wray, George Holland. Private 53572, motor driver from Knightsbridge, Chelsea, missing in action, 23 March 1918. (165)

Yates, John. Lance Corporal 231112, fruiterer aged 21 from Tynemouth, missing in action, 31 March 1918. (180)

Youll, Matthew. Private 38575, licensed victualler, Queen's Head Inn, Thornley, missing in action, 24 March 1918. (167)

Headstone of William Wilson at Bard Cottage Cemetery, Boesinghe. (*Gaynor Greenwood*)

Courts Martial,
11th DLI, 1915–1918

Details are from The National Archives, WO 213/6–26, listed in date order, by name, rank, date of court martial, place, charges, sentences and any notes.

Bousfield, W. CSM, 1 November 1915, at Laventie, drunkenness, reduced to the ranks, mitigated to Lance Corporal.

Hamilton, W. Private, 3 November 1915, at Laventie, striking an officer, imprisonment one year with hard labour, suspended.

McCormack, M. Private, 12 November 1915, at Laventie, striking an officer and drunkenness, eighteen months' hard labour, suspended.

Forsythe, R. Private, 20 January 1916, in the field, absence, imprisonment with hard labour, three months, suspended.

Kelman, A. Private, 13 March 1916, Cassel, miscellaneous S.40, FP1, one month.

Martin, J. Corporal, 6 July 1916, in the field, desertion and drunkenness, reduced to the ranks, not guilty of desertion.

Pickard, J. W. Sergeant, 12 August 1916, in the field, absence, six months' hard labour and reduced to ranks, suspended.

Potts, J. Private, 26 August 1916, striking an officer, two years' hard labour, suspended.

Tyson, Thomas. Private, 16 October 1916, Corbie, absence, twenty-one days' FP1.

Chamberlain, J. Private, 16 October 1916, Corbie, S.40 and S.18.2a, not guilty.

Fox, E. Private, 24 November 1916, S.40, forty-two days FP1.

Roberts, J. W. Private, 9 March 1917, Guillemont, theft, forty-two days' FP1.

Myers, T. H. Private, 13 April 1917, in the field, S.40, not guilty.

Brown, H. Private, 29 May 1917, in the field, striking an officer, twenty-eight days' FP1.

Mulroy, A. Private, 11 July 1917, in the field, S.40, one years' hard labour, suspended.

Mead, J. Private, 16 July 1917, Dieppe, offence against an inhabitant and miscellaneous, not guilty.

Kinnafick, C. Private, 29 September 1917, in the field, absence, eighty-four days' FP1.

Hughes, J. Corporal, 16 January 1918, in the field, absence, twenty-one days' FP2 and reduced to the ranks.

Howard, R. Private, 1 March 1918, in the field, S. 40, fourteen days' FP1, loss of two months' pay, remitted to loss of one month's pay.

Snowball, R. Private, 12 March 1918, in the field, absence, eighty-four days' FP1.

Hudson, M. Private, 10 April 1918, in the field, disobedience to Sergeant, eighty-four days' FP1, remitted to fifty-six days.

Scott, J. Private, 25 May 1918, in the field, S.40, fourteen days' FP1.

Dodd, L. Private, 13 June 1918, S.40, in the field, fifty-six days' FP1.

Rose, C. Private, 23 September 1918, in the field, insubordination, fourteen days' FP1.

Chapman, J. F. Private, 16 November 1918, in the field, absence, ninety days' FP1.

Wilson, C. A. Private, 18 November 1918, in the field, insubordination, twenty-eight days' FP1.

Hodgson, D. Corporal, 13 December 1918, in the field, absence, reduced to ranks.

Kelly, R. Corporal, 13 December 1918, in the field, absence, reduced to ranks.

Index